Beckett an

MANCHESTER
1824

Manchester University Press

Beckett and nothing

Trying to understand Beckett

Edited by
DANIELA CASELLI

Manchester
University Press

Manchester and New York

distributed in the United States exclusively by Palgrave Macmillan

Published by Manchester University Press
Oxford Road, Manchester M13 9NR, UK
and Room 400, 175 Fifth Avenue, New York, NY 10010, USA
www.manchesteruniversitypress.co.uk

Distributed in the United States exclusively by
Palgrave Macmillan, 175 Fifth Avenue,
New York, NY 10010, USA

Distributed in Canada exclusively by
UBC Press, University of British Columbia, 2029 West Mall,
Vancouver, BC, Canada V6T 1Z2

British Library Cataloguing-in-Publication Data is available

Library of Congress Cataloging-in-Publication Data is available

ISBN 978 0 7190 8784 4 paperback

First published by Manchester University Press in hardback 2010

This paperback edition first published 2012

Printed by Lightning Source

Contents

List of figures

All are drawn translations by Bill Prosser from the *Human Wishes* manuscript with the king permission of Edward Beckett.

List of contributors

Jonathan Bignell is Professor of Television and Film and Director of the Centre for Television Drama Studies at the University of Reading. Among Jonathan's recent publications are *Big Brother: Reality TV in the 21st Century* (Palgrave Macmillan, 2005), *The Television Handbook*, third edition (Routledge, 2005) (with J. Orlebar), *Popular Television Drama: Critical Perspectives* (Manchester University Press, 2005) (ed. with S. Lacey), *An Introduction to Television Studies* (Routledge, 2004), *Media Semiotics: An Introduction*, second edition (Manchester University Press, 2002), and 'How to watch television?: pedagogy and paedocracy in Beckett's television plays', in *Samuel Beckett Today / Aujourd'hui*, 2005, and 'Beckett at the BBC: the production and reception of Samuel Beckett's plays for television', in L. Ben-Zvi (ed.), *Drawing on Beckett: Portraits, Performances, and Cultural Contexts* (University of Tel Aviv, 2003).

Peter Boxall is Reader in English at the University of Sussex. He is the author of *Since Beckett: Contemporary Writing in the Wake of Modernism* (Continuum, 2009), *Don DeLillo: The Possibility of Fiction* (Routledge, 2006), *1001 Novels You Must Read Before You Die* (Cassell, 2006), *Endgame and Waiting for Godot: A Reader's Guide to Essential Criticism* (Palgrave Macmillan, 2003), editor of *Beckett/Aesthetics/Politics* (Rodopi, 2000) and co-editor of the *Year's Work in Critical and Cultural Theory*. He is the editor of *Textual Practice*.

Enoch Brater is Kenneth T. Rowe Collegiate Professor of Dramatic Literature at the University of Michigan. Among his works on

Beckett are: *Essential Samuel Beckett* (Thames & Hudson, 2003); *The Drama in the Text: Beckett's Late Fiction* (Oxford University Press, 1994); *Beyond Minimalism: Beckett's Late Style in the Theater* (Oxford University Press, 1987; 1990; 2000); *Why Beckett* (Thames and Hudson, 1989); *Beckett at 80 / Beckett in Context* (Oxford University Press, 1986); *Approaches To Teaching Beckett's* Waiting for Godot (Modern Language Association, 1991); *Around the Absurd: Essays on Modern and Postmodern drama* (University of Michigan Press, 1990); *The Theatrical Gamut: Notes for a Post-Beckettian Stage* (University of Michigan Press, 1995).

Daniela Caselli is Senior Lecturer in Twentieth-Century Literature and Culture at the University of Manchester. She is the author of *Beckett's Dantes: Intertextuality in the Fiction and Criticism* (Manchester University Press, 2005), *Improper Modernism: Djuna Barnes's Bewildering Corpus* (Ashgate, 2009). Her articles on modernism, Beckett, Djuna Barnes and critical theory have appeared in *Textual Practice, Critical Survey, Samuel Beckett Today / Aujourd'hui* and *The Journal of Beckett Studies*.

Mladen Dolar is Professor of Philosophy at the University of Ljubljana. Co-founder of the Ljubljana School of Psychoanalysis, he is the author of studies on Hegel, aesthetics and psychoanalysis, of *A Voice and Nothing More* (MIT Press, 2006) and, with Slavoj Žižek, *Opera's Second Death* (Routledge, 2002).

Terry Eagleton is Professor at the University of Lancaster. Among his recent publications are *Reason, Faith, and Revolution: Reflections on the God Debate* (Yale University Press, 2009), *Trouble with Strangers: A Study of Ethics* (Wiley Blackwell, 2008); *The Meaning of Life: A Very Short Introduction* (Oxford University Press, 2007), *How to Read a Poem* (Blackwell, 2006), *Holy Terror* (Oxford University Press, 2005), *After Theory* (Penguin, 2004), *Sweet Violence: The Idea of the Tragic* (Blackwell, 2002), *Literary Theory: An Introduction* (Oxford: Blackwell, 1996).

Matthijs Engelberts is Lecturer in French at the University of Amsterdam. A long-standing editor of *Samuel Beckett Today / Aujourd'hui*, he has published widely in the field of Beckett Studies both in English and in French.

Catherine Laws is a musicologist and a pianist specialising in contemporary music. Much of her research centres on the relationship between music and language, with a particular focus on the work of Samuel Beckett and composers' responses to his texts. She has published a range of articles on these topics and is currently completing a book on Beckett and music. Catherine is currently a Research Fellow at the Orpheus Institute in Ghent, and an Associate Lecturer at University College Falmouth (Dartington).

John Pilling is Emeritus Professor of English and European Literature at the University of Reading, where for many years he directed the Beckett International Foundation and edited the *Journal of Beckett Studies*. He still serves on the editorial boards of *JOBS* and *SBT/A*. Among his many books on Beckett are *Samuel Beckett* (Routledge and Kegan Paul,1976), *Frescoes of the Skull: The Later Prose and Drama of Samuel Beckett* (with James Knowlson, Grove Press, 1979), *The Ideal Core of the Onion: Reading Beckett's Archives* (with Mary Bryden, Beckett International Foundation, 1992), *The Cambridge Companion to Samuel Beckett* (Cambridge University Press, 1994), *Beckett Before Godot* (Cambridge University Press, 1998), *Beckett's* Dream *Notebook* (Beckett International Foundation, 1999), *A Companion to* Dream of Fair to Middling Women (Journal of Beckett Studies Books, 2004), *A Beckett Chronology* (Palgrave Macmillan, 2006).

Bill Prosser is a Senior Research Fellow at the University of Reading, working on a research project entitled 'Beckett and the Phenomenology of Doodles' funded by the Leverhulme Trust. Prosser worked for many years as an illustrator for, among others, *The Times*, *The Sunday Times*, *The Observer*, *Vogue*, *Elle*, *New Scientist*, *The Listener*, Penguin Books, Oxford University Press, BBC Publications and Blackwell. Selected recent exhibitions include: 'Samuel Beckett: The Irish European', Museum of Reading, 2006; 'Human Wishes', Bob Kayley Studio Theatre, University of Reading (which accompanied the world premiere of Beckett's *First Love*), 2006; 'Drawings', Ashmolean Museum, Oxford, 2005; 'Naked', Royal West of England Academy, Bristol, 2004. In November 2006 he showed several of his Beckett drawings in Paris as part of the celebrations that marked Beckett's centenary.

Laura Salisbury is a RCUK Research Fellow and Lecturer in Modern and Contemporary Literature at Birkbeck, University of London. She has published on Beckett and comedy, Irish jokes, poststructuralist ethics and on the work of Michel Serres. She is co-editor of *Neurology and Modernity* (Palgrave Macmillan, 2009) and is currently researching studies on late modernism and on the relationship between modernism and neurology.

Russell Smith is Lecturer in English at the Australian National University, Canberra. His research interests are in critical and cultural theory, modernist and contemporary literature, Australian literature and visual arts, and Samuel Beckett. His work on Beckett has appeared in *Samuel Beckett Today / Aujourd'hui*. He has edited *Beckett and Ethics* (Continuum, 2009) and he is co-editor of the *Australian Humanities Review*.

Stephen Thomson is Lecturer in English at the University of Reading. His work on critical theory and comparative literature has appeared in *Parallax, Cultural Critique* and *Comparative Literature*. He has published on Beckett in *Samuel Beckett Today / Aujourd'hui*. He is currently working on a monograph on sleepwalking.

Derval Tubridy is Lecturer in English and Visual Culture at Goldsmiths, University of London. Her Ph.D. for Trinity College, Dublin, explored the relationship between language, subjectivity and the body in the prose and drama of Samuel Beckett. Author of *Thomas Kinsella: The Peppercanister Poems*, she has also published on Beckett's prose and drama, Jasper Johns, James Joyce, Irish poetry and philosophy and literature. Her research has been funded by the Fulbright Commission and the British Academy. An abstract painter, she has exhibited in Ireland and Britain. She is currently working on a book called *Art after Beckett*.

Shane Weller is Reader in Comparative Literature and Co-Director of the Centre for Modern European Literature at the University of Kent. He has published on European modernism, postmodernism and literary theory, with a particular focus on Samuel Beckett, Maurice Blanchot, Paul Celan, Jacques Derrida, Martin Heidegger and Friedrich Nietzsche. He is the author of *Literature, Philosophy,*

Nihilism: The Uncanniest of Guests (Palgrave Macmillan, 2008), *Beckett, Literature, and the Ethics of Alterity* (Palgrave Macmillan, 2006) and *A Taste for the Negative: Beckett and Nihilism* (Legenda, 2005).

Acknowledgments

My gratitude goes to all the contributors, for their hard work and patience, and to Edward Beckett, for his kind permission to use manuscript material.

All unpublished material and Bill Prosser's 'drawn translations' have been reproduced by kind permission of Edward Beckett, the Estate of Samuel Beckett.

The photograph on the cover is reproduced courtesy of Jonathan P. Brater.

Daniela Caselli

Foreword
Nothing new

Terry Eagleton

Postmodernism is supposed to be averse to grand narratives, but it has at least one of its own. According to this tall tale, Western culture manifests a continuous belief in a free, self-determining human subject, one that takes itself to be at the centre of the universe and is transparently present to itself. Only recently, so the story goes, have we come to realise that the human subject is diffuse, decentred, constituted to its roots by cultural and material forces. The all-powerful autonomous subject has been humbled and chastened in our time, dislodged from its imperial sovereignty and unmasked as no more than the ephemeral product of (and here one may choose) language, culture, history, the unconscious and so on.

There is something in this myth, as there is something in most myths which have convinced enough people for a long enough time. One is puzzled, however, to find the champions of heterogeneity telling such a drearily homogeneous tale. Can one really trace such a uniform conception of the subject all the way from Descartes to Davidson? And if we can, what becomes of the notion of history as text? The truth is that this buoyant, replete, self-fashioning subject is one of several strands of reflection on subjectivity within Western culture, and by no means always the dominant one. Take, for example, the lineage of Christian thought which passes from Augustine to Aquinas and on to contemporary theology. For this legacy, God lies at the core of the human subject, as the power which enables us to be ourselves. Yet he is not an entity, principle, creature, substance, life-force, individual, exist-ent being or spiritual essence. Though he is said to be personal, he cannot be hypostasised to 'a person', in the sense that Paris Hilton is arguably a person.

From the standpoint of entities and substances, God is pure nothingness. He is not a 'being' but the ground of possibility of any form of being whatsoever. He cannot be counted up along with other phenomena. God and the universe do not make two. He is a sublime abyss of infinite negativity; and to claim that human beings are his creatures is to claim that they, too, are shot through from end to end by nothingness. St Augustine was perhaps the first great thinker to propose this thesis. If God, as Thomas Aquinas argues, is closer to us than we are to ourselves, and if God is no sort of thing at all, then what is most definitive about the human animal is pure negation. It is negativity which makes us what we are. To be a subject, as opposed to being a tin of caviar or a hat stand, is to elude definition and slip through the net of language. Subjectivity is the ceaselessly frustrated act of seeking to leap on our own shadows, or trying to see ourselves seeing something. The subject consists in no more than a constantly failing attempt to grasp itself. It represents a gaping hole in reality. It is the askew, unnameable, out-of-joint factor which prevents the field of the real from ever being fully totalised.

The greatest of all negative theologians of the medieval period, the Irish monk John Scottus Eriugena, understood this very well, and Samuel Beckett took an interest in his work. Creation for Eriugena is a great spiral of self-referential signs with a void at its centre, rather like Joyce's *Ulysses*. God is entirely unrepresentable, and so is the human subjectivity which signifies our participation in his Being. We have perfect self-knowledge, Eriugena remarks, only when we recognise that we do not know who we are.[1] So much for self-transparency. As a later Irish theologian, the eighteenth-century Archbishop King, observed, 'all finite beings partake of nothing, and are nothing beyond their bounds'.[2] Another Irish bishop, George Berkeley, famously commented that, when it came to the Irish, something and nothing were near allied. There was little you could teach the Irish about negativity (one thinks of another Protestant clergyman, Jonathan Swift), and Samuel Beckett is a modern inheritor of this distinguished narrative.

The liberal-humanist subject which supposedly lies at the centre of Western civilisation is above all autonomous. Its freedom lies not only in its emancipation from external constraint but in its strenuous self-determination. To determine, of course, means etymologically speaking to set limits; and to be free is to set one's own limits, rather than submit to those imposed by another. Freedom is not freedom from determination, but self-determination. There may well be some such noble conception in the mighty liberal heritage which passes from John Locke to John Stuart Mill; but it stands at odds with the religious belief which has shaped Western culture for a much longer period. We have just seen that, as Aquinas argues, God is the power which enables us to be ourselves. He is not the obstacle to our freedom, but the ground of it. It is by our dependence on him that we come into our own. Dependency, as in all authentic love, is not the opposite of self-determination but the condition of it. If we fell out of God's hands we would be mere automata. Only by participating in his own life of pure freedom can we be free ourselves.

In this sense, the theological tradition recognises that human dependency is ontologically prior to human freedom, and is in some sense the precondition of it. In this, it runs contrary to the notion of the self-moving subject. What characterises human animals most obviously is what characterises all other animals, namely their dependence on Nature, biology and their carers. Unless human infants are tended and nourished, they will die very soon after birth. Indeed, it is well known that human animals, because of what Lacan calls their 'premature' birth, are considerably more dependent on their fellows than, say, calves or piglets. If this is one way in which we differ from our fellow creatures, the other is that our peculiar form of belonging to the world allows us in the end to be more independent of Nature and biology than they are. We are determined in such a way as to be self-determining – self-determining to a much greater degree than slugs or goldfish, which is what we mean by claiming that humans are historical beings. They have the peculiar capacity to make something of what makes them. And this capacity is nowhere more evident than in language.

Sigmund Freud taught us that our primordial dependency is so intense that sundering these bonds is bound to induce a convulsive crisis. Subjectivity is born in trauma. And this trauma persists into our adult life as a festering wound within the psyche, dragging our perceptual and instinctual apparatus out of true and ensuring that we will never wholly recover from the torrid psychical melodrama of our early years. Only the young dream of maturity. Psychoanalysis is the secular world's version of theology in all kinds of ways, but never more so than in its perception that what meagre degree of autonomy we can negotiate for ourselves must be within the context of a deeper dependency. This is indeed a fact about us which the liberal legacy has ignored to its detriment.

If psychoanalysis is a science of anything, it is a science of desire, or of that which fails to find satisfaction. But here, once again, theology has pre-empted it. If desire is what hollows us into non-being for Jacques Lacan, it is just the same for Thomas Aquinas. In his *Summa Theologiae*, Aquinas argues that human beings can never be identical with themselves because desire is the very essence or organising principle of their being. Since to desire is to lack, what makes us what we are is an absence of being. For Aquinas, unlike Lacan, this hankering is ultimately one for God, which is to say that it is the inscription within us of a sovereign good for which we cannot help yearning. The nothingness of God can be felt at work in his subjects in the negativity of desire, which is always an empty excess over and above any specific object. Desire is just the way that the good is built into our material bodies and seizes us independently of the abstract will. It is what orientates our existence, a penchant or predilection which is radically prior to choice. Choice does not go all the way down, whatever marketing executives may imagine. The will for Aquinas is not a strenuous impulse but a primary orientation of our being. We have a natural bent towards well-being, an ineradicable interest in our own flourishing. We cannot choose not to choose the good, however much we might define or distort the notion. Our appetite for what Aquinas calls *beatitudo* or happiness is not in itself optional, any more than our appetite for food is. It is the way our bodies are biased and ballasted towards what is desirable.

Aquinas sees a kind of contradiction here. It is natural for us to desire happiness, but equally natural for us not to attain it, as self-divided, time-torn creatures who are chronically unable to coincide with ourselves. Desire for Aquinas is infinite, just as it is for his psychoanalytical successors. Dissatisfaction is our normative condition, and the perfection we seek would signal the death of our humanity. The only sort of human body which coincides with itself is a corpse – though Aquinas in fact refuses to call a corpse a body. He sees it instead as the remains of one. The Thomist view of the human condition is remarkably similar to the Lacanian one, shorn of its tragic dimension. For the Freudians, the human creature is the neurotic animal – which is to say that, because a degree of repression is essential for us to operate, human beings are sick with desire. For Aquinas, the desire which depletes us into non-being is consummated in the love and knowledge of God, who is both cause and object of it.[3] The self is exiled and unhoused, and in Augustine's words in the *Confessions* will never rest until it rests in its Creator. For Lacan, the bleak truth of humanity consists in persisting doggedly in our exile, refusing to give up on our desire, and renouncing all ideological consolation. Lacanian ethics are a form of ascetic otherworldliness without God.

The semi-myth of the autonomous subject must necessarily reckon without those two mighty champions of early modem rationalism, Hobbes and Spinoza. Thomas Hobbes is an out-and-out determinist; so is Benedictus de Spinoza, for whom freedom is no more than the ignorance of necessity. Nature and humanity for Spinoza are facets of a single system and are governed by the same laws; so that the forces which mould human passions are also those which ordain the fall of a leaf. Men and women are thus far from being autonomous agents, and only the common people labour under this vulgar delusion. It is because they are oblivious of the causes of their own actions that they can entertain the agreeable fantasy known as liberty. Even God is not free to do whatever takes his fancy. He is determined by his divine nature every bit as much as a goldfish is determined by its goldfish-like nature. True freedom lies not in trying to break free of these inexorable laws but in recognising them for what they are and accepting in Stoical spirit that they could not have been different.

If the great rationalists like Spinoza, Hobbes and Leibniz are in grave doubt about the self-determining subject, so are the great empiricists. What is affirmed ethically of the subject – that it can master its own destiny – is at odds with what is claimed of it epistemologically. For as far as knowledge goes, the subject of empiricism is purely passive. For the greatest of British philosophers, David Hume, the mind is simply a receptacle of sensations and perceptions from the 'external world', a phrase which Ludwig Wittgenstein professed himself to have trouble in understanding. But there is no one of these sensations, Hume writes in a celebrated passage, which represents what one might call the self:

For my part, when I enter most intimately into what I call *myself*, I always stumble on some particular perception or other, of heat or cold, light or shade, love or hatred, pain or pleasure. I never catch *myself* at any time without a perception, and never can observe any thing but the perception. When my perceptions are removed for any time, as by sound-sleep; so long am I insensible of *myself,* and may truly be said not to exist.[4]

The repeated italicisation of 'myself' begins to sound increasingly ironic, rather as the phrase 'For my part' is calculatedly mock-modest. If all knowledge resides in the senses, then how could we ever know that immaterial principle called the self which is supposed to weld our various sensations together? And how therefore can we answer the question of why this particular sensation is mine rather than yours? My selfhood cannot be simply a random assemblage of experiences, since all these experiences have something in common, namely that they happen to me. But when I search for this 'me', all I find is this or that discrete experience. The self would seem to be beyond knowledge, just as the form which coheres the various parts of a work of art appears to be invisible. At least, however, this invisible aesthetic form gives itself *in* the various parts, which would not seem to be true of human experience. How then can empiricism account for the coherence and continuity of the subject? Are we really made anew in every moment? Is the fact that this pain is mine rather than yours contingent rather than necessary?

The postmodern bogeyman of the discrete, sharply individuated, self-moving agent is beginning to look a little thin. It starts to look even thinner if we turn to Immanuel Kant, whose work is among other things a response to Hume's scepticism. In his *Critique of Practical Reason*, Kant certainly posits a free, self-determining human subject, as the foundation of his liberal ethics; but it follows from what he has argued in the *Critique of Pure Reason* that this admirably self-responsible subject must be entirely unknowable, both to itself and to others. All we can actually know is the phenomenal world; the subject, by contrast, is a noumenal affair, impenetrable to reason. We know that we are free because we catch ourselves acting that way out of the corner of our eye; but this can never be theoretical knowledge.

What is most precious about the human subject, then, slips through the net of language and presents itself as the purest enigma. Since the subject is no kind of object, it is not 'in' the world at all. It can be regarded only as a perspective on the world, which cannot itself be objectified. Ludwig Wittgenstein will revisit this case in his *Tractatus Logico-Philosophicus*, a work for which the self is no more part of the world than the eye is included within its own field of vision. The task of the philosopher is simply to draw a line around what can be said, leaving all the most important topics unspoken.

At the highpoint of its mastery, then, the modern subject confronts itself as a void. Subjectivity is bound to elude itself in the very effort to objectify itself. In its unfathomable, inarticulable depths, the human subject is an illustration of what the eighteenth century knows as the sublime. It is a formidable black hole at the centre of the cosmos. It has a triumphant edge over all the purely phenomenal objects around it; but, since it can find no reflection of itself in any of these non-subjective things, it suffers a permanent crisis of identity and risks imploding catastrophically upon itself. Where it is most self-assured, it is also most solitary. The modern subject is a manic-depressive or bipolar affair, pitched ceaselessly from the most euphoric self-assertion to an anguished sense of its own vacuity. That it cannot be defined is both its delight and its disaster. It needs some kind of other to confirm its own identity; but, since that other also poses a threat to its autonomy, its instinct is to erase the very otherness which might tell it who it is. This is one reason why the subject is self-blinded at the very peak of its powers. It is both all and nothing, omnipotent and enslaved; and Karl Marx will have something to say about the historical grounds of this remarkable contradiction.

The dialectical legacy from Hegel and German Idealism to Marx and the Frankfurt School has its own way of puncturing the myth of the self-sufficient subject. What it teaches is that there can be no identity without non-identity – which is to say that every identity works by an in-mixture of otherness, subsisting only in relation to what it is not. To speak of identity is already to speak of a structural opening to otherness, rather than of the self-enclosure which is supposedly characteristic of the autonomous subject. Indeed, as the nineteenth century wears on, that dimension of otherness becomes more and more minatory. With Schopenhauer, it takes the form of the voracious Will, which installs itself at the core of our being like some virus or malevolent force, and which is absolutely alien to our happiness and well-being. There is now a power within us which constitutes the very kernel of the self yet is stonily indifferent to us. Subjectivity is what we can least call our own. If Schopenhauer dubs this force the Will, Freud and Lacan will later give it the names respectively of the unconscious and the Real. For Nietzsche, too, Will (though in his case Will-to-Power) is all there is. Both subjects and objects are grammatical fictions, mere spume on the wave of a force which is far more fundamental than either of them. Selfhood is simply another of those ontologically groundless categories of which, however, we have some pragmatic need, and which we therefore posit to augment our flourishing. For Kierkegaard, the self is thrown into perpetual crisis by that relationship to the Other known as religious faith.

We are still no nearer, then, to tracking the liberal-humanist subject to its lair. That it exists somewhere is not to be doubted; but both Marx and Freud rudely dislodge it from whatever sovereignty it still clings to, as the former insists that all the most vital social processes go on 'behind the backs' of the agents involved, and the latter demonstrates that the ego is the mere tip of the vast, submerged iceberg of the unconscious. It is, as Freud remarks, no longer master of its own house. The forces which go into the making of the subject must necessarily be absent from its experience, thrust violently underground, if it is to operate coherently. Repression, in short, is good for us. The subject is therefore never at one with itself, and will bear the wound of this original trauma permanently inscribed within its identity. Louis Althusser will later adapt this model to develop a new theory of ideology. The tragedy of the subject for Jacques Lacan is that there is no single signifier in which it could express itself whole and entire, so that the subject is consequently doomed to hunt for itself along a potentially infinite chain of signifiers, all of which are merely placeholders or metaphors for it. For the subject to articulate itself in a signifier is thus for it to lose itself at that very moment, in a perpetual flickering of presence and absence. The subject, so to speak, disappears down the crevices between its various signifiers, scattered and strung out along an unending chain of meaning, and can be detected only as a kind of low rumbling noise in the hinterland of its own speech.

The most ominous form of negativity for both Freud and Lacan, however, is not this essential inarticulacy but *Thanatos* or the death drive. At the centre of the self we find installed a pure negativity, one which wishes to dismantle the ego and return us to the security of non-being. Nothing is more invulnerable than nothing. The scandalous secret of the human subject is that it actually desires its own destruction, harbouring as it does in its depths a sublimely annihilating force which would reduce it to nothing. It would not perhaps be too hyperbolic to claim that for psychoanalysis, the truth of the subject is death – a claim which brings that theory close to the thought of the Heidegger of *Sein und Zeit,* for whom human existence is always at some level being-towards-death. Adapting Heidegger's categories, the Sartre of *Being and Nothingness* sees consciousness, or the *être pour soi,* as a pure kind of *néant* or negativity. Since to be conscious is always to be conscious of something – since consciousness, in phenomenological jargon, is 'intentional' – there can be no content to subjectivity in itself, which is a practice rather than a substance. For him as for Lacan, we find a pure void or abyss in the inmost reaches of the self. Moreover, our very historicity is a matter of negation, as we continually annul one situation in an empty surge forward to another. This, one might suggest, is the Sartrean version of desire.

What can this Cook's tour of Western philosophy tell us? Simply that the fractured, non-originary, decentred subject did not first see the light of day with modernism, or postmodernism, or poststructuralism. It is not as though there is a single identifiable break between the full, self-present, self-originating subject of, say, the classical realist novel, and the lean, eviscerated creatures of Samuel Beckett. There is, to be sure, a kernel of truth in this suggestion. Roughly speaking, the former kind of subject belongs to capitalism in its buoyant liberal, Enlightenment and industrial heyday, while the latter is far more typical of its later, darker, corporate, crisis-wracked phase. The liberal-humanist subject is secretly the subject of the era of production (including self-production); whereas the so-called decentred subject can be seen as belonging either to the epoch of consumption, consisting as it does in a dispersed network of libidinal desires, or as reflecting the deflation and alienation of the subject under twentieth-century capitalism. But this linear conception, while true as far as it goes, is too simple in itself. It overlooks among other things the extent to which the subject and non-being were associated long before Beckett or Eliot or Kafka burst upon the scene.

A key text here is Joyce's *Ulysses*. In what one might call the surface or 'phenomenal' text of the novel – the day in Dublin – both Stephen and Bloom would seem the familiar, sharply individuated characters of realist fiction, of which the novel is among other things a monstrous parody. The intellectual and the petty bourgeois both appear autonomous and self-motivating enough. From the viewpoint of the novel's Homeric subtext, however, they are no more than functions of a plot which is taking place altogether elsewhere, one which shows up their apparently free actions to be rigorously determined by an invisible network of forces. Or, to put the point in Marxist terms: an old-style individualism lingers on; but, in the new world of monopoly rather than liberal capitalism, it is corporate, anonymous, less tangible forms which covertly call the tune.

It is a familiar case that Beckett's Ireland never really bred the kind of developed liberal, capitalist, middle-class culture which makes for a thriving literary realism. What middle class the country could boast of was small, subordinate and to some extent ethnically alien to the great mass of small tenant Gaelic farmers. Liberal individualism never flourished in traditional Irish culture, which is one reason why Oscar Wilde proved so scandalous to it. An individualism which was commonplace in the urban, Protestant, middle-class, metropolitan nation was audaciously subversive in its agrarian, communalist, Catholic colony. Whereas the commonsensical British tend to believe in a substantive private self beneath the public mask, Wilde and Yeats adhered to the truth of masks themselves. Identity was less an essence underlying the mask than what was constructed by it. One thinks also of the mid-nineteenth-century Irish poet James Clarence Mangan, with his flaxen-coloured wig, waxen, Andy-Warhol-like complexion, outsize green spectacles, false teeth, two bulky umbrellas (one for each arm), exotic hat and bottle of tar water, a man whose whole identity was mask-like and calculatedly inauthentic, rather like his poetry. For all of these writers, the distinction between mask and reality could be dismantled: the truth of the self, if any such grandiose entity could be said to exist in Irish culture, could be expressed only through a device or persona. For Wilde in particular, selfhood is protean, pliable and pluralistic, endlessly reinvented rather than brutely given. If this makes him a postmodernist *avant la lettre*, it also harks back to a turbulent Irish history in which identity is always doubled, precarious and unstable. Postmodernists tend rather callowly to celebrate this condition; the Irish were aware of just how painful it could be.

Much of that pain is transmitted through the work of Samuel Beckett, a man who sprang from a declining social class in Ireland which at the time of the founding of the Free State was regarded by a good many nationalists as amounting to little or nothing. That little or nothing is also Beckett's writing, which is as slim as is compatible with (just) existing, and which purges all trace of what one might call the expressive personality. Subjectivity is relentlessly mechanised and externalised, as it often is in Swift. There is no modish celebration of the fragmented subject in Beckett; there is rather a sense that, however dire such a condition may be, it is probably preferable to viewing the self as the robust agent of its own destiny. Beckett is averse to that conception partly because he came to consciousness in a colonial culture that was in the process of achieving collective self-determination, and as a middle-class Protestant intellectual felt estranged from that project; but he is also suspicious of it because, in a world after fascism, self-affirmation has too sinister an infinity with mass murder. It is as though all action after Auschwitz is garbage. Better to suffer the pains of self-dispossession than court the perils of dominion. One must back the beggar man against the king. Only by some extreme form of *kenosis* or self-emptying could one expiate the crimes which flow from an inflated sense of human agency, both fascist and Stalinist. You cannot answer those crimes with vigorous actions of your own (though Beckett the *maquisard* did exactly that), since to do so would be to remain within the same noxious frame of reference, make a move within the same lethal game.

This, as it happened, proved too gloomy a perspective. What brought Hitler to his knees was a collective action, and the same was to happen forty years later with neo-Stalinism. There is a limit to what Hegel called the labour of the negative, as is evident, too, in the case of deconstruction. The stark, solitary, scooped-out subject, for all its imaginative fertility, is not the only response to the Pozzos of this world. Even so, it figures in Beckett as a kind of negative utopia. A world of diminished subjects whose language is only ever an inch or so from silence is at least a non-injurious one, since men and women in this attenuated sphere lack even the kind of agency they would need to skewer one another. By the same token, however, they lack the kind of agency which might enable them to resist such atrocities, which cannot be said of the real-life Beckett. In a kind of imaginative homeopathy, the problem becomes the solution: the sadly dwindled state to which twentieth-century barbarism has reduced men and women is also a prophylactic against the powers which have brought them so low. You cannot pick a quarrel with the wellnigh-dead. The point of the death drive is to save us from the unseemly buffetings of this world by returning us to an inanimate, pre-egoic state; and Beckett's characters are somewhere en route to this deeply desirable goal, some of them rather more advanced along the path than others. But since there is no death in his work, just as there is no end to writing and no closure to consciousness, these characters are not yet able to take refuge in this immortal sanctuary altogether, but are caught like the living dead in some twilight or subliminal state, unable quite to shake off the long disease known as life however much they are falling apart at the seams.

What Beckett shares with the post-structuralists is a fear of determinacy. In the wake of Hitler and the Gulag, there is something profoundly disturbing about the *proposition*. It belongs to a grammar of violence. Too many have perished of absolute truth in the modem age. Certainty can be lethal, but irony and ambiguity can act as antidotes. To deconstruct the proposition is a political move, and for Beckett the word 'perhaps' is an anti-fascist weapon. By the time of Jacques Derrida, this nervousness of the determinate has become a wellnigh pathological aversion to it, so that the emphatic or impassioned begins to look incorrigibly vulgar. It is true that too much belief can make you ill, but so can too little. One can die of scepticism, like Martin Decoud in Conrad's *Nostromo*, just as surely as one can drown in a surfeit of doctrine. *Pace* the Derrideans, indeterminacy is not always on the side of the political angels. There are times when conviction is preferable to confusion. The vacant subject is not always more progressive than the replete one. One should not encourage a dogmatism of undecidability. There is a creative sort of nothingness, which as in Beckett consists in a sense of the extreme frailty and finitude of the human, and which is the foundation of any authentic ethics or politics. There is also the negativity of the nihilist, for whom the very idea that one value might be more precious than another provokes a cackle of relativist laughter. It is hard to see how this particular form of nothingness can resist the insolence of power.

The radical-Protestant deity is a hidden God, one who has turned his hinderparts to the world. His withdrawal then provokes a crisis of neurotic uncertainty in his subjects, akin to Vladimir and Estragon's anxiety about the coming of Godot. Despite its delight in ritual, *Waiting for Godot* is a profoundly Protestant text, and not only in its austere rejection of papist frippery. If the Other is inaccessible to us, how do we know that he has recognised us for what we are? How, as the Lacanians inquire, are we to recognise recognition? Would such recognition be a specific kind of act, or are we being acknowledged all the time without knowing it? How would we identify Godot in any case, were he to come? Has he arrived already? Did the two tramps mistake the name 'Godot' for 'Pozzo'? Ambiguity is curse as well as blessing. It may retrieve us from the clutches of the autocrats, but only at the cost of plunging us into a state of chronic ontological anxiety. If Beckett is decisive about at least one thing, it is that this, in the end, is the only choice. One may admire the starkness of this dichotomy without signing on for it.

Notes

1 See Dermot Moran, 'Wandering from the path: *navigatio* in the philosophy of John Scottus Eriugena', *The Crane Bag Book of Studies*, 2:1 and 2 (Dublin: Blackwater Press, 1978), p. 244–51.

2 William King, *Sermon on Predestination* (Dublin, 1709). See also *Archbishop King's Sermon on Predestination*, ed. Andrew Carpenter (Dublin: Cadenus Press, 1976), p. 143.

3 See Stephen Wang, 'Aquinas on human happiness and the natural desire for God', *New Blackfriars*, 88:1015 (May 2007), 322–34.

4 David Hume, *A Treatise of Human Nature* (London: Routledge, 1985), p. 300.

Introduction
Beckett and nothing: trying to understand Beckett

Daniela Caselli

> Best worse no farther. Nohow less. Nohow worse. Nohow naught.
> Nohow on.
>   Said nohow on. (Samuel Beckett, *Worstward Ho*)
>
> In unending ending or beginning light. Bedrock underfoot. So no sign
> of remains a sign that none before. No one ever before so – (Samuel
> Beckett, *The Way*)[1]

What not

On 21 April 1958 Samuel Beckett writes to Thomas MacGreevy
about having written a short stage dialogue to accompany the
London production of *Endgame*.[2] A fragment of a dramatic dialogue, paradoxically entitled *Last Soliloquy*, has been identified as
being the play in question.[3] However, John Pilling, in more recent
research on the chronology, is inclined to date *Last Soliloquy* as
post-*Worstward Ho* and pre-*What Is the Word*, on the basis of a
letter sent by Phyllis Carey to Beckett on 3 February 1986, on the
reverse of which we find jottings referring to the title *First Last
Words* with material towards *Last Soliloquy*.[4] If we accept this new
dating hypothesis, the manuscripts of this text (UoR MS 2937/1–3)
– placed between two late works often associated with nothing –
indicate two speakers, P and A (tentatively seen by Ruby Cohn
as Protagonist and Antagonist) and two ways in which they can
deliver their lines, D for declaim and A (somewhat confusingly)
for normal.[5] Unlike Cohn, I read A and P as standing for 'actor' and
'prompter', thus explaining why the text is otherwise puzzlingly
entitled a soliloquy and supporting her hypothesis that the lines

'Fuck the author. Fuck all authors' underline the rehearsed quality of the suicide.

There are three holographs of this incomplete text: MS 2937/1 is the longest version, consisting of four sheets of paper, with a substantial section of the third page, numbered 2 in the manuscript, crossed out; this is followed by a single sheet in which both MS 2937/3 and MS 2937/2 appear, the latter placed at the bottom of the page. MS 2937/3 contains four exchanges between P and A, while MS 2937/2 consists of five lines, no longer attributed to any of the two speakers. This dialogue laboriously stages a theatrical death by drinking poison, rehearsed by A and prompted by P (as quoted below, the initials A and P are inconsistently followed by a full stop).

In a letter of 26 April 1980, as S. E. Gontarski and Antony Uhlmann remind us,[6] Beckett responded to Joseph Chaikin's request for permission to adapt *Stories and Texts for Nothing* by suggesting staging a single 'Text for nothing' as follows: 'Curtain up on speechless author (A) still or moving or alternately. Silence broken by recorded voice (V) speaking opening of text. A takes over. Breaks down. V again. A again. So on. Till text completed piecemeal. Then spoken through, more or less hesitantly, by A alone. Prompts not always successful, i.e., not regular alternation VAVA. Sometimes: Silence, V, silence, V again, A. Or even three prompts before A can speak.' This staging, ultimately rejected by Chaikin, was, in Beckett's words of 5 September of the same year, a method 'valid only for a single text. The idea was to caricature the labour of composition.'[7] It is tempting to read *Last Soliloquy* as such a caricature, as if Beckett were following his own suggestions for the staging of a 'text for nothing', doomed, for reasons different from those of Chaikin, to be in turn rejected and jettisoned. P can be read as the gatekeeper of the letter of the text (he twice threatens to leave A if he does not 'stick to the book') and of the intended meaning ('A (D) All man can. Have with myself away. (Pause. N.) With myself away. / [erased words] What you suppose that means? / P. Nothing left but to away with yourself.'). Nevertheless, the letter of the text is itself far from self-evident in the words of P, missing as they do the defining verb which would equate suicide with the 'nothing left': 'Nothing left but to away with yourself' as opposed to 'Nothing left but to do away with yourself'. Later, an exasperated A wants to have done with the lines and with himself away and adduces as his excuse to accelerating the process the fact that nobody 'will know'; P, however, replies that the author will. At which point the 'Fuck the author. Fuck all authors' line is delivered (as if it were not a line), and P then leads the attention back to the text. The manuscript stages the complex relationship between text, hidden and yet all-pervasive authorial control, P and A as different kinds of interpreters, and the possibility of an audience and its reactions. The process of 'having with oneself away', of swooning or dropping and putting an end to this drivel about what and what not is a double staging, where the register alternates between the normal and the declamatory; both are, however – to borrow from Shane Weller's discussion of nihilism in Beckett – *du théâtre*.[8] The author is evoked as a menacing and potentially displeased entity by P, but is otherwise absent; the text has a letter and yet needs to be interpreted, and discussed, by two very different readers such as A and P are; and A dutifully plays the role of the actor in search of a stable interpretation for the lines he is supposed to deliver.[9] Eager to find an explanation, or a meaning, this typology of actor has become a familiar figure in Beckett criticism, in which Beckett's repeated refusals to provide psychological explanations for his characters' behaviour are legendary.[10]

Last Soliloquy is a good example of a text belonging to the grey canon that has recently been receiving increased critical attention,[11] a text that was, until not long ago, nothing for most people aside from specialists. It is also a text that rehearses some of the central preoccupations with nothing that a number of scholars have identified in Beckett and that this volume wants to both analyse further and question. It does so by engaging with 'little' nothings, 'what nots', and having these partial, temporary, unsatisfactory 'nothings' enter into a dialogue that threatens to turn them into something else. *Last Soliloquy* is, I would argue, a text that 'returns to the scene of its betrayals', from its very opening lines: 'A (D) I am done. All? I – / P Have. / A (N) What? / P Have done. I have done. / A: Better one. Stronger.' This 'abandoned work' echoes incipits from *Waiting for Godot* (E: 'nothing to be done') to *Endgame* (C: 'Finished, it's finished, nearly finished, it must be nearly finished') via the desire for exhaustion of the *Texts for Nothing* and some of the *Fizzles*. However, it also, and perhaps more heavy-handedly than both *Worstward Ho* and *What Is the Word*, reads as a 'caricature of the labour of composition', and in this respect Cohn's analogy

with *Catastrophe* and *Fragment du théâtre II* stands: 'Ten words
two mistakes', P drily points out to A, forcing him to take it from
the top, hindering the progress toward the drinking of the goblet of
poison.[12] In line with much of the canon, the text exploits the fact
that (as Denise Riley has pointed out in a book which characterises
Beckett's late monologues as 'a stoical embodiment of sheer utterance set against pathos') 'there's humour in the not quite dead.
Out of a satirical weekly, Freud clipped a joke about the old adage:
"Never to be born would be the best thing for mortal men." – But,
adds the philosophical comment in *Fliegende Blätter*, this happens
to scarcely one person in a hundred thousand.'[13] The echoes of
previous works are generated at a dizzying speed in this text, from
the 'what not' structure of *Watt* to the oral pleasure in the repetition of 'swoon too soon', paralleling Krapp's delight in the round-
ness of his spools ('Spool! [*Pause*] Spooool! [*Happy smile. Pause
. . .*]'). Almost a compendium of how Beckett's theatre – moving
towards an ever-increasing paring down – deals with nothing, this
text also mounts an 'approach to nothing that is to be produced
in performance', which, as Stephen Thomson argues in Chapter 4
below on *Footfalls*, 'operates not by the simple removal of things
but by their interaction, their "busy life", even by their addition'.[14]
Rather than being merely a stripped down 'stoical utterance' this
soliloquy is focused on the relation between the what not and the
not what. The difference between 'What not if not what' and 'What
not if not what not' is presented as the difference between getting
the (invisible original) script right or wrong; but, unlike the actor,
we do not seem to have a prompter who can guarantee – however
infuriating that may also be – our interpretation of the text, and
are left with that movement back and forth 'by way of neither' that
John Pilling, Stephen Thomson, Derval Tubridy, Laura Salisbury
and Peter Boxall discuss from different perspectives in the course
of this volume:

P. (prompting) Then what?
A. Then what? What not? If not all what not? What not done? What
    if not all done not done? What? What not? (N.) What now?
P. (prompting) What not if not . . .
A. (N.) Not what?
P. (prompting) What not.
A. (N.) What not if not what not?
    [. . .]

What is remarkable in this manuscript is also the comic eager-
ness of the actor not only to have done with this 'drivel' but also
to 'drop dead' by quickly (too quickly for P) quaffing the poison
from his theatrical goblet. In line with the rest of the Beckett
canon, however, such ending can never quite take place, and the
piece ends with the actor alternating his swooning and dropping
'too soon' with the prompter's fantasy of fame and acclaim. Not
unlike what happens in *What Where*, the text voiced by the speakers repeats the movement of the text itself: A questions P on the
sense that 'what not if not what not' makes, and P. comically and
enigmatically replies:

P   Did all sense what he didn't.
A   Couldn't.
P. Right. What couldn't he didn't.
A. Didn't couldn't.
P. Right.
    (Pause)

This last soliloquy for two voices makes us unsure that we have
actually heard the 'last words first' uttered: the last words of
the soliloquy seem to be 'what not if not what not?', declared,
as above, to be the correct version by P, who is, however, soon
losing his credibility as a guide, having just assented to A's 'didn't
couldn't' and thus given up on his reading of the letter of the (for
us invisible) script. Furthermore, in line with the paradox of the
title, the last words could be seen as being 'cue me in darling'
(which is the last line in MS 2937/1), or, if we were to really
'stick to the book', the lonely letter P, hanging in mid-air after the
last line. This literal reading, however, unlike what P promises
to A, is no guarantee against being abandoned, no matter how
faithful to the text we remain. *Last Soliloquy* attacks the vanity of
actor ('fuck the author'), the fantasies of the prompter ('Ovation')
and that of 'the labour of composition'. By having A asking again
for the cue and leaving P dangling in mid-air, the text indicates
that the labour is indeed not finished, even after the hypothesised
curtain has dropped, like the actor himself. MS 2937/2 sums up
the situation in four brief lines, echoing the smile (although that
was 'toothless for preference') at the end of *That Time*: 'Smile
first. / Smile? / (from text) Long smile. / (Smile off). Quaff. /
Drop.'

Little nothings

On 26 April 2006, to mark the occasion of Beckett's centenary, *The Onion* published an article under the title 'Scholars discover 23 blank pages that may as well be lost Samuel Beckett play'. Parisian scholars – the article claimed – 'uncovered a small stack of blank paper', 'the latest example of the late Irish-born writer's genius'. A 'natural progression from his earlier works, including *Breath*, a 30-second play with no characters, and 1972's *Not I*, in which the only illuminated part of the stage is a floating mouth', these blank pages are allegedly praised by literary scholar Eric Matheson for 'the bare-bones structure and bleak repetition of what can only be described as "nothingness"'.[15] The spoof article identifies and mocks what is by now often taken to be the defining, almost clichéd characteristic of Beckett's work: its engagement with 'nothing', or, as the *Onion*'s Sartrean inflection has it, Nothingness.[16] Ironising on the industry spinning around this Beckettian 'very little, almost nothing', *The Onion* also attacks the way in which 'crrrritics!' (a classic Beckettian insult in *Waiting for Godot*, matched only by 'architect' in the French version) project their fantasies of an all-controlling genius on to this nothing.

To dig up a jettisoned, unfinished, and paradoxical text such as *Last Soliloquy* may appear as dangerously encroaching on *Onion* territory; and yet I would argue that it helps us to reflect precisely on the ways in which trying to understand Beckett's engagement with nothing can cast some light on issues at the forefront of contemporary discussions of his work. Indeed, it can help us to see how *The Onion*, by qualifying nothing in Beckett as a cliché, places itself firmly on the side of common sense by claiming to be able to 'rigorously distinguish between clichéd and non-clichéd readings of an *oeuvre* [. . .] in which the nature of cliché is itself both thematized and problematized'.[17]

'Nothing' has been at the centre of Beckett's reception and scholarship from its inception. Beckett criticism was characterised in its early stages by a sustained attention to nothing as a philosophical concept. As Peter Boxall has pointed out, 'initial responses to Beckett's drama by critics such as Vivian Mercier and Martin Esslin and the important work by Hugh Kenner and Ruby Cohn arguably responded to Beckettian nothing rather in the manner that Georges Duthuit approaches the inexpressive "predicament" suffered by Bram van Velde'.[18] Attention to nothing (perhaps more than anywhere else in Esslin's much debated notion of the 'theatre of the absurd') has often been directed towards a basic condition of humanity, so that a 'groundlessness of being' is soon metamorphosed into 'the ground of Beckett's writing, that an uncompromising expression of the meaningless of the human condition becomes the expressive occasion of his work, and of the experience of being more generally'.[19] In Alain Robbe-Grillet, for instance, being is read as having a nothing at its core, with Beckett as the playwright able to stage such nothing, to give it a material shape. The importance of this tradition cannot be underestimated, since – as Stephen Thomson points out in Chapter 4 below on the late theatre – recent theories on the increasing importance of Beckett's theatrical image over drama still address the preoccupation with nothing on stage.[20] To see the late theatre as pared down to almost nothing and favouring image and movement over dialogue, is to follow in the steps of a tradition that privileges 'nothing' on stage while exposing that the nothing that critics such as Martin Esslin, Vivien Mercier and Alain Robbe-Grillet had perceived in *Waiting for Godot* and *Endgame* was far too full of somethings.

Theodor Adorno, who in his 'Trying to understand *Endgame*' (1958) argued that the nothing which characterises the Beckett stage (and page) could not be read as a content, exploded (possibly even before it had become an ingrained critical tradition) the comforting association between Beckett and existentialism which characterises, one may argue, some of the early work on Beckett, but which is still an important legacy in Beckett studies (and not always a disabling one, as anyone who teaches Beckett is quick to discover). For Adorno, 'drama cannot simply take negative meaning, or the absence of meaning, as its content without everything peculiar to it being affected to the point of turning into its opposite'.[21] This is why for him Sartre's conventional theatre delivered nothing as a message, thus reducing theatre to 'a clattering machinery for the demonstration of worldviews';[22] unlike Sartre's *pièces*, Beckett's plays resisted – through their form and structure – having their nothing transformed into something. 'We are not beginning to . . . to . . . mean something?' Hamm asks Clov in *Endgame*, turning upside-down the assumption that something on stage can mean nothing, even in plays in which 'nothing happens, twice', as Vivien Mercier famously said of *Waiting for Godot*.

Nothing remains a central preoccupation in the criticism after Adorno; no critical tradition has been able to disengage from the

problem of nothing in Beckett, and for good reasons, even if sometimes, as P. J. Murphy has recently argued, this happened at the
expense of being able to trace 'alternative dimensions of his work
of a more affirmative nature.'[23] What happens to nothing, however,
is distinctly different in those critics who, marking a break with
previous humanist readings of Beckett, started looking at nothing
both as a possibility and as a problem, such as Steven Connor,
Leslie Hill, Thomas Trezise and Carla Locatelli.[24] Both texts and
performance cease to be, in these critical contribution, 'a place
where nothingness yields itself up to expression'[25] and, focusing on
how the human occurs in Beckett under the sign of disavowal, see
nothingness as part of a subjectivity unable to coincide with itself.
With hindsight, the danger for critics working within a humanist tradition was that of turning 'the human' into an allegedly
knowable and shared entity, which could flip its negativity into a
positivity precisely thanks to this essential quality. Similarly, the
danger of some criticism produced within a tradition interested in
decentred subjectivities and negative self-reflectivity was that of
hypostatising in the past scholarship a fullness that was probably
never quite as solid as one might have wished. This is, in brief,
Eagleton's position with regards to the history of philosophy in the
foreword to this volume; such a critique, in turn, can be suspected
of caricaturing postmodernists and post-structuralists as card-
carrying Derrideans more interested in the opacity of their own
and other's writing than in the painstaking business of elucidation
which remains an essential trait of this criticism.[26] Beckett's work,
one can say after Connor in 1988, 'seems to undermine not only
the particular claims of his individual critics, but the more general
claims upon which they often rest and from which they derive their
authority'.[27] As most of the critics mentioned here already made
clear in the early 1990s, however, even this self-reflective form of
resistance in Beckett's work cannot be, in turn, metamorphosed
into a stable value, as interventions focused on nihilism[28] unsaying
and 'unwording',[29] negative space in Beckett's theatre,[30] irony,[31]
Zen,[32] the body[33] and authority[34] have demonstrated.

All done unsaid

The all-controlling eye of the invisible author, able to tell the difference between 'what not' and 'not what' in the soliloquy even if

nobody else can, is both a comic and a serious staging of one of the main paradoxes of the Beckett canon. Analysing the ways in which Dante appears in the Beckett oeuvre, I have argued that Dante is assumed as a source of literary and cultural authority while also participating in the texts' sceptical undermining of authority.[35] This point can be extended beyond Dante, and, as *Last Soliloquy* makes clear, applies to repetition, parody and 'caricature' of Beckett's own texts too. *Last Soliloquy* can be read both as a pared-down version of Beckett's late theatre, advertising an especially parodic take on the movement towards finishing, and as an exercise in accretion, where the textual lives of 'not', 'what not' and 'nothing' are collected, from *Murphy* to *Watt*, from *Godot* and *Endgame* to *What Is the Word*. In a much less lyrical register than either *Worstward Ho* or *What Is the Word*, *Last Soliloquy* implicates itself and the main actors of its theatre (author, prompter, actor, audience) as sources of authority which undermine authority (the 'labour of composition'). Through its back and forth movement, these jettisoned pages endorse and resist what is tempting in Beckett, that is, not only filling in the nothing, or turning it into something, but also project and apply this nothing to a figure, to the image of Beckett the author, whose giant black-and-white pictures reproduced on the banners lining central Dublin were looking down on us during the April 2006 Irish Literature Festival celebrating the centenary of his birth. The black-and-white reproductions of the rather stark and forbidding face of the author claimed to be recognising the nothing at the core of Beckett, indeed claimed to be faithful to it through their employment of a minimalist style that is however far from being 'immune from the grip of commodity aesthetics'.[36] By going for the 'critically minimal' as if it were a product to be possessed and marketed, rather than laboured for, the iconic presence of the author seemed to be watching us to see if we ever wanted, like A in *Last Soliloquy*, 'to swoon too soon'.

This cultural phenomenon mirrors the problems encountered even by those critics who have scrupulously avoided seeing negation, nihilism and nothing as containers to be filled with a philosophical meaning or mere disabling mechanisms that force the reader into silence. In many instances, a resistance to both these positions is accompanied however by the notion of an author too complex, too skilful, or – we could say with an adjective that has always been circulating in Beckett studies, even if often under the sign of disavowal – too *good* to be reduced to any one system. Like most Beckett scholars, I share a hard-won appreciation of his oeuvre, of its complex mechanisms of recuperation and resistance, but I remain intrigued by how the Beckett oeuvre, through its paradoxical fidelity to nothing, produces critical approaches which aspire to putting an end to interpretation: in this instance, the issues of authority, intertextuality and context, which this volume tackles via 'nothing'.

These are, I would argue, central problems at the forefront of Beckett studies today. By retracing the history of Beckett studies through 'nothing', this volume is also a way of taking stock of the present moment in Beckett studies. Criticism is to some extent linked to an economy of the new (as it was, albeit in less neo-liberal forms, even before the scholarly field took on late capitalist forms of exchange) which intrinsically clashes with a Beckettian poetics in which 'the sun' shines 'having no alternative, on the nothing new'[37] and in which even the negation of the new has a textual history that negates its inauguratory function.[38] Bearing this in mind, P. J. Murphy in his *Beckett's Dedalus: Dialogical Engagements with Joyce in Beckett's Fiction* claims that the two most fruitful ways forward in the field have been renewed understanding of historical specific contexts and engagements with what Peter Boxall describes in this volume as 'influences and legacies'.[39]

The issue of nothing, because of its simultaneous protean malleability and stubborn resistance, has given rise in this volume to discussion of historically specific contexts and issues of intertextuality (both in Beckett and in artists who have turned to his work). 'Context' is a word seemingly impervious to any possible form of attack: how could we not welcome more specific historical research that places Beckett within the history of film, of television, of Ireland, of music, of visual art? Jonathan Bignell's Chapter 7 in this volume looks at the material history of televisual production and places the aesthetic concerns of Beckett's television plays within a nuanced context that takes into account the formation of ideas of television aesthetics, appropriateness and economical concerns. Matthijs Engelberts's contribution (Chapter 9) digs up reviews and comments within cinema studies and popular film publication in order to use 'nothing' as a category to interrogate the fraught relation between cinema and literature in *Film*, thus providing a historical context for Bignell's previous work on authority in *Film*.

Catherine Laws (Chapter 10) discusses the nexus between nothing and silence in order to analyse the specific relations between music, sound, and hearing from *Dream of Fair to Middling Women* to *Ghost Trio* and *neither*. Russell Smith (Chapter 11) goes back to biographical narratives (a former no-no of a certain critical tradition) and mobilises them in order to see how Beckett can speak to contemporary criticism aiming at recuperating affect in literature and culture. This is seen as a viable notion able to overcome some of the dead-ends of post-structuralism without forgetting how these have been fruitful forms of critique to widely held humanist assumptions. Bill Prosser (Chapter 5) looks at something that has remained a 'nothing' within the Beckett canon so far: his doodles as they appear in the *Human Wishes* manuscript. Prosser uses them to interrogate aesthetic theory and questions a reading of doodles which sees them simply as a means to guess the psychological state of the author or his hidden motivation. By devoting detailed attention to these little nothings that seem to deflect attention from themselves while being the outcome of boredom, Prosser provides us with a new context in which to rethink the role of marginality, tedium and relations between the textual and the visual in the canon. Enoch Brater (Coda), in his brief personal recollection in which the complex, funny and even melancholic sounds of nothing resonate, also provides us with a context in which a memoir becomes a history of interpretation. Terry Eagleton, in the foreword to the volume, revisits the debates around Beckett as the twentieth-century writer able to undo both the liberal-humanist subject as 'the subject of the era of production' and the 'so-called decentred subject'. Analysing Beckett's protestant and middle-class Irishness and his historical and geographical locations, the foreword polemically shows the dangers of reading Beckett as annihilating subjectivity, as turning subjectivity into nothing. Focusing on the ambivalent attitude of the Beckett oeuvre towards nothing, Eagleton maintains that there is 'no modish celebration of the fragmented subject in Beckett' and that, if Beckett 'shares with the post-structuralist a fear of determinacy', 'ambiguity is a curse as well as a blessing' in his work.[40]

In this respect, these pieces contribute to a renewed interest in context in Beckett studies. But, if context seems an approach beyond reproach, it is not without pitfalls. If the importance in Beckett of the familiar, the material, the domestic, the situated cannot be underestimated (as indeed it has been), the notion of context can nevertheless act as the promise of full meaning, of 'restoring' the Beckett oeuvre to its 'heart', to adapt *Dream*'s sarcastically sweetish expression.[41] Context, in other words, can promise to finally deliver a solid materialism that the Beckett oeuvre seems instead stubbornly to both promise and rebuff. This is why the contributors to this volume treat history (the history of music, television, film, philosophy and materiality itself) as a set of complex, if not necessarily unstable, narratives. These narratives demand, just as the primary texts do, careful scrutiny and analysis in order not to be simply turned back either into supplements to texts which continue to prove too disquieting or into replacements for some form of solidity which the notion of the human has, for quite a long time, been unable to provide. To trace contexts for Beckett's peculiarly variable nothings does not, in other words, let us off the hook: we still have to carry on that labour of interpretation that David Cunningham has persuasively argued, after Adorno, to be of central importance,[42] and that John Pilling describes in Chapter 7 as 'the relationship between "not", "need", "nothing" and . . . "going on"'. Also, to find a context, and to argue for the importance of a context in the awareness of the difficulties that any historical narratives presents us with, does not take us back to a crass form of relativism. As Laura Salisbury's Chapter 12 demonstrates, to argue for the real is very different from stubbornly asserting that the real is there for all to see.

Context, therefore, cannot be the panacea to a Beckett criticism 'bogged down' both by the difficulty of being able to say something about Beckett's nothing and by the fact that this lack of mastery easily flips over into yet another form of mastery, this time projected on to the author. This volume, through contributors such as John Pilling, Laura Salisbury, Mladen Dolar, Shane Weller, Peter Boxall, therefore focuses – through attention to variable incarnation of the nothing in Beckett – on the issue of value in Beckett. These authors look at what we could broadly define as influence in Beckett, from the role of Beckett's fascination with neurology (Salisbury) to his engagement with philosophy (Dolar; Weller), from the role of self-repetition in the oeuvre (Pilling) to the ways in which Beckett's nothing has been trasmuted and put to use by writers such as Sebald and Coetzee (Boxall).

The relation between intertextuality and the recourse to manuscript study is one at the core of a reconsideration of 'nothing'. As Stephen Thomson has argued, the crucial and painstaking work of manuscript studies 'raises some curious critical quandaries': in the words of Dirk Van Hulle, 'drafts open up interpretive possibilities that cannot be perceived in the final version, and yet they form an "underlying" presence. Whether or not the knowledge of these presences is necessary or even relevant to a richer understanding of the final version is perhaps not the most crucial issue.'[43] If the effort should not necessarily be aimed at reinstating cut material to produce an Ur-text, then it is essential to explore how the 'very little, almost nothing' we have in front of us – the result of a process of distillation, of cuts as opposed to accretion (as Dolar points out in his chapter) – promises to be of value.[44]

By looking at intertextuality in Beckett, the volume wants to tackle this sort of critical investment; this is not to dispute – as our practice makes clear – the central role of manuscripts in the oeuvre, but to avoid using manuscripts (and context, and authority) as a way of bringing interpretation to a close. To put it slightly differently, we are at a critical point in Beckett studies in which new textual resources should not be let to 'speak for themselves' but should be recognised as part of that interminable process of interpretation which characterised the published canon. I have argued elsewhere in favour of a reading of manuscripts that brings to the fore issues of marginality at the centre of the Beckett canon, rather than relegating them as a marginal which can constantly be recuperated as origin.[45] Smith, Salisbury, Dolar, Boxall, Tubridy, Weller and many other contributors to this volume (among them myself in this Introduction) employ letters, manuscripts and interviews not only because these prove their points but also because they are part of a wider reconsideration of value and the limits of interpretation in the oeuvre. However, in this volume neither intertextuality (or even the more affectively invested 'influence') nor context are simply welcomed with the sigh of relief that seems to have characterised their recent critical reception. They do not allow us to finally stop worrying about issues that elude the aesthetics and let us go back to good, honest, uncomplicated spade work: critics as diverse as Pilling, Cohn and Connor have always known that archive work was never that. Persuasive literary criticism has always, be it labelled humanist or post-structuralist, built its argument on the close reading of texts, be they published or in manuscript form. The archive may interestingly complicate the picture, but it does not simply bring us back to the comforting stability of authorial intentionality. When Mladen Dolar (Chapter 3) traces, through the relation between Beckett and nothing, the relation between voice and stone in Sartre and Beckett, we are reminded precisely of the importance of the history of an idea, even the ideas of context, influence, and history. When Laura Salisbury (Chapter 12) talks about the history of materiality through that of neurology and brings the two into a dialogue sustained by Beckett texts, letters and notebooks, she is arguing against the collapse of a history of materiality into a materiality of history that can simply be taken for granted. When Peter Boxall (Chapter 2) theorises a future for the study of Beckett's legacies he is, at the same time, interested in the constant problem of value in the oeuvre. A value which – because it cannot be assigned *a priori* to a certain position – derives from not knowing where you are 'with' Beckett and may even point to a reconsideration of the place of ethics in literary criticism. When John Pilling draws a history of 'not' within the Beckett oeuvre, he reads the notebooks to *Watt* as part of an interminable 'going on without in Beckett', which cannot be stopped.

The last line of the self-translation of *Je suis ce cours de sable qui glisse* reads 'My peace is there in the receding mist / when I may cease from treading these long shifting thresholds / and live the space of a door / that opens and shut'.[46] Perhaps the nothing peculiar to Beckett lies there: the peace is in the indefinite place of the receding mist, the wish is to cease 'trading these long shifting thresholds' and to live in a paradoxically impossible space, not immune, however, from a dialectic movement. Like in the case of the strip of light in *Footfalls*, it is important, when staging our critical theatres of the Beckett oeuvre, not to let this impossible 'space of a door / that opens and shut' grow a landing around it.[47]

Notes

1 Samuel Beckett, *The Way*, first published as 'Crisscross to infinity' in *College Literature*, 8:3 (1981). This alternative title, Ruby Cohn points out, was 'foisted on Beckett'. Holographs and typescripts of *The Way* are held at the HRC, with photocopies at UoR. See UoR MS 3218. Ruby Cohn, *A Beckett Cannon* (Ann Arbor: University of Michigan Press, 2001), p. 269.

2 John Pilling, *A Samuel Beckett Chronology* (Basingstoke: Palgrave Macmillan, 2006), p. 140.

3 *Ibid.*, p. 140, and Ruby Cohn, *A Beckett Canon*, p. 241. See also C. J. Ackerley and S. E. Gontarski, *The Grove Companion to Samuel Beckett* (New York: Grove Press, 2004), p. 309.

4 I would like to thank John Pilling for generously sharing this information.

5 Cohn, *A Beckett Canon*, p. 241. Although 'N.' is used in the body of the text to indicate the 'normal' tone of voice, at the top right of page 1 of the manuscript we read: 'D = declaim A = Normal'.

6 S.E. Gontarski, 'From unabandoned works: Samuel Beckett's short prose', *Samuel Beckett: The Complete Short Prose 1929–1989* (New York: Grove Press, 1995), p. xvi; Anthony Uhlmann, *Samuel Beckett and the Philosophical Image* (Cambridge: Cambridge University Press, 2006), p. 51.

7 Gontarski, 'From unabandoned', p. xvi.

8 Shane Weller, *A Taste for the Negative: Beckett and Nihilism* (Oxford: Legenda, 2005), p. 170.

9 There is no indication of the gender of either P and A in the manuscript, but the role of the heroic solitary actor places A quite firmly in a masculine position.

10 Perhaps a less well-known instance in this genealogy is Beckett's letter to Alan Schneider of 21 November 1957 regarding *Endgame*, recently discussed by Matthew Feldman. After recalling his thoughts on the pre-Socratics, Beckett interprets the Sophist paradox of the 'Heap and the Bald Head' and refers to the 'Old Greek'. Alice and Kenneth Hamilton, in *Condemned to Life: The World of Samuel Beckett* (Grand Rapids, MI: Erdman 1976), propose the identification of the 'Old Greek' with Eubulides (linked with Alexinus). Beckett could easily in his memory of Whilhelm Windelband's *A History of Philosophy* (New York: Macmillan [1893] 1907) have confused Eubulides and the more often touted Zeno; see Windelband, p. 89. 'One purpose of the image throughout the play', Beckett writes, 'is to suggest the impossibility logically, i.e. eristically, of the "thing" ever coming to an end. "The end is the beginning and yet we go on." In other words the impossibility of catastrophe. Ended at its inception, and at every subsequent instant, it continues, ergo can never end. *Don't mention any of this to your actors!' No Author Better Served: The Correspondence of Samuel Beckett and Alan Schneider*, ed. Maurice Harmon (Cambridge, Mass. and London: Harvard University Press, 1998), p. 23; emphasis mine. See also Matthew Feldman, *Beckett's Books: A Cultural History of Samuel Beckett's 'Interwar Notes'* (London: Continuum, 2006), p. 32.

11 In addition to the classic work by John Pilling, C. J. Ackerley, Mary Bryden and James Knowlson, see *Samuel Beckett Today / Aujourd'hui: Notes diverse holo* (special issue on the Trinity College Dublin manuscripts), eds Matthijs Engelberts, Everett Frost and Jane Maxwell, 16 (2006); Daniela Caselli, *Beckett's Dantes: Intertextuality in the Fiction and criticism* (Manchester: Manchester University Press, 2005); Dirk Van Hulle (ed.), *Beckett the European* (Tallahassee, FL: Journal of Beckett Studies Books, 2005) and *Manuscript Genetics: Joyce's Knowhow, Beckett's Nohow* (Gainsville, FL: University Press of Florida, 2008); Matthew Feldman and Mark Nixon, *Beckett's Literary Legacies* (Newcastle: Cambridge Scholars Publishing, 2006).

12 Cohn, *A Beckett Canon*, p. 241.

13 Denise Riley, 'But then I wouldn't be here', in *Impersonal Passion: Language as Affect* (Durham: Duke University Press, 2005), pp. 105–13, pp. 3 and 106. Sigmund Freud, 'Jokes and their relation to the unconscious' (1905), *Standard Edition of the Complete Psychological Works of Sigmund Freud*, ed. James Strachey, vol. 8 (London: Hogarth Press, 1964), p. 57.

14 In this introduction, I am referring to portions of longer incarnations of Thomson's and Boxall's chapters.

15 *The Onion*, 42:17 (26 April 2006).

16 On how the link between Beckett and nothing, and, more specifically, between Beckett and nihilism, has been placed in the realm of 'public consciousness' as opposed to that of criticism since the time of Esslin's early writings, see Shane Weller, *A Taste for the Negative*, p. 6. For a popular history of nothing, see John D. Barrow, *The Book of Nothing* (London: Jonathan Cape, 2000). See also Hélène Cixous's *Le Voisin de zéro: Sam Beckett* (Paris: Galilée, 2007) a book poised between the academic and the impressionistic, which produces a troubling familiarity between critic and writer, as suggested by the 'Sam' sported in the title. Forthcoming in English as *Zero's Neighbour*, trans. Laurent Milesi (Cambridge: Polity, 2009).

17 Weller, *A Taste for the Negative*, p. 20. Elizabeth Barry, *Beckett and Authority: The Uses of Cliché* (Basingstoke: Palgrave Macmillan, 2006).

18 See note 13. See also Peter Boxall, *Contemporary Writers in the Wake of Modernism* (London: Continuum, 2009) and *Samuel Beckett: Endgame and Waiting for Godot* (Basingstoke: Palgrave Macmillan, 2000). I tend to see Ruby Cohn as doing something quite different from the other critics mentioned, such as John Fletcher. See for instance Beryl Fletcher, John Fletcher, Barry Smith and Walter Bechem, *A Student's Guide to the Plays of Samuel Beckett* (London: Faber & Faber, 1978); John Fletcher, 'The private pain and the whey of words: a survey of

Beckett's verse', in Martin Esslin (ed.), *Samuel Beckett: A Collection of Critical Essays* (Englewood Cliffs, NJ: Prentice Hall, 1965), pp. 23–32; and Ruby Cohn, 'Philosophical fragments in the Works of Samuel Beckett', in Martin Esslin (ed.), *Samuel Beckett: A Collection of Critical Essays*, pp. 169–77.

19 I am quoting from a longer version of Boxall's chapter.

20 S. E. Gontarski, 'Staging himself, or Beckett's late style in the theatre', *Samuel Beckett Today / Aujourd'hui: Crossroads and Borderlines / L'œuvre Carrefour / L'œuvre limite*, eds Marius Buning, Matthijs Engelberts, and Sjef Houpperman, guest editor Emmanuel Jacquart, 6 (Amsterdam: Rodopi, 1997), 87–97. Emphasis added.

21 Theodor Adorno, 'Trying to understand *Endgame*', in Theodor Adorno, *Notes to Literature*, 2 vols, vol. 1, trans. Shierry Weber Nicholsen (New York: Columbia University Press, 1991), p. 242.

22 Adorno, 'Trying to understand *Endgame*', p. 242.

23 P. J. Murphy, *Beckett's Dedalus: Dialogical Engagements with Joyce in Beckett's Fiction* (Toronto: University of Toronto Press, 2009), p. 4.

24 This has been followed, more recently, by the work of Daniel Katz, *Saying I No More: Subjectivity and Consciousness in the Prose of Samuel Beckett* (Evanston, IL: Northwestern University Press, 1999); Anthony Uhlmann, *Beckett and Poststructuralism* (Cambridge: Cambridge University Press, 1999) and *Samuel Beckett and the Philosophical Image* (Cambridge: Cambridge University Press, 2006) and Garin Dowd, *Abstract Machines: Beckett and Philosophy after Deleuze and Guattari* (Amsterdam: Rodopi, 2007).

25 I am quoting from a larger version of Boxall's chapter.

26 Shane Weller discussed both these theoretical positions, using examples from Lukács to Žižek and from Adorno to Badiou. Weller, *A Taste for the Negative*, pp. 6–23.

27 Steven Connor, 'The doubling of presence in *Waiting for Godot* and *Endgame*', in Steven Connor, ed., *New Casebooks:* Endgame *and* Waiting for Godot (Basingstoke: Macmillan, 1992), p. 131. This point has also been taken up by Simon Critchley in *Very Little . . . Almost Nothing: Death Philosophy Literature* (London: Routledge, [1997] 2004). For an in-depth discussion of Critchley's position and its critique, see Peter Boxall Chapter 2 below.

28 Weller, *A Taste for the Negative*; Mladen Dolar, *A Voice and Nothing More* (Cambridge, MA: MIT Press, 2006).

29 Locatelli, *Unwording the Word: Samuel Beckett Prose Works after the Nobel Prize* (Philadelphia: University of Pennsylvania Press, 1990); Leslie Hill, *Beckett's Fiction: In Different Words* (Cambridge: Cambridge University Press, 1990); Steven Connor, *Samuel Beckett: Repetition, Theory and Text* (Oxford: Blackwell, 1988).

30 Enoch Brater, *Beyond Minimalism: Beckett's Late Style in the Theatre* (Oxford and New York: Oxford University Press, 1987); Shimon Levy, *Samuel Beckett's Self-Referential Drama: The Sensitive Chaos* (Eastbourne: Sussex Academic Press, 2002).

31 Ruby Cohn, *Samuel Beckett: The Comic Gamut* (New Brunswick: Rutgers University Press, 1962); Simon Critchley, *Very Little*; Laura Salisbury, forthcoming.

32 Paul Foster, *Beckett and Zen* (London: Wisdom, 1989).

33 Anna McMullan, *Theatre on Trial: Samuel Beckett's Later Drama* (London: Routledge, 2003); Yoshiki Tahiri, *Samuel Beckett and the Prosthetic Body: The Organs and Senses in Modernism* (Basingstoke: Palgrave Macmillan, 2006); Ulrika Maude, *Beckett, Technology and the Body* (Cambridge: Cambridge University Press, 2009).

34 Daniela Caselli, Steven Connor and Laura Salisbury (eds), *Journal of Beckett Studies*, 10:1 and 2 (Fall 2000 / Spring 2001). Reprinted as *Other Becketts* (Tallahassee FL: Journal of Beckett Studies Books, 2002); Caselli, *Beckett's Dantes*; Elizabeth Barry, *Beckett and Authority*.

35 Caselli, *Beckett's Dantes*.

36 David Cunningham, 'Ascetism against colour, or modernism, abstraction and the lateness of Beckett', *New Formations*, 55 (Spring 2005) 104–19, p. 116. See also Caselli, Connor and Salisbury's 'Introduction' to *Other Becketts*.

37 Samuel Beckett, *Murphy* (London: Picador, 1973), p. 5.

38 See John Pilling, Chapter 1 below.

39 *Murphy*, *Beckett's Dedalus*, p. 19.

40 For a radically different notion of the postmodern from that put forward by Eagleton see Slavoj Žižek. See also Shane Weller's detailed discussion of these two approaches in *A Taste for the Negative*. For a specific history of Irish philosophical thought in Beckett, see also Eagleton, 'Beckett and Nothing', in Anna McMullan and S. E. Wilmer (eds), *Reflections on Beckett: A Centenary Celebration* (Ann Arbor: University of Michigan Press, 2009).

41 See David Addyman, 'Samuel Beckett and the treatment of place' (Ph.D. thesis, Royal Holloway, University of London, 2008); Peter Boxall, 'Beckett's negative geography: fictional space in Beckett's prose' (Ph.D. thesis, University of Sussex, 1996).

42 David Cunningham, 'Trying (not) to understand: Adorno and the work of Beckett', in Richard Lane (ed.), *Beckett and Philosophy* (Basingstoke: Palgrave Macmillan, 2002), pp. 125–39, p. 138.

43 Dirk Van Hulle, 'Genetic Beckett studies', Introduction to *Beckett the European* (Tallahassee, FL: Journal of Beckett Studies Books, 2005), pp. 1–9, p. 3.

44 For a wider debate, see Lois More Overbeck and Martha Fehsenfeld,

'In defense of the integral text' and Matthew Feldman, 'Beckett and Popper, or "what stink of artifice": some notes on methodology, falsifiability, and criticism in Beckett studies', *Samuel Beckett Today / Aujourd'hui: Notes diverse holo,* eds Matthijs Engelberts, Everett Frost and Jane Maxwell, 16 (2006), 347–71 and 372–91, respectively. Feldman partially revises his position in 'After "The End" of Samuel Beckett: influences, legacies, and "legacees"', Introduction to Matthew Feldman and Mark Nixon, *Beckett's Literary Legacies* (Newcastle: Cambridge Scholars Publishing, 2006); for a critique of this notion of falsifiability, see Van Hulle, 'Genetic Beckett studies'.

45 Daniela Caselli, 'The promise of Dante in Beckett's manuscripts', *Samuel Beckett Today / Aujourd'hui: Notes diverse holo*, eds Matthijs Engelberts, Everett Frost and Jane Maxwell, 16 (2006), 237–57.

46 Carla Locatelli has recently presented an innovative and persuasive reading of this poem at the 'Beckett in Rome' 2008 international conference, forthcoming in print.

47 See Thomson, Chapter 4 below.

1

On not being there: going on without in Beckett

John Pilling

'The essential is never to arrive anywhere, never to be anywhere . . .'
(Samuel Beckett, *The Unnamable*)[1]

Not much in Beckett is left wholly unaffected by the notion of 'not being there', even though he remains haunted by the self-imposed imperatives of 'going on'. Not being there is only one of 'the problems that beset continuance' of which Beckett spoke in connection with the art and craft of his Israeli friend Avigdor Arikha, to which there can only ever be temporary solutions. The problems derive in large part from what another *hommage* to Arikha embodies as 'Eye and hand fevering after the unself',[2] a text which envisages the '[t]ruce for a space' in which some kind of relief attends a creative act that provides its own aspirin. I take the phrase 'not being there' from the coda (or 'codetta')[3] of the tenth of the *Texts for Nothing*, finished in Paris in August 1951, the 'voice' of which has just decided that in its objective case of 'he', 'he'll have done nothing, nothing but go on'.[4] The 'he' in question, very much in question as it happens (and perhaps precisely because it happens) is one of the 'pale imitations' of me and mine ('the one person') of which the text has earlier spoken,[5] or attempted to speak, with Beckett mindful from the outset – *The Unnamable* having come to a grinding halt more than a year earlier (in January 1950) – that there is 'nothing new' here.[6]

Where, we might ask ourselves, have we heard this 'not' before, given the prevalence of the 'nothing new' (a phrase itself by no means new, since it is being reprised from the opening sentence of *Murphy*, written in late 1935)? Well, there is of course one very striking example at the end of the short story 'Dante and the lobster', first published in the last issue of the Parisian émigré magazine *This Quarter* in December 1932, and subsequently in revised form in the collection *More Pricks Than Kicks* in May 1934. Belacqua is watching his aunt lift the lobster above the pot of boiling water which will kill it. 'Well', thinks Belacqua, 'Well, it's a quick death, God help us all', only for a voice to cut short the ironies and paradoxes of a quick death for all with the stern riposte, from no known source: 'It is not.' This is perhaps the most famous 'not' in the whole of Beckett, with the very position of the riposte, and its violent rejection of a more benign outcome, guaranteeing it maximum attention even in the absence of any designated authority to whom the substantive (or otherwise) declarative claims of 'It is' might be referred.

'Not' is of course not much of a word on which to construct an argument, even when a popular science author, John D. Barrow, can write 380 pages under the title *The Book of Nothing*.[7] 'Not' is, we might go on to say, not much of a *word* at all, since it only really exists, or becomes active, in combinations like 'is not', 'has not', 'was not', 'did not' and such like, or in the less formal, the contracted forms that we find more convenient, 'isn't' and so on, which almost seem to preserve by ellipsis the absence they cannot quite contain. But to say 'becomes active' is perhaps misleading, since 'not' is surely better described as *reactive*, a qualifier, which cannot act as a qualifier unless and until there is something to qualify, something to react against. As *not* something, it gravitates in the opposite direction to something, *towards* nothing. As such, it is more a gesture than a word, yet it is nonetheless felt to be a fact, and quite as much of a fact as what it qualifies, much like 'nothing' in number theory and practice. Beckett's *Watt* tells us: 'the only way one can speak of nothing is to speak of it as if it were something'.[8] 'Not', then, *is* something, even as it gestures towards nothing. It may or may not be trumpeted as '*that something itself*' in the overheated manner of the Joyce essay of 1929,[9] but it is the something that we use, in English, to designate nothing; and of course all languages (even though they use different words) do much the same thing. 'Not', a naturally re-active word, is a word full of potential, playing an active role in an 'art of negation'. It is, of course, only one weapon among many, but it is obviously one of the most effective weapons we have to subvert what has already been written, rendering it either less said, unsaid, or, in

Beckett's own late coinage, 'missaid' ('Say for be missaid', we read in *Worstward Ho*). And, though 'not' is undoubtedly extremely effective in an immediate and local context, there is of course no limit to its effects in the longer run. 'Not' occurs dozens and dozens of times in Beckett's first sustained prose fiction *Dream of Fair to Middling Women*, and even seems to possess a kind of generative power when, as often, a cluster of 'not's lurks, as it were, in the margins of a text unusually preoccupied with 'the problems that beset continuance' (there are three in close proximity on 89, five, surrounded by other negative indicators, on 92–3). But the extreme case I have in mind is *Watt* (1941–45), which uses the formula 'Not that . . . for he [or, more often, 'it'] was not' hundreds and hundreds of times, the formula thereby becoming one of (and perhaps the major) contributor to the book's curious and distinctive elusiveness, which many readers find tiresome and/or alienating.[10] 'Not' is even to be found in *Watt*'s 'Addenda', in the poem, or piece of doggerel, beginning 'Watt will not / Abate one jot',[11] a relic surviving from one of the six notebooks in which *Watt*, before it became *Watt*, was written.

There are differences, and a gap of at least ten years, between the 'not' of 'Dante and the lobster' and the 'not's of *Watt*. The former is notable principally for its dramatic force, its immediate impact; the latter instances render a materially physical text metaphysically immaterial. In 'Dante and the lobster' the effect is one of surprise. But surprise is the least durable aesthetic phenomenon, and can only really occur once if the short story writer wants to keep his distance from O. Henry. In *Watt* the formula acts as an enabling element. Rather than terminating the business of writing, it furthers it, requiring the writer to 'go on' by producing more. Yet the very circularity of the construction, with a 'not' at either end frustrating negotiations, is also a kind of 'not' in itself, a *disabling* element. Precisely because of the circularity we find it peculiarly difficult to get beyond the surface of the statement and access the 'true' substance towards which it appears to gesture. In short, 'not' (like Knott) is one of the somethings which enable *Watt* to get going, and to keep going, even as it disables the reader's 'natural' desire to get a grip on what is happening, thereby rendering that very desire of questionable status.

Beckett was no theorist. But when, in the summer of 1938, he jotted down some abstract thoughts on how art is produced, or produces itself, he spoke of a 'creative autology' (*autologie créa-trice*) and envisaged two needs ('Les deux besoins').[12] What are these two needs? First, the 'besoin d'avoir besoin', the need to have a need, or the need to have need, let's call it, *the need to need*. Secondly, the 'besoin dont on a besoin', the need of which one has need, the need one wants, the need experienced as an appetite in a context of lack or want, let's call it *the need one needs*. (In German, as Beckett well knew, the word 'Not' designates a need, the need, need pure and simple; and the six months in Germany had left Beckett hyper-aware of need and want.) But only when he came to *Watt* could he explore the ambiguities of the two needs. Late in part three of *Watt*, on the point of leaving Mr Knott's house, Watt reviews what he knows of 'the nature of Mr Knott himself': 'For except, one, not to need, and, two, a witness to his not needing, Knott needed nothing, as far as Watt could see. [. . .] And Mr Knott, needing nothing if not, one, not to need, and, two, a witness to his not needing, of himself knew nothing. And so he needed to be wit-nessed. Not that he might know, no, but that he might not cease.'[13] This is perhaps the *locus classicus* in Beckett for the relationship between 'not', 'need', 'nothing' and . . . 'going on'.

With Beckett not given to 'new ground', however, there are other ways in which similar elements recompose themselves. 'The forms', Malone tells us, 'are many in which the unchanging seeks relief from its formlessness'.[14] One such form is the September 1976 text *neither*, sometimes thought of (though Beckett did not think of it) as a poem. The title tacitly answers to two needs, being either n*i*ther or n*ee*ther according to taste, and the text opens up with a movement 'to and fro' as if it might just as well have been called 'Between'. The movement envisaged is 'from impenetrable self to impenetrable unself / by way of neither', and as such invites com-parison with the *hommage* for Arikha. In *neither* there is no talk of nots or needs or nothings in what reads like a version, or perver-sion, of the philosophical 'law' of the excluded middle. The two opposed terms ('self' and 'unself') are both said to be 'in shadow', although the shadows permit the identification of 'the one gleam or the other'. As *either* shadows *or* gleams the two opposed terms are also 'refuges', as Mr Knott's house was, for Watt, in a way. But once the 'to and fro' movement is stilled, they diminish and disappear, in a kind of verbal equivalent of the *diminuendo al niente* in music. In their absence the 'way of neither' occupies the space: 'absent for good / from self and other / [. . .] then gently light unfading on that unheeded / neither'. Whatever 'neither' may be, it is conceived of as a variant on the 'refuges', but (unlike them) an 'unspeakable home'. This 'home' is 'unspeakable' because it is neither one thing nor another, but somewhere between them. Not so much, then, an 'excluded' middle as an 'included' one, included but unspeakable.

Beckett had dealt with something similar to this some fifty years before, at the very beginning of his writing career, in a more declarative manner. Always 'on [his] way', he was 'never much of a one for new ground' (in *From an Abandoned Work*, a text ending 'my body doing its best *without* me').[15] In the programmatic third section of *Dream of Fair to Middling Women* ('UND', an appendix masquerading as the pivot of the whole) Beckett half-heartedly attempts to sum up the essence of his *alter ego* Belacqua, what (to adapt *Watt*) we might wish to call 'the nature of [Belacqua] in himself': 'At his simplest he was trine [a kind of three-in-one]. [. . .] Centripetal, centrifugal and . . . not. Phoebus chasing Daphne, Narcissus flying from Echo and . . . neither.'[16] Neat or not neat, there it is, or is not. Hence Beckett's next 'move': 'The dots are nice don't you think?' The dots are *not* 'nice' in the sense we intend when we ask of someone 'did you have a nice time?', but rather in the sense found in the phrase 'a nice distinction', a fine line separating things which are almost the same, but not the same. The distinction being drawn is between categories which can be stated, contrasted, in every sense of the word staged (like 'impenetrable self' and 'impenetrable unself'), and a third category, which is really a *non*-category rendering all categorisation whatsoever suspect. Beckett knows full well that the dots are not 'nice' (in the 'agreeable' sense of the word), but a kind of obstruction, or (as in the postwar art criticism on Geer and Bram van Velde) an *empêchement*.[17] Any attempt to transform a looming and shapeless absence into a cut-and-dried presence, a nothing into a something, is foreclosed.

In the non-category 'neither' one is 'without' (in a state of need, or outside any category), but without what? Perhaps the 1969 text we know in English as *Lessness* supplies an answer. This was originally written in French as *Sans*. 'What', we may ask ourselves, 'is *Sans* without?' Beyond what is obvious – there is, for example no 'plot' in the accepted sense – this study in 'disorder' pits a rudimentary 'little body' against a *mise en scène* ultimately seen as a 'figment' of the imagination. The text circles in upon itself via repeated motifs randomly generated and distributed, as if words had a life of their own. This is a way of 'going on' whilst 'not being there', but a more abstract example than, say, that supplied in the 1975 play *Footfalls* by the voice of Mrs Winter, asking 'What can you possibly mean, Amy, to put it mildly? Amy: I mean, Mother, that to say I observed nothing . . . strange is indeed to put it mildly. For I observed nothing of any kind, strange or otherwise. I saw nothing, heard nothing, of any kind. I was not there. Mrs W: Not there? Amy: Not there.'[18] Like the woman in *Rockaby* and the grey-heads of *Ohio Impromptu*, these are not so much figures as (to adapt *Lessness*) 'figments'.

It is no accident that Beckett should have gravitated near the end of his writing life towards the virtual worlds of celluloid and television, media particularly adapted to the conjuring up of images and to vanishing them away. But Beckett's fascination with 'figments' can be traced also by way of a 1974 poem in French beginning 'hors crâne . . .' ('something there' in its more expansive English version).[19] In the French poem the 'crâne' or skull is described (compare both *Lessness* and *neither*) as the 'abri dernier', the last refuge. This skull occupies a kind of median position (a 'tympanum' the Unnamable would say: 'on the one hand the mind, on the other the world, I don't belong to either')[20] between the 'dedans' and the 'dehors', the inner and the outer, the 'two needs' perhaps, which we might re-inscribe as the 'without' and the 'without which nothing'. The poem floats the idea of 'something there': 'quelque part quelquefois / comme quelque chose'. The English version, by contrast, seems to point in the opposite direction. After a 'sound so brief / it is gone and the whole globe', there is 'in the end' (or in the end there will be) 'nothing there'. This brief sound is the aural equivalent of what will in a still later (1986) poem be a 'Brief gleam'. But both are what Arsene, in his 'short statement' in *Watt*, would call 'sites of a stirring beyond coming and going, of a being so light and free that it is as the being of nothing'.

For a final illustration, or a final sounding, I turn to an example of 'going on' from a text that, for most readers, is 'not there' in the special sense that it has never been published, having been jettisoned in the 'tidying up' that permitted *Watt* to emerge and to, in some sense, be. At the start of the third of the notebooks towards *Watt*, under the date of 5 May 1942, Beckett engaged in the kind of *reculer pour mieux sauter* strategy which he had already decided, in

Dream, could only ever be *reculer pour mieux enculer*.[21] This is how
to bugger yourself, or, how to bugger yourself up:

> The creative consciousness is double and obscure. Double and
> obscure when it acts, double and obscure when it receives.
>   Its acting is a receiving, its receiving an acting.
>   When it acts it receives its own act, when it receives it acts on the
> act of another.

At this point Beckett steps back, as it were, to admire his own
handiwork, and wryly adds: 'God saw that it was good. Paul de
Kock [popular late nineteenth-century French novelist, beloved
of Molly Bloom] also.' God's single, once-and-for-all act of creation ('Let there be light! And there was light') has here become
'double and obscure' in a to-and-fro between re-creation and
de-creation.

A few lines below this Beckett tries to 'fail better' (as he was later
to put it in *Worstward Ho*) by shedding a little more light on what
has thus far been 'obscure' or merely obscured:

> When it acts it receives its own act.
>   It accepts & suffers it.
>   It accepts & suffers itself.
>   It is its own accepting & its own suffering. In the act is the accept-
> ing and its continuance the suffering.

Of the many double aspects here I would want to stress the one
which is contained in the last of these oddly declarative propositions, where there is, on the one hand, 'the act', and, on the other,
'its continuance'. This is not creation *ex nihilo*, but (as the next
entry indicates) a response to 'something there':

> In the Creation is the ?

Perhaps at this point Beckett was reminded of his own 'definition'
of art in his review of *Intercessions* by Denis Devlin in the last pre
war issue of *transition*, almost exactly four years earlier: 'pure
interrogation, rhetorical question less the rhetoric'.[22] For here the
'something there' is nothing more than a question mark, the mark
of 'not being there'; and even without an answer there is no alternative to 'going on', irrespective of the conditions and constraints
that threaten the continuance of the enterprise.

Notes

1 Samuel Beckett, *The Unnamable*, in *Trilogy: Molloy, Malone Dies, The Unnamable* (London: John Calder, 1959), p. 341.
2 Samuel Beckett, *Disjecta: Miscellaneous Writings and a Dramatic Fragment*, ed. Ruby Cohn (New York: Grove Press, 1984), p. 152.
3 Samuel Beckett, *Dream of Fair to Middling Women* (Dublin: Black Cat Press, 1992), p. 113.
4 Samuel Beckett, *No's Knife* (London: Calder and Boyars, 1967), p. 121.
5 *Ibid.*, p. 120.
6 *Ibid.*, p. 119.
7 John D. Barrow, *The Book of Nothing* (London: Jonathan Cape, 2000).
8 Samuel Beckett, *Watt* (London: John Calder, 1963), p. 74.
9 Beckett, *Disjecta*, p. 27.
10 Beckett, *Watt*, p. 64ff.
11 *Ibid.*, p. 250.
12 Beckett, 'Les deux besoins', in *Disjecta*, pp. 55–7.
13 Beckett, *Watt*, p. 202.
14 Beckett, *Malone Dies*, in *Trilogy*, p. 198.
15 Samuel Beckett, *From an Abandoned Work*, in *No's Knife*, p. 139, p. 142 and 149; my emphasis.
16 Beckett, *Dream*, p. 120.
17 Beckett, 'Peintres de l'empêchement', in *Disjecta*, pp. 133–7.
18 Samuel Beckett, *Footfalls*, in *Collected Shorter Plays* (London: Faber & Faber, 1984), pp. 237–43, p. 243.
19 Samuel Beckett, *Collected Poems in English and French* (London: John Calder, 1977), pp. 62–3.
20 Beckett, *The Unnamable*, in *Trilogy*, p. 386.
21 Beckett, *Dream*, p. 120.
22 Beckett, *Disjecta*, p. 91.

2

Nothing of value: reading Beckett's negativity

Peter Boxall

The first section of Samuel Beckett's novel *Watt* depicts Watt's journey to and arrival at Mr Knott's house, an establishment in which Watt is to feel for the first time in his life at rest. When Watt arrives at his destination and settles himself, like Beauty's father enjoying the hospitality of the Beast, at Mr Knott's kitchen table, he meets Knott's manservant Arsene, whom he is to succeed in Mr Knott's employment. As Arsene prepares to leave in order to make way for Watt, he delivers a long speech in which he describes to Watt the peculiar homecoming that is in store for him. 'How it all comes back to me', Arsene remarks, comparing Watt's prospective period at Mr Knott's with his own just drawing to a close. The 'dark ways', he says, are now 'all behind' him, and he has before him 'rest in the quiet house'. For him now, he goes on,

> there are no roads, no streets any more, you lie down by a window opening on refuge, the little sounds come that demand nothing, ordain nothing, explain nothing, propound nothing, and the short necessary night is soon ended, and the sky blue again over all the secret places where nobody ever comes, the secret places never the same, but always simple and indifferent, always mere places, sites of a stirring beyond coming and going, of a being so light and free that it is as the being of nothing.[1]

To have arrived in such stillness, to have been delivered to the midst of such rest, Arsene enthuses, is to have been 'proffered all pure and open to the long joys of being himself, like a basin to a vomit'. 'Having oscillated all his life between the torments of a superficial loitering and the horrors of disinterested endeavour', Arsene reflects, 'he finds himself at last in a situation where to do nothing exclusively would be an act of the highest value and significance'.[2]

This moment in Beckett's writing, at which the prospect of doing nothing is accorded both value and significance, might be thought of as a turning point. Beckett's earlier protagonists Belacqua and Murphy were fond of indolence, and enjoyed after their own fashion the delights of inactivity, but this moment in *Watt* is arguably one in which Beckett's work for the first time seeks to orient itself to nothinghood as a generative principle, and to develop a form that not only accommodates itself to this 'being of nothing' but is in some way derived from it, drawing its value and significance directly from an encounter with the 'nothing' that both Arsene and Watt find they are contracted, under Mr Knott's employment, to 'do'. At this moment not only can one glimpse the birth of the 'nothing to be done' that opens *Waiting for Godot,* and in a sense inaugurates Beckett's career as a dramatist, but one can hear here the first stirring of works that would not arrive at their own stilled thresholds for decades to come – works such as *Come and Go,* and *Stirrings Still.*[3] It is as if here, as Watt settles himself at Mr Knott's kitchen table, jostling against the shades both of Grimm's fairy tales and of the fictions of the Big House, he is initiated by Arsene into a doctrine of nothinghood that is also Beckett's initiation into the negative writing practice, the literature of the unword, that becomes his signature, and that marks his departure from the Joycean fictions that had characterised his early period.[4]

Such an encounter with a nothingness which has significance and value, however, both stages a certain Beckettian becoming – as if here in contemplation of the 'being of nothing' both Beckett and Watt find themselves in their 'midst at last, after so many tedious years spent clinging to the perimeter'[5] – and poses a difficulty that Beckett's writing in a sense never overcomes. For if the relentless effort to give expression to nothingness and meaninglessness might be thought of as the central task of Beckett's writing, it is also the case that this is a task in which Beckett is doomed endlessly to fail. As the double genitive in my title suggests, to propose a 'nothing of value' is at once to ascribe value to nothingness, and to declare an absence of value, and this paradoxical contradiction between the simultaneous assertion and negation of value accompanies any attempt to make nothingness significant, to ascribe to it qualities or quantity, to 'weigh absence in a scale', or to 'mete want with a span'.[6] This is of course a conundrum with which Watt himself has much fun, and which diverts him for a considerable amount of the time he spends in Mr Knott's establishment. The 'incident', for example, of the Galls father and son, in which the said Galls come to Mr Knott's house in order to tune the piano, is comically tormenting for Watt because it requires him to confront, and to try to articulate, his sense that the 'incident' was in some sense unconsummated, that, happening, it nevertheless failed to happen, taking place as it does in the empty midst of Mr Knott's nonbeing. 'What distressed Watt' the narrator explains,

> in this incident of the Galls father and son, and in subsequent similar incidents, was not so much that he did not know what had happened, for he did not care what had happened, as that nothing had happened, that a thing that was nothing had happened, with the utmost formal distinctness.[7]

Watt 'could not accept', we are told, that 'nothing had happened, with all the clarity and solidity of something'.[8] The incident itself – 'a piano tuned, an obscure family and professional relation, an exchange of judgements more or less intelligible'[9] – becomes a 'purely plastic' manifestation of a central unhappening, a kind of unnameable occurrence at the heart of things that is somehow formally represented by the arrival of the Galls father and son. The skill that Watt tries to learn at Mr Knott's is one which will allow him to negotiate the relation between the nothingness that resides at the heart of Mr Knott's establishment and those 'outer meanings'[10] in which such nothingness finds itself expressed, without either corrupting Mr Knott's nothingness by contact with the forms that give it expression, or allowing himself and his surroundings – including the Galls father and son – to fall into that unnameable vacuum which it is the job of Watt and of the narrator Sam to relate, to commit to words and forms. But this skill proves elusive to Watt; 'to elicit something from nothing', the narrator reflects, 'requires a certain skill, and Watt was not always successful, in his efforts to do so'.[11] Watt learns eventually 'to accept that nothing had happened, that a nothing had happened, learned to bear it and even, in a shy way, to like it',[12] but the suggestion is that this learning, this bearing, this shy liking, does not constitute a resolution of the contradiction between something and nothing – or the development of a capacity successfully to 'elicit something from nothing' – but rather demonstrates the birth of a certain willing-ness to live in the midst of its impossible demands. In the dramatic dialogues between Beckett and George Duthuit, Beckett suggests that the painter Bram Van Velde is faced with the kind of dilemma that so exercises Watt – that he is confronted with the demand that whilst there is 'nothing to express', he is nevertheless obliged to express, and so, as a consequence, the content of his painting must in some sense be a nothingness made something, an expression of the impossibility of expression. Duthuit, in responding to what he calls Beckett's 'fantastic theory' of inexpressive art, suggests that the means of resolving this difficulty is simply to suggest that the 'occasion of his painting is his predicament', and that an art which is 'skewered on the ferocious dilemma of expression',[13] is one that becomes 'expressive of the impossibility to express'.[14] Beckett responds that 'No more ingenious method could be devised for restoring [the artist] safe and sound to the bosom of saint Luke',[15] but the burden of his unserious argument in the dialogues is that this kind of critical reconciliation between expression and inex-pression, between something and nothing, is a premature recon-ciliation that shields us from the ferociously unthinkable relation between the nameable and the unnameable in which it is Watt's perhaps dubious privilege to dwell during his stay with Mr. Knott. Beckett's writing does not incubate that skill that Watt sets out to learn, does not constitute a nothingness made palpable, but rather performs an endlessly failed reaching for a nothingness which gives rise to the work, which the work seeks endless to name, but which remains also forever beyond the grasp of those forms which are its only manifestation. When Malone declares epigrammatically that 'the forms are many in which the unchanging seeks relief from its formlessness',[16] he suggests just this kind of unending back to front striving, in which an unchanging formlessness comes to birth in a series of Beckettian forms which can only embody such formless-ness by disavowing it, by denying its only defining characteristic. Beckett's formlessness, like that of *The Unnamable*'s uncharacter Worm, dies at the moment of its birth into form; delivering it kills it, bringing it into being condemns it to death.

None of this, of course, is news. On the contrary, it might be argued that the question of the relation between form and form-lessness, between something and nothing, is that which has deter-mined the passage of Beckett's reception from the 1950s to the present day. The problem that Beckett has addressed in his writing, and that Beckett studies has addressed in seeking to develop a critical discourse that is adequate to the philosophical and hermeneutic challenge represented by his work, is how to calculate the value of the nothingness that Watt discovers with Mr. Knott, without either doing violence to such nothingness by translating it into somethingness, or falling into the silence and inarticulacy that is the only faithful response to the apprehension of 'the being of nothing'. Each of the various phases of Beckett criticism, I would suggest, can be characterised in terms of how they respond to this central problem, the problem that Simon Critchley describes in much broader philosophical terms as the 'problem of nihilism'.[17] The way in which Beckett's nothingness is accorded value can be seen as an index to the critical mode in which he is approached. The shift from the humanist urge to recuperate Beckett's negativity under the figure of a *condition humaine,* to the deconstructive tendency to see Beckett's undoing as symptomatic of a more general failure of language to adequately represent the human, might be the most legible shift in the critical approach to Beckett's negativity. But there are several other critical approaches that have evolved through this history, and in each case one might argue that the value of Beckett's negativity is a key to the way in which he is read. Theodor Adorno, for example, has famously argued that Beckett's nothing represents is the unnameable remains of a critical art, the last remaining expression of negative autonomy in the midst of what Adorno calls the 'total society'. Similarly, to characterise an Iserian understanding of Beckett's writing in relation to reader response theory would require us to calculate the value that Iser gives to Beckett's negativity; to catch the precisely Blanchottian cast of Blanchot's reading of Beckett requires an attentiveness to Blanchot's address to Beckett's unnameability; to approach Deleuze's articulation of Beckettian exhaustion in his signal essay 'The exhausted' is to hear the ways in which 'Language III' gives expression to silence; to understand Cavell's reading of Beckett's *Endgame* requires an approach to a Beckettian version of Wittgensteinian silence; and so on.[18]

So, it is possible to read Beckett's readers in terms of their understanding of negative value. But if Beckettian nothingness might give rise to the critical traditions that grow up around his work, nourishing them like good soil, it is also the case that such negativity constantly challenges the critical discourses it provokes, undermining their claims to authority, emptying them of explanatory power at the moment that it endows them with it. This is what lies behind Simon Critchley's analysis of Beckett's 'resistance to interpretation', a resistance that Critchley discovers in his own reading of Beckett's relation to nihilism. 'The Writings of Samuel Beckett', Critchley writes,

> seem to be particularly, perhaps uniquely, resistant to interpretation. To speak from the vantage point of a conceptual framework, an interpretive method or any form of metalangauge, is, at the best of times, a hazardous exercise with regard to those texts regarded as 'literary' [. . .]. However, the peculiar resistance of Beckett's work to philosophical interpretation lies, I think, in the fact that his texts continually seem to pull the rug from under the feet of the philosopher by showing themselves to be conscious of the possibility of such interpretations; or better, such interpretations seem to lag behind the text which they are trying to interpret; or, better still, such interpretations seem to lag behind their object by saying too much: something essential to Beckett's language is lost by overshooting the text and ascending into the stratosphere of language.[19]

There is something about Beckett's singular attitude to nothingness, something about the way that nothingness resides at the heart of his work, as it lies at the heart of Mr Knott's establishment in *Watt*, that renders interpretation peculiarly empty, that dismantles the critical apparatuses that one brings to it, that turns the assumptions that one makes about the value of reading inside out. Indeed, Critchley's own response to the challenge of Beckett's 'meaninglessness' suffers just this paradoxically surplus lag, this tendency to say at once too much, and not enough – almost nothing. When he claims that 'the task, the labour of interpretation – of interpretation respecting the determinate negation of meaning enacted by Beckett's work – is *the concrete resurrection of the meaning of meaninglessness*',[20] one experiences the same peculiar emptying of a claim that occurs whenever Beckettian nothingness is put to critical work. To valorise Beckett's meaningless as an 'achievement', the 'achievement of the ordinary',[21] is to have one's own system of value exposed to the peculiar undoing effect of Beckett's logic, as Critchley knows. Rather than using such a system or 'metalanguage' to develop a reading of Beckett – to assess its value, to concretely recreate his meaninglessness – it is as if Beckett's writing reads one back, demonstrating the vanishing point of one's own reading practices whilst refusing to yield itself to interpretation. It is perhaps this quality, this kind of reverse interpretation, that leads to Derrida's famous reluctance to read Beckett, to expose deconstruction to Beckett's deconstructive gaze. Beckett is an author, Derrida says in an interview with Derek Attridge, 'to whom I feel very close, or to whom I would like to feel myself very close; but also too close',[22] and it is precisely this proximity, this sense that Beckett's writing takes on the qualities of s/he who reads him, that causes one to brush up against a kind of inclusive limit to reading, a limit to interpretation, for Derrida a limit to deconstruction. He has been able, Derrida says, to respond in some fashion to a number of other writers, to Kafka, Joyce, Celan, Artaud – he has been able, with these writers, 'to risk linguistic compromises'.[23] As he puts it, 'I have given myself up to them'.[24] But this giving up is not possible in relation to Beckett, because it would threaten a kind of annihilation, a disintegration of a reading practice which comes unspeakably home to itself in the text that it reads. 'This wasn't possible for me with Beckett', Derrida says, 'whom I will thus have "avoided" as though I had always already read him and understood him too well'.[25]

The approach to Beckett's negativity, then, has defined a number of the critical discourses that have sought to account for his work, whilst also producing the dismantling of such discursive structures, as Watt finds that his language is dismantled as he comes nearer to the emptiness marked by Mr Knott. This double effect does not in any sense render the history of reading or nonreading of Beckett's work valueless. On the contrary, the peculiar aporetic effects that occur at the threshold between Beckett and his readers stage a certain stalled becoming of Beckett's writing, whilst also allowing for a reflection on the limits of critical reading. But it does mean that the question of value in Beckett has proved difficult to measure or to quantify, or to articulate critically. It is this difficulty that has contributed to the perception that Beckett's writing is somehow uniquely resistant to criticism and to thought – a perception that is perhaps the dominant feature of his reception. It has been clear to many, for example, that his writings have a political and ethical valence – a simple glance at the contexts which Beckett's work have addressed testify to this – but it has seemed a constituent part of Beckett's politics and of his ethics that they resist or evade expression, both in the writing itself and in the critical languages that account for it. Derrida remarks in his interview with Attridge that a 'certain nihilism is interior to metaphysics (the final fulfilment of metaphysics, Heidegger would say) and then, already, beyond'.[26] In Beckett, nihilism is brought to the point of an expression which reveals this interiority, but only by putting it under a certain erasure, stating the productive value of nothing whilst finding its own expressive power negated in the process ('All I say cancels out', the narrator of *The Calmative* declares, 'I'll have said nothing').[27] 'With Beckett in particular', Derrida says, the 'two possibilities' – the interiority of nihilism and its location in or deferral to the beyond – 'are in the greatest possible proximity and competition. He is a nihilist and he is not a nihilist'.[28] The history of Beckett criticism has been, to a degree, an attempt to live up to these two proximate and competing possibilities, and in seeking to do so the criticism has traced the limits of critical thinking, often by failing to think what the texts seem to enable us or provoke us or require us to think. But what I want to argue here – and this is the main claim of this chapter – is that we are now entering into a period in the reception of Beckett's in which a new set of possibilities for the articulation of Beckett's negativity are beginning to make themselves felt. This new period or phase, I would argue, is one that is enabled by a growing awareness both of Beckett's debts and of his legacies, and one that is informed by a much stronger and deeper body of knowledge than was previously available both about the ways in which Beckett's thinking interacts with a number of traditions that he inherits, and about the ways in which those who come under his influence interact with the legacies that he passes on. Daniela Caselli's book *Beckett's Dantes: Intertextuality in the Fiction and the Criticism* and Matthew Feldman's and Mark Nixon's collection *Beckett's Literary Legacies* are two examples – from either end as it were – of this new concern with tracing intertextuality and influence in and through Beckett's work.[29] One of the effects of this new development is to suggest ways in which the kind of proximity that Derrida finds so disabling – the closeness which leads reading practices to become one with and negated by the work that they seek to read – might be in some sense deflected, to introduce the kind of distance in which reading might take place, in which nothingness might yield to an expression which is not immediately negated or cancelled out or, as *The Unnamable*

has it, 'invalidated as uttered'.[30] When Derrida reads Beckett, he
suggests, he finds in his writing a kind of mirror, as Murphy finds
himself mirrored in Mr Endon's gaze in *Murphy*. The proximity that
Derrida invokes in his failure to read Beckett is given an uncom-
fortable, and peculiarly erotic, form when Murphy seeks to look as
deeply as possible into Mr Endon's eyes. 'Kneeling at the bedside',
the narrator writes,

> the hair starting in thick back ridges between his fingers, his lips,
> nose and foreheads almost touching Mr Endon's, seeing himself
> stigmatized in those eyes that did not see him, Murphy heard words
> demanding so strongly to be spoken that he spoke them, right into
> Mr. Endon's face, Murphy who did not speak at all in the ordinary
> way unless spoken to, and not always even then.
> 　'the last at last seen of him
> 　himself unseen by him
> 　And of himself'
> 　A rest.
> 　'The last Mr Murphy saw of Mr Endon was Mr Murphy unseen by
> Mr Endon. This was also the last Murphy saw of Murphy.'
> 　A rest.
> 　'The relation between Mr Murphy and Mr Endon could not have
> been better summed up by the former's sorrow at seeing himself in
> the latter's immunity from seeing anything but himself.'
> 　A long rest.
> 　'Mr Murphy is a speck in Mr Endon's unseen.'[31]

This passage is the first of several in Beckett's writing which dwell
on the peculiar sense that seeing, like reading, requires a degree of
distance. Murphy's hunger to find himself recognised by Mr Endon,
his desire to penetrate into the emptiness that he imagines resides
behind Mr Endon's cornea, results here of course in an approach
only to his own image, 'horribly reduced, obscured and distorted',[32]
a self-regard that is also an unseeing. Proximity here destroys the
conditions that might allow for vision, that might allow us to see
across a divide or a gulf between one person and another, creating
instead a kind of short circuit in which what one looks at becomes
a simple reassertion of what one already is, and in which precisely
the empty gulf between discrete things, what Belacqua and Watt
think of as the 'interval' or musical pause,[33] is eradicated. This
scene in *Murphy* predicts the scene in *Krapp's Last Tape*, in which
Krapp remembers lying in a drifting punt with his lover:

I asked her to look at me and after a few moments – [*Pause.*] after
a few moments she did, but the eyes just slits because of the glare.
I bent over her to get them in the shadow and they opened. [*Pause.
Low.*] Let me in.[34]

And again, in *Company*, the scene reappears, somewhat modified:

You are on your back at the foot of an aspen. In its trembling shade.
She at right angles propped on her elbows head between her hands.
Your eyes opened and closed have looked in hers looking in yours.
In your dark you look in them again. Still. You feel on your face the
fringe of her long black hair stirring in the still air. Within the tent
of hair your faces are hidden from view. She murmurs, Listen to the
leaves. Eyes in each other's eyes you listen to the leaves. In their
trembling shade.[35]

On each of these occasions, the erotics of contact and of proximity
give way to a kind of failure, in which the trembling possibility of
company, of being two, returns to the assertion of solitude. The
perception of an affinity, like that affinity between Beckett and
Derrida, leads to a closeness which destroys such affinity. The
phrase 'Eyes in each other's eyes' might suggest a romantically
unifying gaze, but it also suggests something of the mush and the
stench of a biological decomposition, a decomposition of the apparatus of vision, which requires the eyeball – the 'globe' as it is most
often called in Beckett – to remain whole and sealed, unsullied by
penetration by another.

This kind of failure of vision, then, in which the other becomes
a reflection of the self, might be thought of as analogous to the
failure of reading that Derrida experiences in relation to Beckett.
The emptiness that inhabits Beckett's writing, its lack of content,
suggests and provokes an affinity with the reader, allows the
reader to find his or her self reflected in Beckett's work, as reader
and listener reflect each other in *Ohio Impromptu*, as Murphy is
reflected in Mr Endon. This emptiness, this pallor, allows for and
provokes such affinity, but it is also just this negativity that is eradicated as affinity gives way to stifling proximity, to a becoming one.
Attention to the question of influence and of inheritance, however,
allows for a more oblique gaze, allows for a play of seeing and of
reading in which the gulf, the interval, between reader and listener
might be left open, as the doors and windows in *Ghost Trio* remain
'imperceptibly ajar'.[36] If the nothingness that inhabits the interior

and the beyond of Beckett's writing might have value, ethical and political as well as aesthetic value, then it may be that this oblique gaze offers a means of glimpsing such value, of apprehending it in its arrested state without either making of it a something, or finding one's own reading annulled by contact with it.

To begin to gesture towards such possibility here, in fact, I will focus quite specifically on some of the ways in which Beckett's own gaze has been reflected in recent work by J. M. Coetzee and W.G. Sebald – in Sebald's and Jan Peter Tripp's striking work *Unrecounted*, and in Coetzee's recent essay on Beckett, 'Eight ways of looking at Samuel Beckett'. In Sebald's and Tripp's *Unrecounted*, Beckett's is one of the gazes that is captured in Tripp's extraordinary series of lithographs, which focus tightly on the stilled, unblinking eyes of a number of people and animals, who seem to look at us through letterboxes, posting their gaze from somewhere on the other side of the page.[37] In Beckett's portrait, his eyes are depicted in close up, shining glassily in a bird like fashion, as he looks past us and slightly to the right, over our shoulder. In Coetzee's essay, Beckett's gaze is evoked not visually but verbally, where Coetzee likens Beckett's gaze to that of Kafka. 'It helps to have a piercing gaze', Coetzee writes, 'and Beckett had his own variety of piercing gaze. Like photographs of Kafka, photographs of Beckett show a man whose inner being shines like a cold star through the fleshly envelope.'[38] Both Coetzee and Sebald and Tripp, then, dwell on Beckett's gaze, and in both instances his gaze is invoked partly to celebrate its capacity to penetrate, to pierce or puncture what Coetzee calls the 'fleshly envelope'. In both cases, also, this capacity to cut through flesh is thought through a particular and strikingly resonant relation between human and animal, as if the power to look that these writers find in Beckett allows him not only to shine through his own flesh but also to pass through the species barrier, to achieve the kind of communication or interaction between radically different beings that seems so signally to fail in that recurring mirrored gaze that is first unseeingly shared by Murphy and Mr Endon.

In Coetzee's essay, the piercing quality of Beckett's gaze is imagined in relation most overtly to the whale – to the white whale of Melville's *Moby Dick* – and more implicitly to the bird, to the apprehension of the blackbird that is summoned in Coetzee's title reference to Wallace Steven's poem 'Thirteen Ways of looking at a blackbird'. The relation between human and whale is cast, by Coetzee, in terms of unbroken whiteness, the whiteness of the whale and the whiteness of the cells and rotundas in which Beckett's creatures are immured. 'One image', he writes: 'the white wall of a cell in which we find ourselves imprisoned, which is also the white wall constituted by the huge forehead of the whale. If the harpoon is cast, if the harpoon tears through the wall, into what does it tear?'[39] To be enclosed in a cell, in a white ring of bone, is to be locked into a consciousness that cannot cross that white blankness – the unbroken blankness of page as well as of bone, the 'dumb blankness, full of meaning' that Melville ascribes to whiteness in *Moby Dick*.[40] 'In their white cells', Coetzee writes,

> Beckett's selves, his intelligences, his creatures, whatever one prefers to call them, wait and watch and observe and notate [. . .]. Why do these creatures not grasp their harpoon and hurl it through the white wall? Answer: because they are impotent, invalid, crippled, bedridden. Because they are brains imprisoned in pots without arms or legs. Because they are worms. Because they do not have harpoons, only pencils at most. Why are they cripples or invalids or worms or disembodied brains armed at the most with pencils? Because they and the intelligence behind them believe that the only tool that can pierce the white wall is the tool of pure thought.[41]

Here, Beckett's bodies are seen as impotent beings locked inside themselves, unable to cross that white wall that divides human from the human, human from animal. They do not have harpoons, the harpoon that might tear through the white wall. But what they do have, Coetzee suggests, is the piercing capacity of thought, that capacity that evidences itself, at the close of Coetzee's essay, in Beckett's penetrating gaze, and that is harnessed also in his writing, the writing that corrupts the blank whiteness of the page. It should be stressed that Beckett's creatures find, 'despite the evidence of their eyes, that the tool of pure thought fails again and again';[42] Coetzee here is not arguing that thought alone can transform our conditions, can bring down the barriers that separate human from human and human from animal. But what he does seek to give expression to here is the possibility of a form of seeing or imagining that can stage an open if failed relationship between beings that maintains them in their otherness rather than returning them to blank sameness – the form of seeing that is imagined by Wallace Stevens as he crafts his ways of looking at the 'eye of the blackbird'.[43] Coetzee declares that Beckett's people do not have harpoons, perhaps forgetting or repressing the fact that Malone does indeed have a harpoon of sorts, and that he uses this to pierce, to puncture the pages upon which he writes his narrative (and in a limited sense Beckett's novel), as if writing for Malone is a kind of puncturing. 'The exercise book had fallen to the ground', Malone writes. 'I took a long time to recover it. I had to harpoon it. It is not pierced through and through, but it is in a bad way'.[44] For Malone, writing with his pencil and puncturing his exercise book with a harpoon are part of the same process, part of the same failed attempt to allow writing to destroy and thus to exceed the conditions of its own production, to tear down the wall and the page that separates Ahab from the whale. It is perhaps this capacity for writing to summon the erosion of the barriers that hold consciousness in place, that enclose us with our subjecthood and within our species, that is quietly suggested by the pen that is given as a gift to Malone's character Saposcat by his clumsily adoring parents. The pen, of course, is 'A Bird', and 'a bird, its yellow beak agape to show that it was singing adorned the lid' of the cardboard box in which Mr Saposcat plans to present it to his son.[45] If the suggestion here is that the pen might give sound to that mute singing, as Moran seeks to recognise and communicate with his wild birds at the end of *Molloy*, to 'understand their language better',[46] then it is certain, as Coetzee suggests, that such a hope will fail. Sapo's blackbird will remain mute, thought and writing cannot penetrate the wall that separates you from me, cannot allow the indecipherable, unimaginable thinking of the whale to flood into our own thought. But what Coetzee seeks to put into a kind of motion in his essay is a series of oblique relations, between texts, between writers, between humans and animals, that allows the possibility of an interaction between them, that allows for the kind of impossible surplus that Beckett's writing produces to open its own, imperceptible threshold in which radically different beings might enter into some sort of unspoken colloquy.

Sebald's engaging of Beckett's gaze suggests a similar set of associations between penetrating vision and the possibility of a form of communication across insuperable barriers – across the barrier between humans and animals as well as that between the living and the dead. If Tripp's lithograph suggests something bird like about Beckett's gaze, something unmistakably aquiline, then the verse that accompanies the image builds on this association. 'He will cover / you with his / plumage', the text reads, '& / under his wing then / you will rest',[47] suggesting that Beckett is looking at us here from the other side of the wall that separates human from bird, as if he is looking back at us from an animal future, rather than towards us from a human past. Beckett becomes part here, in all his peculiar animality, of a series of images that reach across Sebald's writing, and that stage an insistent, mute conversation between distant intelligences imprisoned in their cells. Sebald's novel *Austerlitz* is shot through with close-up photographs of the gaze of animals, which regard us, like Beckett, from the other side of a barrier or final border. The novel opens famously with the narrator's visit to a nocturama, in which he is struck by the open gaze of the nocturnal animals, rather as Murphy is compelled by Mr Endon's 'prodigiously dilated pupils',[48] the pupils that become great gaping black holes that fill the field in *Worstward Ho*, 'Inletting all. Outletting all.'[49] Sebald's novel includes a series of photographs of the animals' eyes, composed as Tripp's lithographs are composed, around which the text declares that

> all I remember of the denizens of the Nocturama is that several of them had strikingly large eyes, and the fixed, inquiring gaze found in certain painters and philosophers who seek to penetrate the darkness which surrounds us purely by means of looking and thinking.[50]

This relation between the gaze of the animal and that of the painter, philosopher, poet, emerges again and again in *Austerlitz*, and across Sebald's writing, where it suggests both the imprisonment of the thinker and his or her capacity to transform such imprisonment into a liberation, as if the barrier itself (of cage, of page, of personhood) becomes an open threshold, or is pushed imperceptibly ajar. Much later in the novel, Sebald and his companion Marie see a group of deer in an enclosure whose collective gaze, like that of the animals in the nocturama, is reproduced photographically in the text. Marie, Austerlitz recalls,

> particularly asked me to take a photograph of this beautiful group, and as she did so, said Austerlitz, she said something which I have never forgotten, she said that captive animals and we ourselves, their human counterparts, view one another *à travers une brèche d'incompréhension*.[51]

It is this capacity to regard the other across such a breach – a breach at once absolutely impassable, and strangely, delicately navigable – that characterises the relation between human and animal in *Austerlitz*, and that characterises Beckett's gaze as it is imagined in Sebald. The narrator of *Austerlitz* remarks, of his perception of a similarity between the gaze of Wittgenstein and that of Austerlitz, that

> whenever I see a photograph of Wittgenstein somewhere or other, I feel more and more as if Austerlitz were gazing at me out of it, and when I look at Austerlitz it is as if I see in him the disconsolate philosopher, a man locked into the glaring clarity of his logical thinking.[52]

This extraordinarily delicate play of likeness and singularity, of an intelligence whose locked imprisonment is woven into his freedom from enclosure, whose apprehension of solitude is also a kind of company, is central to the ways in which Sebald negotiates the boundaries that hem us in, that position us in bodies, in time and in space. Sebald develops a poetics which allows the experience of incarceration, in all its horror and its unwavering certainty, to produce a kind of almost unthinkable freedom, as if he has found a language in which to bring the other side of every limit, of every barrier or border, to the point of expression.

So, both Coetzee and Sebald, in different ways, bring Beckett's gaze into a kind of intertextual economy which works to coax the nothingness that inhabits being, and the gulf or breach that intervenes between beings, to a borderline perceptibility. Where Derrida's non-reading of Beckett tends to find itself so closely identified with him that it falls under the erasure produced by Beckett's self-cancelling logic, the play of glances here between Beckett, Sebald and Coetzee opens the ethical possibilities of Beckett's poetic thinking – its ethical value – to a new kind of legibility, a new kind of mensuration. One of the figures in which this impossible thinking, this benighted illumination, finds itself most resonantly expressed is that of visible darkness, a figure which links those who inherit Beckett's legacies with those who pass legacies on to him. In both Coetzee's novel *Slow Man* and Sebald's novel *Austerlitz* the possibility of visible darkness grazes the surface of the text in relation to the work of photography, the bringing to visibility of an image in the darkroom. The protagonist of Coetzee's novel reflects that his greatest pleasure was always in darkroom work. As the ghostly image emerged beneath the surface of the liquid, as veins of darkness on the paper began to knit together and grow visible, he would sometimes experience a little shiver of ecstasy, as though he were present at the day of creation.[53]

Coetzee's protagonist here catches a distinct echo from *Austerlitz*, where Austerlitz tells the narrator that

In my photographic work I was always especially entranced [. . .] by the moment when the shadows of reality, so to speak, emerge out of nothing on the exposed paper, as memories do in the middle of the night, darkening again if you try to cling to them, just like a photographic print left in the developing bath too long.[54]

In both of these instances, the narrators are interested in the way in which photography brings a nothingness, a kind of darkness, into the light, and in both instances it is possible to hear a set of resonances echoing back, through Beckett, to Dickinson and to Milton. The difficult idea of visible darkness, or as Clov has it 'light black',[55] is something that stirs time and time again in Beckett's writing, most notably perhaps in *Company*, where we are told that the faint narrative voice sheds a 'faint light', that 'Dark lightens while it sounds', making the 'darkness visible'.[56] Perhaps the clearest reference at this point in *Company*, the most reputable and well known source of such visible darkness, is book 1 of John Milton's *Paradise Lost*, where the poet captures wonderfully the unthinkable horror of hell by declaring that the flames that burn eternally there do not give off light, but rather shed a 'darkness visible'.[57] This reference also helps darkly to illuminate the Miltonic structure of *Company*, and to bring to light the Miltonic resonance of the narrator's uncertainty about whether Beckett's creature rightly belongs 'in the same dark' as his creator.[58] But the echo I want to focus on here, as this chapter draws to a close, is not from Milton but from Emily Dickinson, a writer with whom I suggest, without any evidence, Beckett has an extraordinarily rich and unspeakable affinity, as though he had always already read her and understood her too well. Dickinson, like Beckett, and like Sebald's and Coetzee's narrators, is entranced by the thought of visible darkness, of lightening black, and the idea stirs in her poetry, as it does in Beckett's. The example I will refer to here is from her poem 'From Blank to Blank', a poem in which it is possible to see the seeds of Beckett's oeuvre:

From Blank to Blank –
A Threadless Way
I pushed Mechanic feet –
To stop – or perish – or advance –
Alike indifferent –

If end I gained
It ends beyond
Indefinite disclosed –
I shut my eyes – and groped as well
'Twas lighter – to be Blind'[59]

Both Beckett and Dickinson, I suggest, catch something from Milton when they imagine the possibilities of a light darkness, a vision that is won from blindness, but Dickinson's thinking of such possibilities seems to me much closer to Beckett's than Milton's is, so close, indeed that they shape to merge, to become a single dark. The blanks that inhabit both the deepest interior of this poem and its far beyond offer to disclose the indefinite that simultaneously annuls them, just as Beckett's writing stages at once a glaringly white revelation of nothingness and a submission to its darkness. In both Dickinson and in Beckett darkness and light become bound up in this wonderfully intricate aporetics of statement and negation, the kind of turning that has made the value of Beckett's nothing impossible to quantify. It is not possible to separate these two movements – the light is won from the dark, just as it returns to it, and the extraordinary reach both of Beckett and of Dickinson emerges from the closeness of this coupling. When reading both poets one has to contend with this difficulty, a difficulty that might make of the most careful reading a kind of avoidance. But what I have been trying to suggest here is that the reading of Beckett and Dickinson together, the reading of visible darkness as it sheds its black light in Milton, in Dickinson, in Beckett, in Coetzee, in Sebald, allows us a kind of approach to nothing made something that the direct gaze makes impossible. It is in the almost unthinkable spaces between Beckett and his legators, and between Beckett and his legatees, that the possibility of an imperceptibly open threshold might be glimpsed, in which the indefinite might find itself disclosed, in which that breach of incomprehension that intervenes between human and human, between human and animal, might come to a kind of ethical expression.

Notes

1 Samuel Beckett, *Watt* (London: Calder, 1976), p. 38.
2 Beckett, *Watt*, p. 39.
3 See Samuel Beckett, *Waiting for Godot*, in Samuel Beckett, *Complete Dramatic Works* (London: Faber & Faber, 2006), p. 10.
4 For a reconsideration of the role of Joyce in Beckett, see P. J. Murphy, *Beckett's Dedalus: Dialogical Engagements with Joyce in Beckett's Fiction* (Toronto: University of Toronto Press, 2009).
5 *Ibid.*, p. 39.
6 *Ibid.*, p. 247.
7 *Ibid.*, p. 73.
8 *Ibid.*, p. 73.
9 *Ibid.*, p. 69.
10 *Ibid.*, p. 70.
11 *Ibid.*, p. 74.
12 *Ibid.*, p. 77.
13 Samuel Beckett, *Proust and Three Dialogues with Georges Duthuit* (London: Calder, 1955), p. 110.
14 *Ibid.*, p. 121.
15 *Ibid.*, pp. 121–2.
16 Samuel Beckett, *Malone Dies*, in *Trilogy: Molloy, Malone Dies, The Unnamable* (London: Calder, 1994), p. 198.
17 Simon Critchley, *Very Little . . . Almost Nothing: Death, Philosophy, Literature* (London: Routledge, 1997), p. 12.
18 See Wolfgang Iser, *The Implied Reader: Patterns of Communication in Prose Fiction from Bunyan to Beckett* (Baltimore: Johns Hopkins University Press, 1974); Maurice Blanchot, 'Where now? Who now?', in *The Siren's Song*, ed. Gabriel Josipovici (Brighton Harvester, 1982); Gilles Deleuze, 'The exhausted', in Gilles Deleuze, *Essays Critical and Clinical*, trans. Michael A. Greco (London: Verso, 1998), pp. 152–74; Stanley Cavell, 'Ending the waiting game: a reading of Beckett's *Endgame*', in Stanley Cavell, *Must We Mean What We Say? A Book of Essays* (Cambridge: Cambridge University Press, 2002), pp. 115–62.
19 Critchley, *Very Little*, p. 141.
20 *Ibid.*, p. 27.
21 *Ibid.*
22 Jacques Derrida, *Acts of Literature*, ed. Derek Attridge (New York: Routledge, 1991), p. 60.
23 *Ibid.*, p. 61.
24 *Ibid.*
25 *Ibid.*
26 *Ibid.*

27 Samuel Beckett, *The Calmative*, in Samuel Beckett, *The Expelled and Other Novellas* (Harmondsworth: Penguin, 1980), p. 51.

28 Derrida, *Acts of Literature*, p. 61.

29 See Daniela Caselli, *Beckett's Dantes: Intertextuality in the Fiction and Criticism* (Manchester: Manchester University Press, 2005), and Matthew Feldman and Mark Nixon (eds), *Beckett's Literary Legacies* (Newcastle: Cambridge Scholars Publishing, 2007). See also Matthew Feldman, *Beckett's Books: A Cultural History of Samuel Beckett's 'Interwar Notes'* (London: Continuum, 2006) and Peter Boxall, *Since Beckett: Contemporary Writers in the Wake of Modernism* (London: Continuum, 2009).

30 Samuel Beckett, *The Unnamable*, p. 293.

31 Samuel Beckett, *Murphy* (London: Picador, 1973), p. 140.

32 *Ibid.*

33 Samuel Beckett, *Dream of Fair to Middling Women* (London: Calder, 1995), p. 28. Here Belacqua seeks to live in the space of the 'Beethoven pause', in the 'silences' that obtain 'between you and me'. This desire re-emerges in *Watt*, where Watt expresses his desire to live in the 'interval' between musical bars (Beckett, *Watt*, p. 134). For a discussion of music and nothing, see Catherine Laws, Chapter 10 below.

34 Samuel Beckett, *Krapp's Last Tape*, in Beckett, *Complete Dramatic Works*, p. 221.

35 Samuel Beckett, *Company*, in Samuel Beckett, *Company, Ill Seen Ill Said, Worstward Ho* (London: Calder, 1992), p. 39.

36 See Samuel Beckett, *Ghost Trio*, in *Complete Dramatic Works*, p. 408.

37 W. G. Sebald and Jan Peter Tripp, *Unrecounted*, trans. Michael Hamburger (New York: New Directions, 2004), pp. 78–9.

38 J. M. Coetzee, 'Eight ways of looking at Samuel Beckett', *Samuel Beckett Today / Aujourd'hui: Borderless Beckett / Beckett sans frontiers*, eds Minako Okamuro et al., 18 (2008), 31.

39 *Ibid.*, p. 22.

40 *Ibid.*; Herman Melville, *Moby Dick* (Oxford: Oxford University Press, 1988), p. 199.

41 Coetzee, 'Eight ways', p. 23.

42 *Ibid.*

43 Wallace Stevens, 'Thirteen ways of looking at a blackbird', in Wallace Stevens, *Selected Poems* (London: Faber and Faber, 1965), p. 43.

44 Beckett, *Malone Dies*, p. 209.

45 *Ibid.*, p. 211.

46 Samuel Beckett, *Molloy*, p. 176.

47 Sebald and Tripp, *Unrecounted*, p. 79.

48 Beckett, *Murphy*, p. 140.

49 Samuel Beckett, *Worstward Ho*, in Beckett, *Company, Ill Seen Ill Said, Worstward Ho*, p. 115.

50 W. G. Sebald, *Austerlitz*, trans. Anthea Bell (London: Penguin, 2001), p. 3.

51 Sebald, *Austerlitz*, p. 369.

52 Sebald, *Austerlitz*, p. 56.

53 J. M. Coetzee, *Slow Man* (London: Secker and Warburg, 2006), p. 65.

54 Sebald, *Austerlitz*, p. 109.

55 Samuel Beckett, *Endgame*, in *Complete Dramatic Works*, p. 107.

56 Beckett, *Company*, p. 15.

57 John Milton, *Paradise Lost*, ed. Alastair Fowler (Harlow: Pearson Longman, 2007), p. 64.

58 Beckett, *Company*, p. 19.

59 Emily Dickinson, 'From blank to blank', in *The Poems of Emily Dickinson: Reading Edition*, ed. R.W. Franklin (Cambridge, MA: Harvard University Press, 1998), pp. 222–3.

3

Nothing has changed

Mladen Dolar

In *Whoroscope*, one of his first published texts, the poem which won a poetry competition in 1930, Beckett aims an elaborate blow at Descartes. There is the philosopher of the methodical reduction, the reduction of all supports in the outside world, in perception, in the body, reduction of all supports in questionable inner certainties, safe traditions and evident truths, reduction of both contingency and necessity, external and internal, in order to arrive to the minimal point of certainty, the firm rock of cogito, the prop of the subject from whom all other props have been taken away. But Beckett takes the cogito (the word never mentioned in the poem, as neither is Descartes for that matter)[1] through its reverse, by the angle of irreducible contingency. The cogito is, as it were, inserted back into the body from which it emanates and into the haphazard eventualities of historical circumstance. The Cartesian body depends on its trivial tastes (the notorious eggs which had to be hatched from eight to ten days, no shorter and no longer); the Cartesian mind is preoccupied with the trivial rivalry with its opponents – both illustrious (Galileo, Harvey, Arnauld) and obscure (Anna Maria Schurmann, Weulles). The cogito is thus confronted with this intricate web of trivia, which Beckett assiduously excavated from Adrien Baillet's late seventeenth-century life of Descartes. Descartes, we learn in the notes appended at the end (in the manner of T. S. Eliot, and without which we would be quite lost), 'kept his own birthday to himself so that no astrologer could cast his nativity', but to no avail: three centuries later Beckett cast his horoscope, his *whoroscope*. This is the whoroscope of the cogito, providing this bodiless entity with the contingency of its haphazard moment, reversing its reduction, reducing its reduction in the opposite direction, expanding it into a baroque fresco of poignant fleshy detail and over-elaborate scholarly references, defying the minimalism of the cogito's subjectivity with the maximal expansion of contingency, and confronting its clear and distinct reason with its underside of stupidity.[2]

Whoroscope has ninety-nine lines, but only because the entries for the competition had not to exceed one hundred lines. It mentions some twenty names and refers to a dozen historical occasions, in a florid and heavily overladen idiom. Compare this to the first piece of Beckett's *Mirlitonnades*, some half a century later:

> En face
> le pire
> jusqu'à ce
> qu'il fasse rire

That's all. The opposition between the two poems couldn't have been more drastic. The whole poem has the flavour of a slogan, the shortest possible *profession de foi*, achieved by minimal means. It is as if Beckett has accomplished his own Cartesian reduction, reduction of means and ends, to arrive to his own version of the cogito, which, in its very minimalism, presents a sort of anti-cogito. He strove for the anti-cogito in *Whoroscope*, if one can venture to give this name to his endeavour, but in a way which fell short in its very floridity. The contingent, trivial and historical network in which it was inscribed was perhaps unwittingly still caught in the workings of the cogito, it was but its underside, it fell into its web precisely through the maximal distance it tried to establish from it. The proper way to deal with the cogito was to take the Cartesian route of reduction: Beckett had to take it on his shoulders, reduce to the utmost, to the core, to the minimum, to the bare rock – to arrive at what? Nothing? Almost nothing? It's the 'almost' that is the problem.

First the language. *Whoroscope*, like most of Beckett's early work, is clearly under the long shadow of James Joyce. Every detail has the tendency of being overblown, the language is thick with convoluted ramifications, jokes are too smart, erudite and studious to be funny, each line ransacks the encyclopaedia. But what defined Beckett's subsequent work was precisely a sharp demarcation from this:

> I realised that Joyce had gone as far as he could in the direction of
> knowing more, [being] in control of one's material. He was always
> adding to it; you only have to look at his proofs to see that. I realised
> that my own way was in impoverishment, in lack of knowledge and
> in taking away, in subtracting rather than adding.[3]

The art of subtraction (the concept whose fortune was secured by
Alain Badiou) versus the art of addition, the infinitely expandable
versus the infinitely shrinkable.

> The more Joyce knew the more he could. He's tending toward omnis-
> cience and omnipotence as an artist. I'm working with impotence,
> ignorance. There seems to be a kind of aesthetic axiom that expres-
> sion is achievement – must be an achievement. My little exploration
> is that whole zone of being that has been set aside by artists as some-
> thing unusable – as something by definition incompatible with art.[4]

The art of omnipotence versus the art of impotence, omniscience
versus ignorance.

> With such a program, in my opinion, the latest work of Joyce
> [*Finnegans Wake*] has nothing whatever to do. There it seems rather
> to be a matter of an apotheosis of the word.[5]

The art of apotheosis, the magic of the word versus the art of the
senselessness, 'the literature of the unword', of the drained, barren,
porous, meaningless word (as Beckett put it in the famous letter to
Axel Kaun, written in German in 1937).

> And more and more my own language appears to me like a veil that
> must be torn apart in order to get at the things (or the Nothingness)
> behind it. Grammar and Style. [. . .] As we cannot eliminate language
> all at once, we should at least leave nothing undone that might con-
> tribute to its falling into disrepute. To bore one hole after another in
> it, until what lurks behind it – be it something or nothing – begins to
> seep through; I cannot imagine a higher goal for a writer today.[6]

So the aim of the writer, by definition someone working with
words, is to impoverish his means, to undo his tools; if not to elimi-
nate his means of production entirely, then at least to make them
work against themselves, to counteract the fascination with words
and meaning, to stop producing more and more meaning and to
engage in hard labour towards the senseless.[7] Joyce's art consisted
in producing an overflow, in making meaning proliferate to the
point of its being expanded into infinite floating, a surplus-meaning

which can never be pinned down and whose fascination lies in infinite addition, in the possibility of an eternal $(n+1)$: Joyce's is the art of the always expandable excess propelled by enjoyment-in-language. The meaning is never to be exhausted, for every surplus produces more surplus; thus it seems that Joyce has reached the very matrix of production of meaning, to the point where generations of scholars will have to sweat over the enigmas of his ultimate book for centuries (as he himself had correctly predicted). To be sure, to describe Joyce as the writer of surplus-meaning is misleading, for what is at stake, in his supreme artistry with words, has only in part to do with the overflow of meaning, it also has to do with the overflow of sounds. Language is taken, in one and the same gesture, as a machine for the endless production of meaning and as a web of infinite sound-echoes, reverberations, words contingently echoing other words and finding a surplus of meaning in the very contingent consonances of sounds, in sound contaminations, intersections, cross-cuts, in endless punning. *Finnegans Wake* can be read as an interminable pun, running for hundreds of pages and folded on to itself, each pun breeding more puns, the end rejoining the beginning. Thus Joyce ultimately embodies, in a paramount manner, the Lacanian concept of *lalangue*, an inextricable web of meaning and sound, of the signifier and the enjoyment, where language is not either taken to be the matter of the signifier or simply sound echoes, but is apprehended precisely through their very difference, their incommensurability – their division and their union falling under the same heading in their very divergence. Hence Lacan's own fascination with Joyce, his seeing Joyce as the incarnation of *sinthome*[8] – the word which is itself a pun on symptom (just as *lalangue* is a pun, for that matter) and which immediately breeds more puns on *saint-homme, sinthome madaquin* (*Saint Thomas d'Aquin*), etc. It seems that Lacan wholeheartedly espoused Joyce as the showcase for a certain line of his teaching. But couldn't one argue that following Beckett's way would actually come much closer to the bone of Lacan's teaching? This is the argument I will briefly try to pursue here.

Beckett's art, as opposed to Joyce's, is the art of $(n-1)$. The words have to be deprived of their magic, hollowed, their meaning has to be subtracted from them so that they become scarce and empty, like senseless sounds,[9] reduced to clichés (dead words in a seemingly living language).[10] What has to be explored is how much one can take away, how little will one make do: the vocabulary is contracted, the references reduced to the minimum, the encyclopaedia has to shrivel, and the grammar has to be reduced to the bare necessity (what Beckett called 'the syntax of weakness'). What better means to achieve this, on an external level, than to write in a foreign tongue, with diminished powers of 'expression', voluntarily forsaking the bountiful 'natural' means at one's disposal? To abandon style, to abandon the notorious 'finding one's own voice' that all creative writing courses are after, to write in a voice which is anonymous and impersonal. The minimal internal split, the least difference, so much at the heart of Beckett's endeavour, is externally translated into the split of two languages, two originals for most of Beckett's texts, which play with minimal divergences between the two. One can easily imagine the two writers reading proofs, Joyce relentlessly adding new twists, and Beckett constantly crossing out, deleting sentences, paragraphs, pages. For one there is never enough, for the other there is never little enough.

Language itself is a veil, that was Beckett's insight already in the late 1930s, not the locus of expression, a veil to be pierced, not expanded, not a canvas to paint upon to conjure a new infinite universe. Rather, the veil is there only to get behind it, to what seemingly lies beyond. But what lurks behind the veil? Is there not a treacherous illusion in the very supposition of something lurking behind the veil that one should get to? 'Be it something or nothing', says Beckett, and the oscillation between the two is fundamental. There is no 'something' behind the veil, no thing that one might get to and take hold of by piercing the veil, no thing with any positive features or qualities, no nameable thing, but it is not simply nothing either. The void itself, the nothing, takes on the quality of 'something' without qualities. The action of piercing the language by reducing the words to the function of a minimal split arrives to the minimal inner split of something/nothing, an irreducible split where neither term can be taken by itself. There is something that always comes to supplant nothing, yet something only emerges on the verge of nothing, at the limit of being engulfed by it.

Along with the reduction of language there is the reduction of the body. Beckett's 'heroes' constantly move from relative mobility to increasing immobility. Means of transportation fail and are taken away, legs won't work any longer, eyes go blind, and the body disintegrates, more and more is taken away from it: it is the infinitely shrinkable body in an infinitely shrinkable space. Molloy and Moran are condemned to greater immobility, Malone is dying confined to a small room, the narrator of *The Unnamable* has shrunk to a mere voice whose origin remains uncertain. The heroine of *Happy Days* is buried in the ground to her waist in the first act, to her neck in the second. In *Breath* there is but a breathing in and out, the pure point of emission, not even of a voice in any linguistic or expressive sense, but of a mere breath, the minimal statement possible – not a statement, just a pure enunciation. The voice itself can be externalised and estranged from the body, as in *Krapp's Last Tape*, taken over by a device, a non-bodily point of emission, or else, more tellingly, there can be 'the voice without a mouth', as in the *Texts for Nothing*, so that even the existence of a point of emission is suspended, reduced to being a split into the inner and the outer.

The body is reduced in the same process as words are reduced: it is increasingly mutilated and emaciated, more and more can be taken away from it, it is the body on the verge of dying, on the way to disappearance, to the bodily almost-nothing. On the unending way there, the bodily almost-nothing is epitomised by the voice, the voice gradually not of a person or any nameable entity, but an unnameable source of enunciation. This is the voice at the point of the void, the voice incessantly on the brink of getting lost itself, but nevertheless persevering, tenuously and tenaciously, always recuperating itself at the very point of vanishing.

The reduction of language and the reduction of the body both lead to the voice. After all, the voice is what language and body have in common, it is the point of their intersection, the network of words and meanings has to be underpinned by a point of bodily emission, it is the incongruity of the two that makes their junction, their minimal overlapping, the crossing. It is as if the diminution of the words endows them with a quality which brings them closer to the body, they are reduced to pure voice, that is, the body at its most obstinate when everything else has been removed. They cling to the body in a way that becomes increasingly material, while on the other hand it is as if the flow of words drains the body, it contracts it. There is a mutual and interdependent reduction, a reduction to the point of exhaustion. Exhaustion is something quite different from tiredness, as Deleuze has taught us in his beautiful essay on Beckett, although Beckett's 'hero' is also always tired to the point of death. Being tired implies he is not able to realise the possible, but the point is that 'he exhausts himself in exhausting the possible, and vice-versa. He exhausts that which, in the possible, is not realized.'[11] It is not that the possible is not realised, it is the possible itself that is exhausted, and the exhaustion of the possible is what is at stake in all Beckett's later work. Taking up another of Deleuze's cues, one could say that the reduction of meaning immediately leads to the production of sense (the sense used in *The Logic of Sense*). The less there is meaning, the more sense is produced, from one sentence to another, out of nothing, of almost nothing, with useless remains, vestiges, residues of what once was meaning, in a necessary illusive retroactive supposition. This is why it is an absurdity to take Beckett under the heading of the 'literature of the absurd' – the reduction of meaning can appear as absurd only by the yardstick of the lost meaning, but the point is precisely to be rid of this yardstick so that sense can be made. The two tramps in *Godot* quite literally *make sense*. A sense that relentlessly keeps surprising us, catching us unaware in the midst of meaninglessness, and the point of *Waiting for Godot* is precisely that *Godot comes*, he keeps coming all the time, and, if it seems that he doesn't, it's only because we have been expecting him from the wrong quarters.

Sartre's *Nausea* was the paradigmatic work which took the absurd as its master word:

> The word Absurdity is now born beneath my pen [. . .]. Absurdity was not an idea in my head, or the sound of a voice, but that long dead snake at my feet [. . .]. And without formulating anything clearly, I understood that I had found the key to Existence, the key to my Nausea, to my own life. [. . .] But I, a little while ago, experienced the absolute: the absolute or the absurd [*l'absolu ou l'absurde*]. [. . .] Absurd: irreducible; nothing – not even a profound, secret aberration of Nature – could explain that.[12]

The famous scene where Molloy finds stones on the beach and sets up an elaborate system for sucking them is a sort of response to the opening scene of Sartre's *Nausea*.[13] Both heroes find themselves on the beach and pick up a stone, but the difference between the two scenes couldn't have been more striking. In six points. First of all, in *Molloy* there is not one stone, epitomising stonehood, as in Sartre's *Nausea*, but a multiplicity, a host of stones, yet a multiplicity to be submitted to count, even more, to a careful and complicated combinatory calculus. They are sixteen – the first thing to do with stones is to count them. Second, if the stone immediately inspired disgust in Sartre's hero, if it was the cause of the onset of nausea which will be persistently tormenting him henceforth, then Molloy picks up stones to put them into his mouth, to suck them. If disgust pertains particularly to taste and smell, where its forces are at their most powerful, then Molloy displays the very opposite of disgust, he does the unimaginable: he puts the disgusting thing into his mouth. Disgusting? Let's see what it tastes like, let's taste the existence, not recoil from it – and unsurprisingly he finds it tasteless. *Stones suck*. Third, the stone is a border creature, found on the dividing line between land and sea, and it has the strange property of putting into question the border, most conspicuously the divide between the exterior and the interior. The stone, which is externality itself, is being internalised, sucked; systematically, one by one, each at its appropriate turn, stones are sucked, that is, kept on the verge, at the aperture, at the point of transition, at the limit, as a detachable part of the body, the oral object, the breast turned stone. It is being oralised, and, most significantly, put at the locus of the emission of the voice – and this is a good description of the way the voice functions in Beckett: it is like sucking stones. The stone, the deadest thing there is, is as if integrated into the life cycle, recycled, on the verge of life and death. Fourth, the stone is a practice, it calls for a practice, it is neither an object of contemplation out there nor something inspiring horror when touched: it is something to handle, feel, process, displace, replace, shift, move, shuffle, order – and the whole scene hinges on arranging the stones in the right pecking order, that is, in their sucking order, so that each will be sucked in turn and in equal proportions. *To leave no stone unturned*. Fifth, if for Sartre's hero the stone is metonymised, spreading its properties to other objects and ultimately to the whole of existing things – so that to exist is to be a stone – then here there is only metonymy from stone to stone, from one stone to another: shall I say, each stone 'representing the subject' for another stone? Shuffling stones from one pocket to another, and between four pockets and the mouth, looks like an elementary structuralist exercise in the dialectics of the empty place and the element that comes to fill it. And the point of the combinatory exercise is to exhaust all possibilities of permutation in this metonymy (see Deleuze). Sixth, all stones taste the same, they are tasteless, indifferent, so why suck one stone rather than the other?[14] Well, the stone is the creature of minimal difference, of the difference of the same, the difference of the indistinct, and it is the 'indifferent difference' that counts, quite literally. And the minimal difference of the indistinct will be very much at stake in all Beckett's later work. To the point of indistinction of life and death.

One can sense that the whole exercise is at the same time essential while being completely pointless: 'And the solution to which I rallied in the end was to throw away all the stones but one, which I kept now in one pocket, now in another, and which of course I soon lost, or threw away, or gave away, or swallowed.'[15] So, are we stuck with the futility of it all? Of course we are, but with the meaningless stones a lot of sense has been made, the scene is extremely striking and very funny, both delirious and completely pragmatic (nonsense and no-nonsense, as it were), crucial and trivial in one: one can make do with Sartre's nauseating stone, provided one submits it to the quickly sketched six points; provided one doesn't turn it into substance or seek transcendence.

In Sartre the stone has no meaning, its stupid being there and inertia endow the rest of existence with a stone-like quality – the stone petrifies it and turns it into absurdity. The stone is recalcitrant to making sense, so the hero is overcome by nausea, by a universal disgust with existence, from which he cannot quite recover until the last page. On the other hand, the antidote to this nauseating stony existence is found in the voice, the voice of an American woman jazz singer, and the voice is what offers the possibility of transcendence in the midst of absurdity: it has the power to dispel the nausea. This is a parable of damnation and salvation. With Beckett, the landscape of absurdity has been utterly overturned. The stone and the voice come to occupy the same place, there is no meaning to be recovered from the one or the other, they both have to be sucked so that sense can be made, in the face of the absence of meaning. The immanent transcendence from stone to stone, from voice to voice, is all there is.

The voice in Beckett implies a body, a bodily point of emission and a bodily point of reception, but its location is uncertain.

> I shall transmit the words as received, by the ear, or roared through a trumpet into the arsehole, in all their purity, and in the same order, as far as possible. This infinitesimal lag, between arrival and departure, this trifling delay in evacuation, is all I have to worry about.[16]

The bodily apertures are interchangeable: the mouth, the anus, the ear communicate immediately, it is not a question of their location, they become all-one. There is just the question of time-lag between arrival and departure; words are received and then retransmitted through the orifices, or not even that.[17]

> Yes, my mouth, but there it is, I won't open it, I have no mouth, and what about it, I'll grow one, a little hole at first, then wider and wider, deeper and deeper, the air will gush into me, and out a second later, howling. [. . .] do I feel an ear, frankly now, do I feel an ear, well frankly now I don't, so much the worse, I don't feel an ear either, this is awful, make an effort, I must feel something[18]

The orifices are not only interchangeable but utterly uncertain; not only their location but also their very existence is questionable, the reception and transmission are on the verge of collapsing, yet the very fact that there is voice, the voice which goes on and on, retransmitting words received, or at least their remnants and crumbs, devouring and vomiting words – this fact implies an opening, an opening as such, the juncture of language and body as an opening, appearing at the very point of closure in this closed and shrinking world with no way out.

Where is the voice coming from, this pure voice of enunciation? Is it a monologue someone is proffering to anybody who might be listening? *A bon entendeur salut?* Or is it going on in the head, the interminable rambling of an internal voice? The alternative is itself faulty, the point of enunciation cannot be quite sorted out in that way, it cannot be placed on either side of this roughest of divides.

> I'll have said it, without a mouth I'll have said it, I'll have said it inside me, then in the same breath outside me, perhaps that's what I feel, an outside and an inside and me in the middle, perhaps that's what I am, the thing that divides the world in two, on the one side the outside, on the other the inside, that can be as thin as foil, I'm neither one side nor the other, I'm in the middle, I'm the partition, I've two surfaces and no thickness, perhaps that's what I feel, myself vibrating, I'm the tympanum, on the one hand the mind, on the other the world, I don't belong to either[19]

One couldn't be more precise: the enunciating voice is the very principle of division, itself not on either side and yet on both sides at once, at the intersection of the inner and the outer and unplaceable in that division, the thinnest of foils which connects and separates the two. Beckett's literature, written as literature is, is at the same time the literature of the voice as no other, not only by virtue of its being close to the spoken idiom, but also by being sustained merely by pure enunciation which propels it forward – the voice of enunciation with no other hold or footing, the voice more important than the words it utters. For the words are hollow, contradicting, clueless, digressing: the flow of words is a constant digression without the main line, without a course, its course is a dis-course, undermining itself yet carrying on. This is not a litera-ture of sentences and statements, the statements are trivial, they are not propelled by a will to express, they contradict and retract themselves, they keep getting lost, and what emerges through all this is a literature of pure enunciation, yet an enunciation which most carnally brings forth the body.[20]

There is a traditional way of dealing with the inner voice under the heading of 'the stream of consciousness'. The term, stemming from William James's *Principles of Psychology* (1890), was first applied to Dorothy Richardson's *Pilgrimage*, then to William's brother Henry, and to Joyce, Woolf and a number of other modern-ist writers, thus becoming like a trademark of the modernist novel. As far as Beckett is concerned, the term is misleading and inappro-priate, for the stream of consciousness presupposes consciousness as realm neatly separate from the outside world, and the writer supposedly follows the inner rambling and faithfully records it as a scribe, putting down its meanderings in a raw form as they appear to consciousness before being made presentable and coherent. The whole point with Beckett is that this inner voice maintains itself as unplaceable, at the very edge of the mind and the world, the speech and the body, cutting into both and being cut by both. Its inner split immediately translates into an outer split and vice versa. It is not that the consciousness is incoherent; rather the very line that separates consciousness and constitutes it as such is constantly blurred and indistinct.

The voice is there as a pure enunciation without a subject, or an enunciation in search of a subject, where various modes and levels of enunciation are mixed, heterogeneous voices are inserted. Without hierarchy and usual punctuation, multitude of diverse subjectivities flock together, but they are just so many aborted attempts, pursued for a while and then abandoned, suspended in the flux of the sheer perseverance of a voice. Voice is the anti-cogito. It is at the far end of clear and distinct reasoning, it is quite its opposite, since its point is precisely to undo the distinctions and to introduce the indistinct. The distinct ideas? 'But it is gone clean out of my head, my little private idea. No matter, I have just had another. Perhaps it is the same one back again, ideas are so alike, when you get to know them.'[21] The indistinct rules.[22] The seemingly most self-evident distinctions get blurred and vague ('It's vague, life and death'),[23] the line between life and death is obscured and confused no less than the inner/outer divide. However, it is the indistinct that opens up the space for a minimal difference, a tiny split, which, so to speak, lacks distinction. The rock of cogito is irretrievable rocked at the very opening of *The Unnamable*, in the justly famous first lines: 'Where now? Who now? When now? Unquestioning. I, say I. Unbelieving. Questions, hypotheses, call them that. Keep going, going on, call that going, call that on.'[24] The French original is more poignant and precise at the crucial point: *'Dire je. Sans le penser.'*[25] It is a question not of belief, but of thought, of dissociating the 'I' from thinking. 'Say I. Without thinking it.' Say ego, without cogito. It is an 'I' which doesn't give support to thought, an unthinking 'I', an 'I' without substance, apart from being a vehicle of perseverance, on the verge of vanishing and resurrecting itself from the void. 'I' doesn't think, but speaks, and exists only as long as it goes on talking. Or does it? Is existence the proper term to describe its status? Doesn't the endless talking preclude ever saying 'therefore I am'? Isn't there a being quite different from existence, a locus of being without qualities?

How can talking ever come to an end? If it is endlessly propelled forward by the thrust of sheer persistence, then this prevents the retroactive recuperation of meaning:

> It's an unbroken flow of words and of tears. [. . .] I confuse them, words and tears, my words are my tears, my eyes my mouth. [. . .] it's for ever the same murmur, flowing unbroken, like a single endless word and therefore meaningless [*sans signification*], for it's the end gives the meaning to words.[26]

Ultimately, meaning is produced retroactively, it is the end which endows the preceding words with a meaning, the provisional ending of a sentence, of a section, the final ending of the book, it is always the last element which reshapes the preceding ones and makes them tend toward that end, in both senses. It totalises what went before, words retroactively become teleological, flowing towards their end or goal that reclaims them, salvaging their haphazard and tentative advance with a hindsight seal. This is what Lacan's concept of *point de capiton*, the suture point, tries to account for. But with an unending flow no such point is ever reached, the *point de capiton* seems to be infinitely deferred and suspended, it is not a journey towards some end which would restore meaning. And if the novel has to end at some point, then the last novel of the great *Trilogy* ends on 'I'll go on', on the impossibility of ending, on the utmost ambiguity of ending which doesn't end.

How can talking ever come to an end? With the correlative reduction of words and bodies, the question can immediately be extended into 'How can body ever come to an end?' 'How can life ever come to an end?' Indeed Beckett's 'heroes' are always and increasingly on the brink of death, they keep dying through whole novels and theatre pieces, waiting for death to come as a salvation, they are all 'heroes' who have come to an end of their journey, who have exhausted the possible, and yet they cannot die. They start at the point of the end of their journey, at the point where some *point de capiton* should make sense of their lives, but the end is endlessly receding, it seems that death would rescue them and that this is all they wish for, but in the space of the withdrawing end there is a time-loop: they are caught in a loop which is at the same time an opening of a space, of a sense without any meaning. They reach a rock, not the firm rock of cogito but rather a being on the verge of nothing, they enter into a space of immortality which provides all the salvation needed precisely at the point where there seemed to be a pure nothing to engulf them. The reduction of words, meanings, bodies, their utter fragmentation leads to a nothing, but 'nothing' is but a loop which keeps them going on, nothing is but an 'event horizon', on the edge of the black hole, in which the minimal object emerges, 'the least'.[27]

Immortality is not the good word for this situation, it reeks of damnation and redemption – a more appropriate and less distinguished word is called for. One of the interpreters says of the Beckett 'hero': 'Not able to be immortal, he is *increvable*! [*À défaut d'être immortel, il est increvable!*]'[28] *Increvable*, an excellent Beckettian word, is hardly translatable into English.[29] The dictionary offers 'to kick the bucket' as the trivial expression for dying

– he is not immortal, he just can't kick the bucket. Could one say 'unbucketable'? If I can be excused this questionable pun: could one say that the 'unbucketable' turns out to be 'beckettable'?

This is where one could use another, albeit highly laden, psychoanalytic term, the death drive. For the death drive is not simply a drive towards death, rather quite the opposite, despite some confusion in Freud. It is a drive which itself cannot die, a pure thrust of persistence which cannot be annihilated,[30] it can merely be destroyed from outside, a pure life in the loop of death, emerging on the verge of nothing. Reduction of words and of bodies thus runs into the realm of the death drive, impelled by 'unnullable least' that cannot be reduced and which glimmers on the edge of nothing.

Is this Beckett's way out of nihilism? Is nihilism defeated and overcome in this way, not by clinging to meaning, value, ethical injunctions, creed, belief, world-view, religion, art, hope, which are all prey to the logic of nihilism and its reproduction, but at the point of reducing them to facing this 'object nothing', nothing itself as a mere loop of 'unnullable least', a support of perseverance, an opening of a new production of sense? Or is the alternative itself faulty, the alternative between Beckett the great nihilist and Beckett the great saviour from the abyss of nihilism? If it is naive to see in Beckett the proponent of the absurd and the showcase of nihilism, is it not also naive to take him as the best antidote, as a host of his defenders have tried to do in various ways?[31]

The least – unnullable least? – one could say is: *nothing has changed*. The double meaning of this sentence invokes on the one hand the claustrophobic and static setting of Beckett's writing, a site where seemingly nothing could ever change – already since the first sentence of his first published novel, the justly famous incipit of *Murphy*: 'The sun shone, having no alternative, on the nothing new.' No alternative, nothing new under the sun, from the first sentence on. Nothing could change except for nothing itself, and maybe this could summarize his endeavour: nothing *has* changed, it has changed imperceptibly as we went on, following the erratic narrating voice in its chaotic meanderings, it has appeared, almost without our noticing, that this nothing *is* the new in 'the nothing new' on which the sun shines without alternative. And that perhaps the ultimate paradox in Beckett is that he has operated this incredible feat, a transformation of nothing, he changed nothing – what seems to be immune to any change by definition – and that this shift within nothing has actually changed the very terms of the alternative.

Notes

1　But we do find 'René du Perron' and 'Fallor ergo sum'. Samuel Beckett, *Collected Poems in English and French* (New York: Grove Press, 1977).
2　It reduces it also in the opposite direction of the horoscope, since the last two lines of the poem point to the moment of death: 'and grant me my second / starless inscrutable hour'.
3　James Knowlson, *Damned to Fame: The Life of Samuel Beckett* (London: Bloomsbury, 1996), p. 352.
4　Lawrence Graver and Raymond Federman, *Samuel Beckett: The Critical Heritage* (London: Routledge and Kegan Paul, 1979), p. 148.
5　Samuel Beckett, *Disjecta: Miscellaneous Writings and a Dramatic Fragment*, ed. Ruby Cohn (New York: Grove Press, 1984), p. 172.
6　*Ibid.*, p. 172.
7　For a reconsideration of the role of Joyce in the Beckett oeuvre, see P. J. Murphy, *Beckett's Dedalus: Dialogical Engagements with Joyce in Beckett's Fiction* (Toronto: University of Toronto Press, 2009).
8　Jacques Lacan, *Le Sinthome* (*Le Séminaire XXIII*) (Paris: Seuil, 2005).
9　See for instance, 'Yes, the words I heard, and heard distinctly, having quite a sensitive ear, were heard a first time, then a second, and often even a third, as pure sounds, free of all meaning [. . .] And the words I uttered myself, and which must nearly always have gone with an effort of the intelligence, were often to me as the buzzing of an insect.' Beckett, *Molloy*, in *The Beckett Trilogy* (London: Picador, 1979), p. 47.
10　But that cliché is dead is itself another cliché. 'A cliché is a dead piece of language, of which one cliché might be that it is dead but won't lie down.' Christopher Ricks, *Beckett's Dying Words* (Oxford: Oxford University Press, 1995), p. 78. The subject has now been remarkably explored by Elizabeth Barry in her *Beckett and Authority: The Uses of Cliché* (Basingstoke: Palgrave Macmillan, 2006).
11　Gilles Deleuze, 'The exhausted', in *Essays Critical and Clinical* (Minneapolis: University of Minnesota Press, 1997), p. 152.
12　Jean-Paul Sartre, *Nausea*, trans. Robert Baldick (Harmondsworth: Penguin, [1965] 1972), p. 185; *La Nausée* (Paris: Livre de Poche, 1968), p. 182.
13　Beckett, *Molloy*, pp. 64–9. See also the remarkable article by Denise Gigante, 'The endgame of taste: Keats, Sartre, Beckett', in Timothy Morton (ed.), *Cultures of Taste / Theories of Appetite: Eating Romanticism* (Basingstoke: Palgrave Macmillan, 2004), pp. 183–202.

14 'And deep down it was all the same to me whether I sucked a different stone each time or always the same stone, until the end of time. For they all tasted exactly the same.' Beckett, *Molloy*, p. 69.

15 *Ibid.*

16 Beckett, *The Unnamable*, p. 321.

17 'Saying is inventing. Wrong, very rightly wrong. You invent nothing, you think you are inventing, you think you are escaping, and all you do is stammer out your lesson, the remnants of a pensum one day got by heart and long forgotten, life without tears, as it is wept.' Beckett, *Molloy*, p. 31.

18 Beckett, *The Unnamable*, pp. 353 and 352.

19 *Ibid.*, p. 352.

20 'Not to want to say, not to know what you want to say, not to be able to say what you think you want to say, and never to stop saying, or hardly ever, that is the thing to keep in mind, even in the heat of composition.' Beckett, *Molloy*, p. 27. And: 'Is there then no hope? Good gracious, no heavens, what an idea! Just a faint one perhaps, but which will never serve.' Beckett, *The Unnamable*, p. 336. And: 'and so depart, towards my brethren, no, none of that, no brethren, that's right, take it back [. . .]. And would it not suffice, without any change in the structure of the thing as it now stands, as it always stood, without a mouth being opened at the place which even pain could never line, would it no suffice to, to what, the thread is lost, no matter, here's another.' Beckett, *The Unnamable*, p. 252. There is a whole rhetoric of retraction in Beckett, the constant attempt to take back, make the said unsaid, but this only makes the insistence of enunciation more tenacious.

21 Beckett, *Malone Dies*, p. 207.

22 'coming to the truth of being requires thinking the non-separate, the in-distinct. But what separates and distinguishes e.g. light from darkness, constitutes rather the place of non-being and of the false.' Alain Badiou, 'L'Écriture du générique: Samuel Beckett' in *Conditions* (Paris: Seuil, 1992), p. 335; my translation. See also Andrew Gibson, *Beckett and Badiou: The Pathos of Intermittency* (Oxford: Oxford University Press, 2006).

23 Beckett, *Malone Dies*, p. 206.

24 Beckett, *The Unnamable*, p. 267.

25 Beckett, *L'Innommable* (Paris: Les Éditions de Minuit, 1953), p. 7.

26 Samuel Beckett, *Text 8, Stories and Texts for Nothing* (New York: Grove Press, 1967), p. 111; Beckett, VIII, *Nouvelles et textes pour rien* (Paris: Les Éditions de Minuit, 1955), pp. 167–8.

27 'Least. Least best worse. Least never to be naught. Never to naught be brought. Never by naught be nulled. Unnullable least.' Beckett, *Worstward Ho* (New York: Grove Press, 1983), p. 32.

28 Simon goes on: 'Through the vibration of time he goes towards his death which he never joins, yet carrying it in him.' Alfred Simon, *Samuel Beckett* (Paris: Belfond, 1963), p. 130.
29 Alain Badiou used it in the subtitle of his book on Beckett: *Beckett: l'increvable désir* (Paris: Hachette, 1995).
30 This is where my reading sharply differs from Badiou's, who sees in the death drive merely a morbid preoccupation with death.
31 I must refer here to Shane Weller's most remarkable *A Taste for the Negative: Beckett and Nihilism* (Oxford: Legenda, 2005), which explores this at length. Weller writes: 'To read all of Beckett's "little phrases" as nihilist may well be naïve, but it is surely no less naïve to read them as resistant to nihilism.' Weller, *A Taste*, p. 196.

4

'A tangle of tatters': ghosts and the busy nothing in *Footfalls*

Stephen Thomson

Ends and processes

It has become commonplace to see Beckett's theatre as progressively reducing itself, stripping away inessentials of speech, decor and incident. The plays of the early 1970s – *Not I, That Time* and *Footfalls* – are sometimes thought of as the theatrical endpoint of this process, perhaps even delivering an essence of Beckett, albeit a typically negative essence. The glamour of this reductive élan surely stems in part from its tendency towards zero, and the quasi-Romantic lure of the abyss. One might even look here for the fullfilment of the literature of the unword,[1] in so far as Beckett privileges 'the way that the text is spoken' over the clear articulation of sense.[2] By the same token, what we see cannot be quite nothing, and our attention is drawn all the more to what remains. Thus, according to Stan Gontarski's highly influential account of the late Beckett theatre, as the 'literary' recedes, the 'performative' aspects – the auditory and the visual – come to the fore.[3] Indeed, the auditory itself is readily subsumed under the visual in the idea of the 'stage image'.

> From *Play* onward Beckett's stage images would grow increasingly de-humanized, reified and metonymic, featuring dismembered or incorporeal creatures. It became a theater *finally* static and undramatic in any traditional sense. It is a theater of body parts and ghosts, a theater striving for transparency rather than solidity.[4]

Gontarski concludes emphatically: 'In the theater, there may only be the late Beckett.'[5] Here, it seems we have finally reached a sort of end towards which Beckett was always tending by way of reduction. Viewed in this light, *Godot* or *Endgame* start to appear positively 'baroque',[6] and must be retroactively reduced to fit. From now on, what counts as theatre is a striking disposition of figures in space: they may speak, but what they say is secondary. We may even infer that, in this line of thinking, theatre names what is distilled at the expense of drama. Thus, in a like spirit, Enoch Brater, though dedicated to locating the incipient *drama* in Beckett's prose, warns against theatrical adaptation where 'no *theater image* takes center stage'.[7] Perhaps it makes sense that an oeuvre so insistently dramatic, notably in its use of monologue, should reserve the theatre for something more precise.

The process of reduction as described by Gontarski does not stop at nothing; how could it? Something must be shown. But neither does it end with the process of writing: it does go on during the time of performance, producing a loss of 'solidity' that continues the slide towards nothing. Viewed in this light, the notions of finality and stasis that come with the idea of the stage image need to be complicated somewhat. There are, of course, some quite marked restrictions on movement in the plays of the early 1970s: Gontarski goes on to point out their 'delimited, ritualized' spaces.[8] But even the impressive brutality of the sorts of torture device used to keep Mouth in place in *Not I* should not distract us from the fact that the lips do move. Indeed, such drama as there is consists of their dynamic, syncopated flow of utterance: likewise May's pacing, as Beckett insisted, is the 'essence' of *Footfalls*.[9] This 'essence' would not, in other words, be a thing, but a rhythm, a movement to and fro. This notion has some authorial licence: when asked by composer Morton Feldman to produce the 'quintessence', it is just such a movement that Beckett sketches.[10] In *neither*, as in *Footfalls*, there is also movement between poles, between light and dark, self and unself, 'by way of neither': we are even told that 'unheard footfalls only sound'.[11] Indeed, in this curiously unclassifiable yet surprisingly blunt little piece it is not difficult to read something like a programme for *Footfalls*. The opera text has the advantage in being able to explain the trademark movement in conceptual terms. We see the 'to and fro' as a curious sort of dialectic, chronically bootless, never reaching its end, with the text only ending equivocally in 'unspeakable home'. Yet it is not for all that what we would usually call a negative dialectic. For the 'neither' that punctuates the piece does not so much effect a negation as leave in limbo both positive and negative. If the play is in some measure a performance of essentially the same pattern, it does not explain this: rather it must act it out, produce it as an experience. If *Footfalls* does this, then perhaps the final lights-up on the strip reveals not nothing but 'that unheeded neither'. Even if it all seems to point, and to work, towards nothing, what we have seen is a remarkably busy nothing.

A back and forth movement, then, is crucial to this theatre, even if it is only the beating of time. The ostensively static nature of the stage images of *Not I* and *That Time* may be a decoy, distracting us from a more fundamental rhythm, and threatening to reinstate them in the confident solidity of objects; the very status they are supposed to resist or put in question. One is tempted to add that the problem is aggravated rather than resolved with the introduction of the idea of 'ghosts'. For while the ghost may indeed convey 'transparency', it also recuperates it in an idea that is familiar, ready-made and sufficient to itself. Does naming what we see a ghost not risk being premature, admiring the hoped-for outcome, when what we must endure is the agonising process?

The ghost, nevertheless, is more durable than this line of argument would imply, and its mention in criticism is now almost *de rigueur*. Indeed it has come to encapsulate this period in Beckett's theatre. Notably Ruby Cohn refers to the plays of the 1970s (and *Play*) as the 'post-death plays',[12] and the relevant chapter of James Knowlson's biography borrows the title 'Shades' from Beckett's own for the BBC birthday celebrations of 1976.[13] The text of *Footfalls* itself seems to authorise this identification by introducing a thoroughly anecdotal ghost in May's little tale of her 'semblance' Amy. The 'moon through passing rack'[14] which figures the church candle veiled by the passage of the vaporous Amy, underlines a process of dematerialisation. Yet it does so by conjuring a pointedly generic ghost-story setting. This may, to a certain extent, be an effect of character: May is to be seen as plundering a stock of ready-made ideas. In the Berlin rehearsals, Beckett tells a puzzled but willing Hildegard Schmahl she can imagine May has stored these words, as if written down; yet, at the same time, 'You are composing. It is not a story, but an improvisation.'[15] In some additions to the play text, Beckett himself seems to follow a similar method of composition. So, during the same rehearsals, the 'South door' of the church is replaced by 'Nordpforte', because, says Beckett, it sounds colder.[16] The sheer thematic obviousness of calling Amy's mother 'Mrs Winter' is reinforced rather than diminished.

It is at least curious that a key play in a theatre famously stripped to the bones should not only contain such anecdotal elements, but even add to them during the process of revision. What is more, the generic nature of such additions risks authorising the interpolation of a familiar context that might, given free rein, tend to consolidate the image, bulking it out with the invisible ground of old stories. For though ghosts are not, of course, an everyday occurrence, ghost stories are. Beckett's own attitude towards allowing such explanatory structures to infect his theatre is perhaps inconsistent. According to Billie Whitelaw, in the rehearsals for *Footfalls* he quite happily points to 'a period between dying and grasping the message you're no longer *there*', and instructs her: 'Make it ghostly'.[17] Yet when Alan Schneider asks whether Mouth in *Not I* is to be seen as inhabiting 'some sort of limbo', Beckett rebuts the question with the now-famous formula, 'All I know is the text. [. . .] The rest is Ibsen.'[18] Beckett's theatre may indeed strive after a sort of limbo, the experience of the uncertainty of 'neither'. But, named too confidently, apprehended in too literal a manner, even a nominally spiritual entity like limbo is not immune to the pull of the realist tradition.[19]

The danger of this pull is arguably all the greater in the case of *Footfalls*; not least because more or less explicit reference to ghosts lends itself to thematising the play's procedures, but also because of a certain homeliness in its bedpans, pillows, carpets and so forth. A further door-related revision from the Berlin rehearsals illustrates the delicacy of striking a balance between reduction and anecdote. Beckett added a vertical strip of light in the background, ostensibly to prevent the audience from thinking the play was over at the penultimate fade. But he also suggested that the light might appear to be 'falling through the crack of a door'.[20] To the extent that what is shown is a light and not a door, the gesture is compatible with the notion of a stripped-down aesthetic, and indeed of the spectral. Yet, as an explanation of space it is curiously naturalising, and potentially lays the ground for further naturalisation. In Walter Asmus's version for the *Beckett on Film* project, the anecdote of the door has grown a landing around it.[21] In Asmus's film, the generic and the folksy coagulate around the increased coherence of materially organised space. The ghost of a door has materialised.

Such a vision is rather more encumbered with materiality than that seemingly conceived by Beckett's most acute critics. In *Footfalls*, it is of the essence that the space should be as little as possible given, for space is that which May's pacing is there to, in a sense, create. As Steven Connor has eloquently put it, the body is enacted 'not as presence, but as a spatial process which itself creates space'.[22] Beckett, indeed, criticises Hildegard Schmahl at one point in the Berlin rehearsals for being 'too much in the concrete space of the theatre, not absolutely enough concentrated in May, in this figure'.[23] Ruby Cohn intriguingly links the 'decreasing materiality' of Beckett's stage spaces with his 'unerring' sense of direction in life. As landmarks disappear in the later theatre, Cohn implies, the realisation of space is all the more intensely a question of 'direction'; not just stage directions but the bodily sense of orientation that informs these.[24] May's steps wear down to no trace at all, swallowed in darkness, yet, as Cohn remarks, they give 'radiance to the darkness of eternity'.[25] The ghosted space of the strip ought, at the final lights-up, to be definitively haunted in the precise sense that it is there by way of something now departed; present only as a ghostly excess, a homeopathic memory of form. This is the spectre that we seek well, and though ghostly appearance in terms of speech and costume may contribute to the effect, they also risk becoming something of a dangerous supplement.

By the same token, it should be noted that these critics are not interested in a formal purity entirely at the expense of attention to material. The material rather persists in an uncanny way which a more nuanced apprehension of the ghost than I have hitherto entertained may encapsulate rather well. For if, as may be casually inferred, the ghost serves as a marker of something become less substantial, it is equally true that it is something more substantial than it ought to be. Two insightful, and queerly complementary, comments of Steven Connor will bring out something of this doubleness. In an unpublished article Connor argues that the all-too material foot of earlier Beckett later pales to a more ghostly entity, and 'Nowhere is this spectral as opposed to abject foot shown more starkly' than in *Footfalls*.[26] But equally, in another place, focusing on walking rather than feet, Connor evokes a notion of the reanimation of properly inert matter: 'Rags are perhaps the busy life of decomposition, a dying that walks.'[27] Beckett perhaps makes a similar point, slyly incisive under the guise of practical art direction: of May's costume he notes one 'could go very far towards making the costume quite unrealistic, unreal. It could, however, also be an old dressing-gown, worked like a cobweb.'[28] Crucially, staging *Footfalls* successfully demands that it should be neither. We have, then, a delicate balancing act between the conceptual purity of the space sketched by May's passage and the potential embarrassment of accoutrements that make up the *business* of the play, and produce this form. The reduction model on its own, I would suggest, struggles to articulate this double aspect of the work. For the approach to nothing that is to be produced in performance operates not by the simple removal of things but by their interaction, their 'busy life', even by their addition. In this chapter, I explore these twin headings – of schematic purity that may seem to point towards philosophy, and the clutter of incident and speech that is conventionally the province of literature – and ultimately ask how the two are related in *Footfalls*.

The philosophical stage

The idea that nothing may be the product of addition as well as subtraction makes an appearance in Beckett as early as *Murphy*. After his final and decisive chess game with Endon, Murphy lays his head on the board and shuts his eyes, seeing only after-images.

> Then this also faded and Murphy began to see nothing, that colourlessness which is such a rare postnatal treat, being the absence (to abuse a nice distinction) not of percipere but of percipi. His other senses also found themselves at peace, an unexpected pleasure. Not the numb peace that comes when somethings give way, or perhaps simply add up, to the Nothing, than which in the guffaw of the Abderite naught is more real. Time did not cease, that would be asking too much, but the wheel of rounds and pauses did, as Murphy with his head among the armies continued to suck in, through all the posterns of his withered soul, the accidentless One-and-Only, conveniently called Nothing. Then this also vanished, or perhaps simply came asunder, in the familiar variety of stenches, asperities, ear-splitters and eye-closers, and Murphy saw that Mr Endon was missing.[29]

The hierarchy between an authentic and a derived nothing is ostensibly quite clear. But given the incorrigibly serio-comic mode of *Murphy*, one may doubt whether he really is so lucky as to have encountered the true, singular Nothing. Certainly, the eventual, bathetic coming-asunder seems to favour the somethings-adding-up model. At any rate, the contradistinction between a true Ur-nothing and a merely derived, factitious one which offers only a 'numb peace', along with the linkage of the nothing to a totality of things, may suggest a pastiche, if not specifically of the work of Martin Heidegger, at any rate of something very like it.

In his famous essay 'Was ist Metaphysik?', Heidegger suggests that our everyday definition of nothing – the negation of the totality of beings – cannot be the true one, for the true Nothing ought to precede, and indeed assist at the production of, beings in the first place. There are, nevertheless, instances in our everyday experience that point to the authentic. Profound, objectless boredom, for example, 'removes all things and human beings and oneself along with them into a remarkable indifference',[30] thus negatively intimating things as a totality. Yet such a mood conceals rather than reveals the Nothing. Only in *Angst* do we make contact with the true Nothing, 'at one with beings as a whole'.[31]

Angst is privileged to do this to the extent that it is not an everyday fear in the face of a banal, clearly defined object but an indefinite 'Angst vor . . .'.[32] The ellipsis indicates the radical absence of any object; of *this and that*. As elsewhere in Heidegger, the seemingly casual phrase *das und das* is used systematically, articulating a rhetoric of contempt for the dissipatory nature of everyday consciousness: we disseminate the authentic core of Being by investing it in trivial, anecdotal misattributions. In 'Was ist Metaphysik', however, this *das und das* has a dynamic counterpart in processes which go *hin und her* – to and fro. Indeed, our everyday chatter on nothing which produces its flawed definition – as the negation of the totality of beings – is 'dahin und daher reden'. The two adverbs, decoupled from two idiomatically unremarkable German verbs for aimless chatter (*dahinreden, daherreden*) and put together, produce a single phrase meaning 'to and fro'. This movement is no sooner isolated than it is dramatised in a figure that roves or tramps (*herumtriebt*).[33] Likewise Heidegger says we lose ourselves in the everyday drift (*Dahintreiben*), or in this or that circuit (*Bezirk*) of things;[34] and total boredom is like a silent mist drifting here and there (*hin- und herziehend*).[35] Indeed, philosophical discourse itself risks falling into an empty quarrel over words when it wanders into 'confused talk';[36] or, more precisely, a 'Hin und Her der Rede'.[37]

Faced with this, science must reassert its seriousness, and reject the Nothing as an 'outrage and a phantasm'. Indeed, the translation 'outrage' here is arguably underplayed: 'ein Greuel' suggests more a horror or abomination, crucially pitching 'eine Phantasterei' in the direction of the uncanny.[38]

But if 'science' is scared of the uncanniness of the Nothing, yet 'has recourse to what it rejects',[39] the homely to and fro seems to spook Heidegger's essay in a similarly uncanny manner. Though it is thetically disparaged, the everyday, distorted consciousness is what animates the essay, gives it a narrative. Heidegger's argument absolutely needs this pattern of movement that is said to characterise the everyday's avoidance of authentic experience, because the true Nothing, like the true Being, cannot be a static concept. It must unveil the Nothing gradually and obliquely, through the ostensibly disavowed to and fro that is itself presented as the characteristic movement of disavowal. At times this precarious doubling, whereby the allegedly derived species furnishes the *mise en scène* through which the underived is produced, seems on the brink of cancelling itself out to avow an identity. So, we have no sooner been chided for turning away from the totality of beings, and so from the Nothing, by escaping into the 'public superficies of our existence', than we are told that this very turning away, precisely as a species of negation, does 'within certain limits' the job of the Nothing anyway: 'In its nihilation the nothing directs us precisely towards beings.'[40] Here, an argumentative proposition from earlier in the essay threatens to rebound on Heidegger: 'if the nothing represents total indistinguishability, no distinction can obtain between the imagined and the "proper" nothing'.[41]

In Heidegger's essay, philosophy, or at any rate a scientific notion of philosophy, is explicitly coming up against its limits: it is precisely because something like the nothing cannot be neatly conceptualised, reduced to a point with a clear location, that this incipient theatricalisation is called for. Heidegger's relationship with art and literature is complex and I cannot hope to do justice to it here. But it is worth noting that, elsewhere in the oeuvre, the theatre is explicitly used to stand for an inauthentic acting out that travesties the authentic. When, in *Being and Time*, Heidegger looks for a way into authentic *Dasein*, he takes as his point of departure the call of conscience. This, he says, is a phenomenon which, once rescued from banalisation, may reveal a fundamental operation of, and attestation to, *Dasein*. As things stand, however, the 'call' is mis-understood as discourse, and consequently veiled in chatter. What it says is more properly understood as nothing; not a word, least of all a soliloquy or trial.[42] For one mishears the call of conscience when 'it gets drawn by the they-self into a soliloquy in which causes get pleaded' ('in ein verhandelndes Selbstgespräch').[43] The language of theatre and lawcourt (*Selbstgespräch*, *Verhandlung*)[44] confirms what is elsewhere implicit: the ersatz consciousness of everyday life is a dramatic production.

Though Maurice Merleau-Ponty is arguably not quite so unfor-giving of everyday self-forgetting as Heidegger, his conception of automatic behaviour as a backdrop against which the phenomenal appears is perhaps even more markedly theatrical. For Merleau-Ponty, we need something like an 'espace corporel': our bodies do not so much inhabit an already given space as carry it around with them through an underlying sense of the reach, grasp and pos-sibilities of our members. The 'espace corporel' is the stage space within which we, as necessarily embodied beings, perform. More precisely, it is

> the darkness needed in the theatre to show up the performance, the background of somnolence or reserve of vague power aginst which the gesture and its aim stand out, the zone of not being in front of which precise beings, figures and points can come to light.[45]

Naming the theatre (*la salle*) here is little more than the acknowl-edgement of a persistent, Gestalt-inspired aesthetic whereby Merleau-Ponty opposes *forme* (what appears) to *fond* (backdrop). Reality is a production, and the analysis that seeks to penetrate it is a sort of dramatic reconstruction. To put it rather tersely, Merleau-Ponty's phenomenology does not believe there is anything beyond Plato's cave and its shadowplay. He does occasionally entertain concepts such as a 'primordial silence', but only so as to set up a notional final backdrop against which the apparent silence of 'pure thought' may be revealed as a thoroughly linguistic hubbub ('bruis-sant de paroles') of ready-made phrases that form the 'fond obscur' of language.[46]

Read with a certain bias of attention, then, phenomenology's account of our relation to this factitious nothing, which may even be the only one there is, can be made to yield most of the ingre-dients for the basic situation of *Footfalls*. Not only is there the to-and-fro movement against a backdrop of darkness, but also the apprehension that there is something properly theatrical in this. It is perhaps tempting, then, to see Beckett's theatre as taking philosophy at its word, returning a metaphor to its proper stage. The argument would, however, require some fine distinctions. For one thing, Merleau-Ponty's *fond* is *obscur* not only in the sense that it is dark, but that being so it disappears, modestly doing its bit to make us believe that figures have just appeared on the stage, so annulling our active role as spectators.[47] The manifestation of a true silence or nothing, if we are to believe in such a possibility, would be of another order altogether. Being bored with a play is, let us remember, Heidegger's example of an experience that does not attain even the derived nothing.[48] But critics of Beckett's later theatre have often remarked on the visibility of its darkness, and of its tense relationship with the figures. As Ruby Cohn notes, a darkness 'envelops Beckett's post-death plays'.[49] That is to say, it does not politely recede into the background, or exist in some conceptual beyond, but encroaches on the spectacle, and indeed is part of it. Hence the play is 'wrested from the void'[50] but, in doing so, it 'uncovers a void'.[51] We are thus left suspended between the thickness of things and the nothing: what we see is both, and, as they eat into each other, neither.

To paraphrase into something like the language of Merleau-Ponty, what is staged is not, as is normal, *forme* at the expense of *fond*. But neither are we, nor can we be, offered the nothing at the expense of things. The signature movement here lies in the doubleness of the enveloping darkness: it is menacing and productive. Thus, for Anna McMullan the darkness surrounding Beckett's later plays, and the consequent lack of a coherent world or ideology, opens up 'a semiotic space from which image and then speech will emerge'.[52] Like Heidegger's proper Nothing, McMullan's version of Kristeva's *khora* is productive precisely because it encroaches or even menaces: having an 'area of darkness to surround the stage image means that the image is never "given", but must continually assert itself against the darkness'.[53] Objects thus have to prove themselves; or rather, we are all the more intensely aware of them because they are not objects, in the sense of patient, satisfyingly whole things that offer themselves to us reassuringly. A disembodied mouth hovering in the middle of an infinite blackness takes this perhaps as far as it can go. As McMullan notes, citing Paul

Lawley, Mouth in *Not I* is a part object, a 'no-thing' in that it cannot properly exist on its own.[54] In its uncanny intensity, the object, and theatre, are 'on trial'.

The plays of the 1970s, however, are not exclusively concerned with this physical trial, the passion of a figure against a backdrop of absence. These figures chatter and listen to chatter. Beckett's theatre does not condemn the *Verhandlung* (or *Prozess*) of soliloquy; rather it subjects it to a series of involutions which countenance a more nuanced entanglement of the self in its self than Heidegger's model will allow.[55] A 'Not I' is not a 'they-self' (*Man-Selbst*): the latter is a commonplace, off-the-peg subject that complacently takes itself for an 'I'. Mouth, on the other hand, narrates a third person which struggles to maintain a fiction of impersonality. This trial is not a diversion from a true existence, but the only existence this thing has. The truth, in the sense of what has to be said, appears here only as a pressure on what is said. Thus, 'that time in court', where the compulsion to speak came from without, merges into now: 'now this . . . something she had to tell . . . could that be it? . . something that would tell . . . how it was . . . how she– . . . what? . . had been? . . yes . . . something that would tell how it had been . . .'.[56] The moment is densely self-allusive, suggestive of a range of Beckett voices who are compelled to tell 'how it is', before, with and after, that time and others, but find themselves unable, even under pain of (self-) torture to say for sure what, where.

A tangle of tatters

Yet, as my analysis of Heidegger and Merleau-Ponty has hinted, philosophy is also on trial when its metaphors are acted out on stage. Where philosophy can elect to bleach a metaphor of walking into a pure schema, maintaining the apparently accidentless functionality of algebra or grammar, theatre must take it at its word, flesh it out, and face the consequences of dipping into the accidental. To put this another way, philosophy has to work to do justice to the resistance of brute matter: theatre, on the contrary, must do work if it is to question the givenness of what is there in front of us. The uncanniness of *Footfalls* lies in its refusal to see the *hin und her* of May's pacing as *either* quite everyday or quite transcendent. There has been a notable tendency in recent criticism to insist that it is just this undecidable, uncanny quality in Beckett that poses questions back to philosophy. Richard Lane's collection *Beckett and Philosophy*[57] is very much oriented towards seeing Beckett as related to philosophy, yet not reducible to it. Ulrika Maude's contribution on Merleau-Ponty and Steve Barfield's on Heidegger are alike in seeing Beckett as both convergent with, and crucially divergent from, the phenomenologists. In each case Beckett is seen to share with phenomenology a worrying at the bounds of everyday notions of materiality, yet to refuse the transcendence and authenticity countenanced by Merleau-Ponty and Heidegger respectively. Spectrality figures in both Maude and Barfield as an expression of this suspension between metaphysical categories.[58] Indeed, Barfield goes one step further to describe Beckett's very relationship with Heidegger as 'uncanny'.[59]

Jacques Derrida, when he explains why he cannot write on Beckett, produces a similar doubling of the uncanny, as theme and as relation. This brief but fascinating apology appears in an interview whose title points us towards the uncanny nature of all literature. The phrase 'cette étrange institution', which may be read idiomatically as 'that uncanny institution', recurs elsewhere in Derrida to denote literature's uncanny presentation of a secret that does not exist, that has nothing behind or beyond it.[60] Derrida's most explicit pronouncement on Beckett's text in the interview – that it maintains to an extraordinary degree a tension between nihilist and affirmative impulses – thus makes of him an exemplar of what is true of all literature.[61] Yet, precisely because Derrida feels 'too close' to Beckett, he feels he cannot speak of him, for fear of falling into the 'platitude of a supposed academic metalanguage'. [62] There is, in other words, a temptation to translate the Beckett text into so many philosophical themes, yet to do so would be to annihilate its difference, its singularity, its uncanniness *qua* literature. Derrida's argument is remarkable, then, in that it locates uncanniness both in literature's constitutional equivocation between materiality and transcendence, and in his own curious casting of Beckett as his own personal William Wilson.[63] Derrida confesses he will sometimes take two or three lines of Beckett with students, but finally give up. It is not honest to

> extract a few 'significant' lines from a Beckett text. The composition, the rhetoric, the construction and the rhythm of his works, even the ones that seem the most 'decomposed', that's what 'remains' finally

the most 'interesting', that's the work, that's the signature, this remainder which remains when the thematics is exhausted.[64]

What the gratifying recognition and enumeration of themes misses, then, is a 'rhythm', something dynamic which plays across the whole text. The situation is rather reminiscent of the wager set up with Geoffrey Bennington in the co-authored *Jacques Derrida*.[65] Bennington will try to explain Derrida, to capture his essence, and Derrida's part will be to struggle against being reduced to a matrix of ideas by pitching his writing in a way that will leave the reader constantly in doubt as to whether an anecdote or phrase is a matter of biographical ephemera, or of high philosophical import.

I would suggest that something similar is going on in Beckett's writing for theatre of the period with which I am concerned, and most especially with *Footfalls*. There is a pull towards the theatricalisation of philosophical ideas which will quite easily reward critical comparison. But a countervailing tendency towards a more trivial world of bedpans, lacrosse and clichéd ghost stories must also be attended to. Crucially, the two are not merely discrete forces but are inextricably linked. This, I think, brings us back to the spoken text of the play with renewed attention. There has, as I started by outlining, been a pull towards the 'stage image' as the bearer of meaning, and a corresponding diminution in the importance of speech, encouraged in part by Beckett's own relative lack of concern for full intelligibility. Yet this has never deterred critics entirely from literary criticism. Stan Gontarski's advocacy of the late, performative Beckett goes hand in hand with a commitment to establishing a more rigorous play-text, inscribing changes made in rehearsal, and pencilled by Beckett on to the published text. These changes are, indeed, often additions, extending the play on unaccented, yet pointed, repetition of certain phrases. The 1976 text already repeats 'it all' in this way: the pause that separates the two utterances, and a studied lack of cadence are essential to holding in suspense the incipient 'oirish' idiom of 'it all, it all'.[66] Yet the threat of banality is arguably necessary to avoid the gnomic potential of 'it all'. The effect is picked up with 'sequel' and 'the semblance' in the third part of the new text.[67] Such emendations one might readily agree are concerned primarily with the music of the piece, and with the sense only contingently and secondarily. But when Gontarski's notes cite the mother's reference to 'lacrosse' as an instance of 'the crucifixion imagery of the play',[68] something more like literary criticism is taking place: the banal and the meta-physically inflated intersect uncannily. The point rests on the gloss of 'His poor arm' as the transept of the cruciform church plan cor-responding to Christ's wounded member. The unutterable capitali-sation of 'His', not found in the 1976 edition, may be an attempt to retranslate Beckett's French version, 'son pauvre bras sauveur'.[69] As Pascale Sardin has pointed out, Beckett's French versions of English texts often make religious references more pointedly.[70] Gontarski's glossing even makes a brave attempt to sew Beckett's seemingly capricious pun on the word 'sequel' into other scraps of textual fabric: 'The "tangle of tatters" in May's narrative is her semblance which she seeks well. Amy herself is, of course, another semblance.'[71] Indeed, 'seek well' would seem to be an attempt to retranslate an invention from the Schiller Theater production, where the original 'Epilog' was replaced by 'Folge', which can equally be read as an imperative, an invitation to follow the path of the double.[72]

In light of all this evident care, Beckett's famous letter to Billie Whitelaw may start to seem rather crafty: 'The pacing is the essence of the matter. To be dramatised to the utmost. The text: what phar-macists call excipient'.[73] Whereas the figure of Mouth is a 'purveyor of a stage text', here the pacing would be the active ingredient, and the text a mere vehicle. But the words of *Footfalls* are certainly not any old words. Supposing they had been composed originally as 'excipient', as the bare minimum required to make the walking go, they go over the score, and take on a life of their own. In fact, they show a prodigious capacity to thematise themselves, as well as the action of the play. And no phrase is more inviting and capacious than 'a tangle of tatters' in that it narrates the play's own aspira-tion to produce dematerialising matter, and what is more gives this paradox a comforting generic home in the ghost story. For, as in the example of 'lacrosse', a poise between the glamour of the tran-scendental, and the derisory materiality of rags and wicker rackets, is what *Footfalls* cultivates.

The thickness of the text of *Footfalls*, not least its thuddingly thematic link to ghostliness, is necessary to maintain the indeci-sion of the uncanny; the emergence of the strange within the very heart of the homely. Walking itself, indeed, is capacious of all these possibilities. Indeed, in this respect, literature may be said to

mirror a movement afoot in philosophy. In an enormously suggestive article on what she terms the 'ambulatory uncanny',[74] Susan
Bernstein (with the help of Samuel Weber, Hoffmann, Nietzsche
and others) examines the uncanny nature of the relation of Being
to Nothing in Heidegger. Specifically, just as the opposition *heim-
lich* and *unheimlich* famously collapses into an identity at a certain
point, so does Being (*Sein*) itself intersect with Nothing, in the
sense that it can be no given being (*Seiend*). The dramatic element
of the ambulatory, however, makes its arrival in Bernstein's analysis via a figure straight from a tale of Hoffmann. At a key point
in his essay 'Zur Seinsfrage', Bernstein notes, Heidegger brings in
Nietzsche's notion of nihilism as the 'uncanniest guest' and has
it wandering around the house, haunting the everyday. Of the
uncanny, then, one might say 'it walks', following the model of
Heidegger's 'es gibt'. Walking, for Bernstein, dramatises the impossibility of reducing concepts like being, nothing and the uncanny
to a point, the inevitability of their emerging through the unfold-
ing time of narrative. Thus she speaks of 'the narrative spasms
that allow the uncanny to come forth, over time, never whole',[75]
and 'the syncopated structure which makes it impossible to define
the uncanny'.[76] As in my analysis of 'Was ist Metaphysik?', philosophy's ambivalent turn towards narrative and literature is at
stake. If a philosophical commitment to avoiding the hypostases of
'science' is taken at its word, a humble tale of the marvellous may
even have the last word. So, as Bernstein argues, through 'The
man of the crowd', Poe 'privileges the walking body, the signifying
process, over any interior or meaning which might characterize it
as a whole or replace it as its end'.[77]

And so does *Footfalls*. In these ways, Beckett's late theatre can
be seen to hold a critical, rather than a merely allegorical, relationship with phenomenology. In a curious way, this can be said to
be a more faithful response than would be the mere plundering
of themes: for it is dedicated not to exemplifying or explaining
but to delivering an experience that puts us on the spot. The idea
of reduction is only half the story here: for it tends towards a
notion of essence, and of nothing, that are ultimately philosophy's
problem. If Beckett has something to say back to philosophy it is
emphatically not because he deals in clean, hard concepts shorn
of the contingencies of bodily existence; for neither, in truth, does
philosophy.

Notes

1 Samuel Beckett, *Disjecta: Miscellaneous Writings and a Dramatic Fragment* (London: John Calder, 1983). One might doubt how seriously this scribble to a pen pal, dismissed by Beckett himself as 'German bilge' (*Disjecta*, p. 170), should be taken. Yet the insistently negative moment of Beckett's oeuvre, which can moreover be seen repeated *en petit* in the genesis of any given text, seems to beckon in this direction, and this sets a price on any apparently programmatic statement dealing with the nothing. See also Shane Weller, Chapter 6 below.

2 Walter D. Asmus, 'Practical aspects of theatre, radio and television: rehearsal notes for the German première of Beckett's *That Time* and *Footfalls* at the Schiller Theater Werkstatt, Berlin', *Journal of Beckett Studies*, 2 (Summer 1977), 82–95, 84.

3 S. E. Gontarski, 'Staging himself, or Beckett's late style in the theatre', *Samuel Beckett Today / Aujourd'hui: Crossroads and Borderlines / L'œuvre carrefour / L'œuvre limite*, eds Marius Buning, Matthijs Engelberts and Sjef Houppermans, guest editor Emmanuel Jacquart, 6 (1997), 87–97, 87–8.

4 *Ibid.*, 93. Emphasis added.

5 *Ibid.*, 95.

6 *Ibid.*, 94. See also Ruby Cohn, *Just Play: Beckett's Theatre* (Princeton: Princeton University Press, 1980), p. 17.

7 Enoch Brater, *The Drama in the Text: Beckett's Late Fiction* (Oxford: Oxford University Press, 1994), p. 12. Emphasis added.

8 Gontarski, 'Staging himself', 93.

9 Billie Whitelaw, *Billie Whitelaw . . . Who He?* (London: Hodder & Stoughton 1995), p. 139. See also Asmus, 'Practical aspects of theatre, radio and television', 83.

10 James Knowlson, *Damned to Fame: The Life of Samuel Beckett* (London: Bloomsbury, 1996), p. 631. One can see something like this movement at either end of the oeuvre, in 'Ding Dong' in *More Pricks Than Kicks*, and in *Quad*.

11 Samuel Beckett, *neither*, *Journal of Beckett Studies*, 4 (Spring 1979), vii. But see also Stan Gontarski, 'Editing Beckett', *Twentieth Century Literature*, 41:2 (1995), 190–207. See also Derval Tubridy, Chapter 5 below.

12 Cohn, *Just Play*, p. 53.

13 Knowlson, *Damned to Fame*, p. 635.

14 Beckett, *Footfalls* (1976), in *Complete Dramatic Works* (London: Faber & Faber, 2006), p. 402. This text credits the 1976 first edition but silently incorporates the changes published in *The Theatrical*

Notebooks of Samuel Beckett Vol. IV *The Shorter Plays* ed. by S. E. Gontarski (London: Faber & Faber, 1999).

15 Asmus, 'Rehearsal notes', 86.

16 *Ibid.*, 85.

17 Whitelaw, *Billie Whitelaw . . . Who He?*, pp. 143 and 146.

18 *No Author Better Served: The Correspondence of Samuel Beckett and Alan Schneider*, ed. Maurice Harmon (London: Harvard University Press, 1998), pp. 279 and 283.

19 The reference is usually taken as a direct swipe at realism's mapping of stage space on to domestic space, but the matter of 'limbo' may make one think of a rather more interesting conjunction of *Not I* and Ibsen's last play *When We Dead Awake*.

20 Asmus, 'Rehearsal notes', 88.

21 *Footfalls*, directed by Walter Asmus, filmed in Ardmore Studios April 2000, with Susan Fitzgerald and Joan O'Hara. *Beckett on Film*, produced by Michael Colgan and Alan Moloney (Blue Angel Films / Tyrone Productions for Radio Telefís Éireann & Channel 4: 2001).

22 Steven Connor, *Samuel Beckett: Repetition, Theory and Text* (Oxford: Blackwell, 1988), p. 162.

23 Asmus, 'Rehearsal notes', 88.

24 Cohn, *Just Play*, p. 17.

25 *Ibid.*, p. 57.

26 Steven Connor, 'Scribbledehobbles: writing Jewish-Irish feet', unpublished, online at http://www.stevenconnor.com/scribble/ last accessed 17 September 2008.

27 Steven Connor, *The Book of Skin* (Ithaca, NY: Cornell University Press, 2003), p. 32.

28 Asmus, 'Rehearsal notes', 87.

29 Samuel Beckett, *Murphy* (London: John Calder, 1969), p. 138.

30 Martin Heidegger, *Pathmarks*, trans. and ed. William McNeill (Cambridge: Cambridge University Press, 1998), p. 86; Martin Heidegger, *Wegmarken*, second edition (Frankfurt am Main: Klostermann, 1978), p. 87; *Wegmarken*, pp. 109–10. See also Russell Smith, Chapter 11 below.

31 Heidegger, *Pathmarks*, pp. 89–90; *Wegmarken*, pp. 112–13.

32 Heidegger, *Pathmarks*, p. 88; *Wegmarken*, p. 111.

33 Heidegger, *Pathmarks*, p. 86; *Wegmarken*, p. 108.

34 Heidegger, *Pathmarks*, p. 87; *Wegmarken*, p. 109. McNeill's translation of *Dahintreiben* as 'preoccupations' and *Bezirk* as 'region' misses the suggestion of patterns of movement.

35 Heidegger, *Pathmarks*, p. 87; *Wegmarken*, pp. 109–10.

36 Heidegger, *Pathmarks*, p. 84.

37 Heidegger, *Wegmarken*, pp. 105–6.

38 Heidegger, *Pathmarks*, p. 84; *Wegmarken*, p. 106.

39 Heidegger, *Pathmarks*, p. 84.

40 Heidegger, *Pathmarks*, p. 92; *Wegmarken*, p. 115. On 'nihililation' see also Shane Weller, *A Taste for the Negative: Beckett and Nihilism* (Oxford: Legenda, 2005) and Erik Tonning, *Samuel Beckett's Abstract Drama: Works for Stage and Screen 1962–1985* (Oxford: Peter Lang, 2007).

41 Heidegger, *Pathmarks*, p. 87; *Wegmarken*, p. 109.

42 Martin Heidegger, *Being and Time*, trans. John Macquarrie and Edward Robinson (Oxford: Blackwell, [1962] 1999), p. 318; Martin Heidegger, *Sein und Zeit*, second edition (Halle: Max Niemeyer, 1929) p. 273.

43 Heidegger, *Being and Time*, p. 319, §56 'The character of consicience as call'; Heidegger, *Sein und Zeit*, p. 274.

44 Heinrich von Kleist in particular frequently draws on and reinforces analogies between theatre and court of law.

45 Maurice Merleau-Ponty, *The Phenomenology of Perception*, trans. Colin Smith (London: Routledge & Kegan Paul, [1962] 1981), pp. 100–1; Maurice Merleau-Ponty, *La Phénoménologie de la perception* (Paris: Gallimard, 1945), p. 117.

46 Merleau-Ponty, *Phenomenology*, pp. 183–8; *Phénoménologie*, pp. 214–19.

47 See Merleau-Ponty on the invisibility of the actress (p. 213) and the blind recognition of the spectator (p. 216).

48 Heidegger, *Pathmarks*, p. 87.

49 Cohn, *Just Play*, p. 53.

50 *Ibid.*, p. 57.

51 *Ibid.*, p. 95.

52 Anna McMullan, *Theatre on Trial: Samuel Beckett's Later Drama* (London: Routledge, 1993), p. 9.

53 *Ibid.*, p. 11.

54 *Ibid.*, p. 75; citing Paul Lawley, 'Counterpoint, absence and the medium in Beckett's Not I', *Modern Drama*, 26:4 (1983), 412.

55 See Ruby Cohn's discussion of soliloquy: Cohn considers May's soliloquising a 'fiction', or 'subterfuge for avoiding soliloquy', but a sort of soliloquy none the less. Cohn, *Just Play*, p. 74.

56 Beckett, *Not I*, p. 381.

57 Richard Lane (ed.), *Beckett and Philosophy* (Basingstoke: Palgrave, 2002).

58 Ulrika Maude, 'The body of memory: Beckett and Merleau-Ponty' and Steven Barfield, 'Beckett and Heidegger: a critical survey', in Richard Lane (ed.), *Beckett and Philosophy*, pp. 108–22, p. 120 and pp. 154–65, p. 161, respectively.

59 Barfield, 'Beckett and Heidegger', p. 156.
60 Jacques Derrida, *Papier machine* (Paris: Galilée, 2001), p. 398.
61 Derrida, '"This strange institution called literature": an interview with Jacques Derrida', in *Acts of Literature*, ed. Derek Attridge (London: Routledge, 1992), pp. 33–75, p. 61.
62 Derrida, *Ibid.*, p. 60.
63 My reference is, of course, to Edgar Allan Poe's tale 'William Wilson', perhaps the classic exposition in English letters of the attraction and danger of the Doppelgänger. See Edgar Allan Poe, *The Fall of the House of Usher and Other Writings*, rev. edn (Harmondsworth: Penguin, 2003).
64 Derrida, *Acts*, p. 61.
65 Jacques Derrida and Geoffrey Bennington, *Jacques Derrida* (Chicago: Chicago University Press, 1993).
66 Beckett, *Footfalls*, p. 402.
67 *Ibid.*
68 *The Theatrical Notebooks of Samuel Beckett*, Vol. IV *The Shorter Plays*, ed. S.E. Gontarski (London: Faber & Faber, 1999), p. 286.
69 Samuel Beckett, *Pas, suivi de quatre esquisses* (Paris: Les Éditions de Minuit, 1978), p. 13.
70 Pascale Sardin, 'Beckett et la religion au travers du prisme de quelques textes courts auto-traduits', *Samuel Beckett Today / Aujourd'hui: Beckett and Religion / Beckett / Aesthetics / Politics*, eds Mary Bryden and Lance St John Butler, 9 (2000), 199–206.
71 *Theatrical Notebooks*, p. 286.
72 Asmus, 'Rehearsal notes', 85.
73 Whitelaw, *Billie Whitelaw*, p. 139.
74 Susan Bernstein, 'It walks: the ambulatory uncanny', *Modern Language Notes*, 118:5 (2003), 1111–39.
75 *Ibid.*, 1117.
76 *Ibid.*, 1118.
77 *Ibid.*, 1119.

5

Nothings in particular

Bill Prosser

In 1654 a performance about nothing took place more muscular than Beckett's double-negative *Waiting for Godot* three hundred years later.[1] The seventeenth-century event attracted a similarly expectant yet sceptical audience as that gathered in 1955, but instead of peering at Gogo and Didi it watched Otto Von Guericke pump air from two hollow bronze hemispheres, balanced together rim to rim. With all prepared, two teams of eight shire-horses strained in opposite directions, heaving to pull the sphere apart. It did not move. Unhitching the horses, Von Guericke opened the air-valve and gently separated the two halves.

Nothing comes from nothing, according to Parmenides. Nothing is more real than nothing, posited Democritus. Nature abhors a vacuum, concluded Aristotle. Beckett was earthier in describing how artists might deal with such *horror vacui*: 'If you ask me why the canvas doesn't remain blank, I can only invoke this clear need, forever innocent, to fuck it with colour, if need be through vomiting one's being.'[2]

His explicit imperative echoes troubles over nothing that had persisted until after the Renaissance, with Descartes, for instance, believing that a perfect vacuum was impossible.[3] But the theatricality of Von Guericke's tug-of-war brought to prominence Torricelli's discovery, made several years earlier, of the earth's atmospheric pressure, together with its unwitting, vacuous progeny. By filling a glass tube to its brim with mercury, and then stopping the top with his finger, inverting the tube, placing its end in a mercury-filled bowl and releasing his finger, Torricelli watched the level drop until balanced by air pressing on the mercury in the bowl. As no air could have entered the tube Torricelli reasoned that the gap at its tip must contain nothing. Subsequently, such down-to-earth vacua remained airtight until punctured by quantum theory, where nothing is never present in the topsy-turvy revelations of particle physics.

Although quantum ambiguities swept away the seemingly objective predictions of Newtonian laws, more personally we can all readily acknowledge the subjective paradoxes of everyday life – those that mix emotional and aesthetic worlds into the messy flux of human experience. Empty and full, something and nothing, these are oppositions that can be applied equally to states of both feeling and sensation. Phrases that we feel 'something empty inside' or 'full of nothing' might have been among the Knots untangled by R. D. Laing:

> One is inside
> then outside what one has been inside
> One feels empty
> Because there is nothing inside oneself
> [. . .]
> one remains empty because
> while one is on the inside
> even the inside of the outside is outside
> and inside oneself there is still nothing
> There has never been anything else
> And there never will be[4]

Laing's empathic reflections on the inner-world's hall of mirrors include several allusions to the disturbing presence of nothings. Beckett, on the other hand, is gently upbeat:

> Watt learned towards the end of this stay in Mr Knott's house to accept that nothing had happened, that a nothing had happened, learned to bear it and even, in a shy way, to like it.[5]

Even more focused on our relationship with emptiness is Heidegger's Freiberg lecture series of 1929–30, in which he speaks of a particular type of emotional vacuum: the emptiness of feeling bored. In this state we choose things to do not because they are interesting in themselves but simply to pass the time, '[m]erely so as not to fall into this *being left empty* that is emerging in boredom'.[6] Boredom, Heidegger contends, is when 'something at hand [. . .] *offers nothing*. Being left empty means to be offered nothing by what is at hand':[7]

> Finding himself now alone, with nothing in particular to do, Watt put
> his forefinger in his nose, first in one nostril, and then in the other.
> But there were no crusts in Watt's nose, tonight.[8]

The concept of Nothing, and the disturbances it has to offer,
Heidegger had already addressed in his inaugural lecture 'What is
metaphysics.'[9] Far from being simply an abstract term, Nothing can
be experienced as the Dread felt when our secure, personal world
of individual existence loses its meaning, panicking us towards 'a
sort of "void without ground" [*Ab-grund*], toward a nothingness.'[10]
Dread arising from Nothingness is universal, with boredom just
one of its minor tributaries, caused by being surrounded by things
that are at hand but offering nothing.

His 'ready at hand' describes our generally inattentive, everyday
experiences with things, and boredom, of course, arises in the most
ordinary of circumstances. Factory work, unsurprisingly, is one
cause, and a recent publication, *The Bored @ Work Doodle Book*,
suggests that boredom remains endemic in the email era.[11] The
book promises how aesthetic alchemy can shift universal tedium
into everyday creativity, but turns out instead to offer a series
of tired graphic exercises. Nevertheless, boredom can blossom
into more genuine absent-minded pictorial ingenuity, as one of
the few thoughtful texts written on doodling celebrates.[12] Ernst
Gombrich writes that: '[i]t is the temptation of the empty sheet
of paper [. . .] at a meeting that induces us to enliven the hours
of boredom [. . .] by permitting our pen to play a game of its own
on this licensed playground.'[13] Gombrich was himself a doodler,
albeit a phoney one. On his own admission he 'forged' a doodle
(making it with a purpose in mind) and entered a competition
enticingly billed as a 'Royal Academy for Doodlers' run by the
London *Evening Standard*.[14] Although Gombrich described himself
as 'a terrible doodler', its editors were duped well enough to award
him a prize of ten shillings. The contest cashed in on a worldwide
craze for doodling in the late 1930s following Frank Capra's 1936
film *Mr Deeds Goes to Town*. A comedy, this revolves around Gary
Cooper's amateur musician outsmarting city-slickers set to steal
his inherited fortune. Charged that his obsessional tuba-playing
is a symptom of insanity he argues that everyone has harmless
illogical pastimes, which are even evident here, in the courtroom.
The judge, for example, is an 'O-filler',[15] and the expert witness,

the psychiatrist, covers his notes with grotesque figures. 'It's called doodling. Almost everybody's a doodler. Did you ever see a scratch pad in a telephone booth?'[16]

The *Evening Standard* published only a small proportion from over nine thousand entries, but after the event closed three psychologists gathered all the submissions for exhaustive statistical analysis.[17] On the basis of written information accompanying each doodle, they, too, identify boredom as an important stimulus. This, coupled with impatience, causes the motor tension that results in doodling – an equivalent of 'trembling, fidgeting, or scratching'.[18] Because this agitation exists below ordinary awareness it divides attention: one can both respond to external stimuli and operate on autopilot, achieving the mental semi-detachment necessary for doodling. They suggest that this frame of mind is close to hypnosis, in which repetitive movements are common – though omitting to mention that rocking a child to sleep was once called 'doodling'.[19]

In any case, a deeper association between boredom and drawing can be found by looking once again at Heidegger's 1929–30 lectures. His fascination with boredom is based on our paradoxical response to its relationship with time. We urgently escape boredom (*Langweile*) because time becomes long (*lang*) – a perverse reaction as we hope to live a long life. Boredom, '[w]e wish to know nothing of it' he says,[20] 'the time that drags must be coerced into passing more quickly, so that its being paralysed does not paralyse us'.[21] We need to make sluggish time temporary:

VLADIMIR: That passed the time.
ESTRAGON: It would have passed in any case.
VLADIMIR: Yes, but not so rapidly.[22]

But this effort is not directed against time itself. 'We do not [. . .] stare at the seconds flowing by, in order to drive them on. On the contrary, even though we often look at the clock, we look away again just as quickly. Toward what? Toward nothing in particular.'[23] None the less we are looking for something – anything that will hasten time that drags.

So: we are waiting at a country station, hours before the train. How do we drive time on, pass dragging time?

We look at the clock – only a quarter of an hour has gone by. Then we go off into the local road. [. . .] Fed up with walking back and forth, we sit down on a stone, draw all kinds of figures in the sand, and in doing so catch ourselves looking at our watch again – half an hour – and so on.[24]

Dying of boredom we kill time by dragging pictures in the sand.

Drawing's etymological root is *trahere*, to drag. Its relationship to deep historical time cannot be known. Oliver Sacks describes how a sufferer from Tourette's Syndrome pressed a circular, sensuous mark on the ground around himself with his foot, saying 'I feel it in my bones. I think it's something primal, prehuman.'[25] Territorial markings, pawing the ground, dragging and drawing along can easily be seen as interconnected. Trail, trailer, track, tractive, tractor, traipse (a trailing walk), trait (a short drawn line), trace and tracery, all follow in train. Being slowed down by dragging something along is an experience that is as old as we are. Boredom is when that thing is time itself.

Beckett's ambition towards language, to 'bore one hole after another in it'[26] and, towards his audience, to '"[b]ore the pants off them"',[27] illustrate boredom's etymology. Born colloquially in the eighteenth century, its parents might be the Anglo Saxon *bor*, 'gimlet', the Latin *foro*, 'to bore', or the French *bourrer*, 'to stuff'. 'Stuff them' might be an equally uninterested response from Beckett regarding his audiences' enjoyment. *Ennui*, in English synonymously from around 1750, has a clearer, more vigorous, root, deriving from the Latin *in odio*, 'in hate'.

Adam Phillips writes of 'the great ennui of childhood' as 'the mood of diffuse restlessness which contains that most absurd and paradoxical wish, the wish for a desire'.[28] Heidegger would see this nonsensical ambition as an opportunity: 'how are we to make room for this initially inessential, ungraspable boredom? Only by not being opposed to but letting it approach us and tell us what it wants.'[29]

Despite its minute examination of the 'passionate intensity' of childhood, Phillips believes that psychoanalysis says little about more vague and subtle feelings such as boredom. To redress this omission he, too, identifies boredom as positive. Parents must allow space for it to flourish and not to 'sabotage it by distraction [. . .] It is one of the most oppressive demands of adults that the child should be interested, rather than take the time to find out what interests him. Boredom is integral to taking one's time.'[30]

A similar sentiment is offered by the Tibetan Buddhist master Chogyam Trungpa:

> Boredom is important in meditation practice: it increases the psychological sophistication of the practitioners. They begin to appreciate boredom and they develop their sophistication until the boredom begins to become cool boredom, like a mountain river. It flows and flows, methodically and repetitiously, but it is very cooling, very refreshing.[31]

Doodles spawn here, in the stream of boredom. It repeatedly hatches a teeming population of geometric patterns, organic fantasies, bizarre figures, hybrid animals, daisy-chain margins and merry-go-round calligraphs. Pictorially, these animate the moribund and invigorate the ornamental, becoming inadvertent 'gateways to the imagination'.[32]

Having nothing particular or interesting to do evacuates the mind of impediments to drawing – from mere disinclination to graphic agoraphobia. Practically everybody doodles, Beckett as much as many, and much more than some. His ramble over the given range, and while all are idiosyncratic, as are the drawings of children, none shows any revelatory iconographic peculiarities. He is not an adult Nadia Chomyn or Jonathan Lerman, redefining our expectations. Nevertheless, again like children's drawings, all are worth looking at. This is because the specific properties of each drawing, rather than being appreciated for literary insight or aesthetic innovation, becomes an opportunity for imaginative engagement.

Beckett's most heavily decorated work is the six notebooks that comprise 'Watt'.[33] However, the manuscript of his play that came to nothing, *Human Wishes*, contains his highest concentration of doodled faces and figures, some seventy-seven of them across two consecutive versa pages.[34] All have nothing to do with the drama's narrative, and their relative compactness provides an intriguing opportunity to explore the particulars that result, one hazards, when nothing is on offer – in this case from his ready-at-hand, ready-and-waiting written drama.

The holograph runs to fifteen loose leaves, the second carrying twenty-four small faces and figures that witness his pen and crayon-scrawled text. (The faces and figures vary between approximately 4 mm and 45 mm in height.) Embedded among them a lone pair of disembodied legs scampers frantically, blindly seeking the rest of itself. Three of the five profiles are facing left (the most common direction for right-handed doodlers), while the remaining characters stare straight out at us. Two of the profiles are wearing hats; one face peeks from below a crownless brim as the other shades himself beneath a shock of dark hair. Of the figures, two are seated, one in a three-legged, one-armed, high-backed chair, the other on a quadruped stool. Five are standing facing us, and five have their backs turned. Five stand in profile facing right, five left. One is lying on his tummy facing right, another sprints off towards the left. He, however, is severely impeded by what might be a bursting bagful of mixed soot and engine-oil.[35]

As to posture, five are bow-legged, five arms akimbo. Three, all seen from behind, are bending forward to the right from their waists, peering or shouting. Another has his hands behind his back, a further has his shoved in his pockets. One appears to be doing what would later be known as the twist – knees sharply forward, arms bent, one in front, the other behind. Three figures might be one, in frozen stages of animation. These are drawn as slack S-shapes doing a loose-limbed dance, with pelvis grinding, arms chugging, feet pointing in, out, in. A zigzag snaps between figures one and two, while three esses throb beside the final dancer; snaking after-images from this louche trio.

These three share in miniature concentration the down-turned lips and jutting jaws of determined fruggers. Elsewhere, others seem to be enjoying themselves too, at least up to a point, with five definitely smiling and another wearing the half-grin of benign toleration. Six have their mouths open, the most dramatic showing a frenzied darkened howl, like a miniature hell-mouth, monstrously gummed and fanged (figure 1). Its owner has pinprick eyes like many of his companions, and the remainder have standard cartoon goggles – circles with dots for pupils. These minor variations in ocular description severely limit the possibility for subtle physiognomic expression. Beeded stares can only be emblematically altered by a smile or a frown, like some caricatural Photofit. This leads to a great deal of repetition, but even so there is enough variation in the shapes and proportions of faces to prevent it becoming a significant aesthetic drawback. Once in a while there is a real imaginative fillip that adds character to a specific face, as with the prone figure's nasal hair and pipe chewing (figure 2), or another's tap-handle ears (figure 3).

Figure 1

All wear trousers. Above the waist many are nondescriptly covered, but several sport specific tailoring. One, for example, wears a woolly pullover – strands straggling down his chest and along his arms and shoulders – over a smart collar and tie. Another is tightly fastened inside a four-buttoned, high-collared outfit, and a third flaunts a diagonally ribbed shirt. Many items are patterned with lines running bottom left to top right – the natural rhythm for someone drawing right-handedly – their density giving subtly different tones. Occasionally, these strokes come as short, punctu-ating jabs, describing a coarse, open fabric. Sometimes they will be more discreet and regular, suggesting a much finer weave. In one instance, a single line inside a pair of trouser-legs follows their

Figure 2

contour exactly, giving a neat military stripe. Other accoutrements
are rare. A pouched belt can be seen, and a bespectacled intellectual (figure 4) proudly boasts a large waist-level patch-pocket on
his tight-fitting painters' smock.

Hats are worn by about half the throng. Most are brimmed but
indeterminate – perhaps trilbys, skimmers or pork-pies. One wears
a plaid cap; another a cloche; a third what might best be called
a crumple. Bowlers are not in evidence. Of the bare-headed, one
is definitely bald, and the others coiffured in a range covering
the neatly brushed, static-wired, combed-over, smarmed-down,
slicked-up and bunched. Footwear is similarly variable, with pairs
of lace-ups, Cuban heels and winkle-pickers parading amongst the
generic nondescript boats.

Figure 3

But in sum this collection is merely the *hors d'oeuvre* for the following page. Here Beckett cranks up the number and complexity of figures exponentially, with fifty-three faces and figures loitering and scurrying across two horizontal bands. The first thing one notices is that in the lower strip a doomed trio are crucified; tiny, inky specimens pinned among the seething crowd. Buried within the upper frieze is another nailed figure, outstretched but incomplete – his hands spiked against a beam, his body lopped below the waist.

Figure 4

The miniature people themselves can be grouped in several ways. Those walking, for example, include one walking right, facing front, looking left; two walking left, facing front, looking front; one walking right, facing right, looking right; and one walking right, facing right, looking front. As for those standing, one faces right and looks right; two face front and look left; three face left and look left; and five face front and look front. Others kneel, crouch, lie or hurdle. Two appear to be doing the hornpipe, forearms laterally across chest and back, knees akimbo, head erect. Both share belts, chokers and spiky hair – energetic punk matelot twins. They are smiling, as are arguably nearly half their peers. A further six or seven look nervous, uncertain or quizzical, while one is desperately glum and a couple downright annoyed. A single *volte-face* head reflects the equivocal nature of the group as a whole, summing them up in a Siamese physiognomy of comedy and tragedy: one face smiles breezily, but remains bracketed irrevocably with its partner, stiffly down-in-the-mouth.

Only a fifth or so of mouths are shown open, and an even smaller fraction are framed by beards or moustaches, with forty-eight faces being smoothly shaven. One of these shows a line running round its jowl suggesting five-o'clock-shadow, a graphic economy later to grace Fred Flintstone. Usually figures are again given formulaically dotted eyes, with more than half enclosed in elliptical or circular shapes. Once, as if to prove this rule, a square appears instead. Expressions are slightly more varied on this second page of doodles, as even moving pupils off-centre, which happens on several occasions, can hint at a character's thought or feeling (e.g. figure 5). One woman is speckled with a double dose of dots, one pair where her eyes would be and another, smaller, underneath. The latter might easily be tears, or perhaps simply cheeks ruddy from ardour or embarrassment.

The spread of fingers is also more expressive. Sixteen figures show them distinctly, tiny bananas or thorns rather than a generalised knobble or pad. One pot-belly aims his index pointedly, and several touch their fingers sharply upwards together as if in prayer. Two of those crucified have theirs splayed by the nails hammered through their palms, while the third's droop like trophies of dead birds. The condemned men's naked feet resemble hands too, with long fingers instead of short toes. Nail-heads make button-backed gloves of each pair. Crucifixion's dreadful mechanics ensure that arms end up diagonally stretched, a pose mimicked by one demonstrative figure nearby. More generally upper limbs are drawn either angled or arced, but a few hang limply straight or push rigidly this way or that. Occasionally a figure is animated by alternating a taut arm with one bent – such as the hurdler gallivanting who knows where, gloved hands punching the air.

Once again, it is their clothing that more than anything gives them individuality. Although nearly all wear some kind of trousers, a group of three have on traditional female attire. Each of these women has a narrow, even pinched, waist, and two wear full skirts, one neatly pleated with a hint of apron. Their two blouses are plain. One lady has chosen a smart four-button bodice with a round collar and long sleeves, while her companion, wringing a

Figure 5

cloth, has picked a no-nonsense short-sleeve *corsage*. The third is
dressed in a pencil-slim number that falls vertically from her hips
below a tight belt and a high pointed collar.

Trousers have a more cosmopolitan, or even international, air,
ranging from the historic through the foreign to the sporting,
respectable and workaday. On display are hose, chaps, jodhpurs,
plus-fours, pressed, striped and workman's tied-at-the-knee. One
can only guess at what the gentleman in the belted, ankle-length
trenchcoat is wearing beneath it. Knickerbockers? Pantaloons?
Pyjamas? Mundane details illuminate more ordinary costumes.
Three fastenings clasp each of two jackets and a frock coat. One
of the short jackets, drawn in profile, has its buttons protruding

as a silhouetted row of nipples along a concave torso. A waistcoat, centrally nipped by a single stud, has balancing slash pockets, while a flap-pouched, round-necked shirt or jerkin is buttoned to the throat. Jumpers come both roll- and v-necked, ties bow or Windsor-knotted. The exotic is represented in the forms of a ruff, cravat, doublet, sash and pair of suspenders.

Hats are similarly varied, comprising one sailor's cap, one topper, one mob cap, two helmets (one Norman), two trilbys, two snap-brimmed, two pillboxes, three peaked caps, three pork pies (e.g. figure 6), and four slouches. In addition, one Ascot-worthy confection puffs a billowing veil, and several vagues could be berets. Cutting a dash, the most ornate hairdo is teased into an unlikely but convincing pointillist afro-geometry. This, coupled with a stern Mohican (figure 7), gives the hirsute an adventurous flavour, expanded elsewhere by a doily perm and fringes ranging from the Betty Boop to the foppish floppy. Exaggerating these excesses is the austerity shown by a couple of modest short-back-and-sides. Some have less opportunity for choice, as the brushed-forward, straggled, and windy combed-over sadly testify.

As ever in Beckett, feet cannot be ignored. Laced-up men clump about in pairs of pointed or round-toed shoes, a woman totters on high heels, horses have trotters rather than hooves. Separated from the figures stand two boots with high ankles and block heels, one filled to the brim with ink and the other open as if to air, its bootstrap bobbing.

Harnessing all these characters is a linear dexterity of some material complication. Although drawn, one assumes, with the same fountain pen, line weights vary significantly. This suggests the use of a highly flexible nib, one that can open and close with the variations of pressure Beckett exerted as he drew. As a wider line reads more darkly than a finer, this, added to the spectrum of ink solubility, gives a broad range of tonal variation. To enrich matters further, as already mentioned Beckett has the habit of shading areas for ornamental reasons. One figure's trousers have been very carefully horizontally striped, rather than hastily hatched, and another character has been circumspectly finger-smudged. Proximity of parallel strokes coupled with a full ink reservoir can sometimes cause areas partially to fill in, giving a dark and broken field, pin-pricked with light. The happiest of accidents can also occur however, as when the paper's absorptive qualities

Figure 6

gently filch from an ink edge, resulting in a mohair glow around a jumper or pair of trousers.

Blots are occasionally turned to advantage. One has become the body of a swarthy, seated figure, another the overripe head balancing on a Lilliputian body. The saturated ellipse of an eye, perhaps as a result of blotting, gives a pious profile its hollow, sightless gaze. Sometimes chancy positives turn out to be too good to be true, as in a series where apparently accidental fillings-in under profiled noses make fortuitous moustaches. There are too many to be coincidence

Figure 7

alone, and a degree of nuanced nudging must have occurred. Also
carefully modulated are gradated tonalities distinguishing the three
crosses. Darkest is the central crucifix, leaving its sagging victim
starkly white and, though clothed, nakedly vulnerable. The left-
hand cross is tightly hatched, giving a fifty-per-cent tone, closely
matched by quicker and more random marks on the figure's clothing. The crucifix to the right is the lightest, its sketchy diagonal flicks
giving only a rudimentary shading and texture. Its prey is left bare
too, but as the tonal contrast is negligible he is more graphically
integrated with his immediate environment, despite his desperate
situation.

All figures seem to have been drawn at an even pace: deliber-
ate if not slow. Fillings-in and hatching are sometimes made more

quickly and with lighter pressure, so that less ink reaches the nib, giving paler lines and more control over darkening an area with layered strokes.

At a more abstract level, just as the lilt of Beckett's language is ingrained in its texture, here varied visual rhymes give the pages their formal coherence and grace. For example, the knee-angle of a running figure is replicated in another's elbow, and the U-bend backside and legs of one small canted figure are repeated, at regularly increasing sizes, in three more querulous folk. In addition to the crucifixions, several other figures are nearly symmetrical, faces and heads included. In particular, one has a very neatly applied internal geometry. His horizontal upper arms form the top bar of an inverted isosceles triangle, its sides each fashioned from a forearm linking straight-ahead with an upward femur and its apex poised at his crotch. Elsewhere graphic equilibrium is at play, as pendulum-scoops profile noses, lips and chins, and mirrored armpits balance hosepipe arms.

Mirror writing is here too: 'RHIN" THE BEST STRON', seen backwards. As if in aesthetic sympathy, the diagonal lines that fill HIN reverse their direction from those in other drawings, and slant top left to bottom right. Several other words appear – 'Hole', 'Holelelllll', 'Huussy', 'Hussy' twice, and 'Blifil'. All are more or less elaborated, the ornate 'B' having a double outline scored across at small intervals by short lines that just run over its edges, turning the letter into a diminutive serpentine railway track.

How many of these drawings were made without premeditation? Because of their overlapping components many figures need to have been imagined at least partially in advance. To give a simple example, if an arm is to appear in front of a body, the arm must be drawn first so that the outlines of the body can be interrupted when they reach it and then carry on beyond, giving the illusion that they have been obscured. Not all components are constrained like this. A head can be invented without committing which way its body will point. This can then be drawn in any orientation, sometimes appearing to make the head swivel extravagantly. To a certain extent torsos and legs can be lavishly twisted against each other like this too, the tension between them creating a swirling, tortuous pirouette.

So as to see how a single doodle might have evolved take, for instance, that of a plaid-capped man with his hands on his waist,

Figure 8

viewed from the rear (figure 8). This cove's head could have been composed first, but his arms and hands must have been drawn before his one armpit and the outlines of his torso, as these cease at his sleeves' edges. His shirt cuff, too, with its spot of button or link, could only have been sectioned off after his arm was completed. The evolution of his cap can also be imagined, as the largest, complete, enclosure seems to have been made first, with perhaps the smaller one to its right added next. The six loops that radiate from these two were then joined, amoeba-like, in sequence. The echoing horseshoe marking his legs was drawn after his torso, as it meets this at waist level, with its rhyming inside-leg line added next. Perhaps these broad shapes describing his head and body were complete before any hatching began. In any event, careful diagonal lines that give his pullover its tone and texture would have had to wait their turn until the garment was complete. Clearly Beckett's pen was ripe and flowed freely – sometimes too freely given the picture's bleeds, blots and smudges. But its ink dilution gives added clues to the drawing's chronology. His dense diagonal stokes reveal their drawn direction by their disposition of ink, as more is deposited at the termination of a line, darkening it. Those on this figure were made right to left, being lighter at their right-hand tip.

It is not at all easy to say how much a type of semi-detached pre-meditation played in this. But it cannot be nothing, for otherwise the drawing could not be what it is. Deliberation need only occur an instant before committing a line to paper, as, like all drawing, doodling is a process of give-and-take. The artist responds to what appears, and abstraction glides effortlessly into figuration. First draw any line, add another and it becomes an arm. Draw an enclosure, add two dots and it's a face. Once started, elaboration proceeds in a hinterland between conscious and preconscious processes, with the artist watching what is emerging with surprise as much as directing its 'inarticulate form'.[36] Inevitably drawings are as paradoxical as Winnicott's transitional objects, concurrently made and found.[37]

Invoking the name of a psychoanalyst, particularly one who used drawing successfully in his work with children, suggests that analysing Beckett's doodles to divulge their psychological secrets is the next logical step. However, Beckett himself voices this concern:

The analysis of the relation between the artist and his occasion, a relation regarded as indispensable, does not seem to have been very productive [. . .] the reason being perhaps that it lost its way in disquisitions on the nature of occasion.[38]

Susan Sontag expands on this disquiet by saying that we should avoid interpreting images because to do so is a contamination – a hangover from the excesses of evaluation occasioned by the repositioning of religious iconography in an evolving secular age.[39] In brief, a largely short-term and 'political' tactic has grown into an endemic attitude whereby there is always some kind of discrepancy between the visible work and its meaning. Further, as Maclagan makes clear,[40] this gap has been widened by Freudian theory, which postulates an apparently novel but in fact relatively restricted symbolism that has a degree of overlap with the figurative and emblematic interpretative traditions within art history. Both writers agree that the 'form' of images has been ignored in examinations of 'content', and offer similar recommendations on how this shortcoming might be addressed. These rely first of all upon paying scrupulous attention to the material qualities of pictures. Sontag, for her part, advocates 'acts of criticism which would supply a really accurate, sharp, loving description of the appearance of a work of art', even though this 'seems harder to do than formal analysis'.[41] Maclagan proposes analogous accounts that stay 'close to the observed qualities of the work' and yet 'without undue forcing [. . .] evoke its feel [. . .] differentiate its internal dynamics'.[42]

Seen from these perspectives, Beckett's doodles clearly have nothing to hide. Complete in themselves, they want for nothing, have nothing to prove, nothing to declare, nothing better to do, and strictly in the wider scheme of spontaneous drawings are nothing special, nothing to write home about. Nothing is to be lost by making nothing of them. On the other hand, although they might be next to nothing, made free, gratis, and for nothing, they may not quite be a fuss about nothing – it is difficult to feel nothing for them.

But for those still tempted to speculate on avoiding the viruses and booby-traps that every attempt at detailed psychological analysis contains, nothing is more appropriate than Beckett's cautionary advice to Billie Whitelaw: 'If in doubt – do nothing'.[43]

Notes

1 See Vivien Mercier's famous definition of Godot as 'a play in which nothing happens, *twice*', Vivien Mercier, 'The uneventful event', *Irish Times* (18 February 1956).
2 Samuel Beckett to George Duthuit, 9–10 March 1949, trans. Walter Redfern, in S. E. Gontarski and Anthony Uhlmann, (eds), *Beckett After Beckett* (Gainesville: University Press of Florida, 2006), pp. 18–21.
3 Visual arts have their own dilemmas. For example views with nothing in common, such as the fifteenth-century discovery of the vanishing point and late-twentieth-century high modernism's deification of flatness. In the former Nothing is taken as the ultimate focus in representing three dimensions, so that the picture-plane vanishes, while the latter's metaphysical purity relies on the immutability of a painting's surface. Postmodernism leaves nothing to chance, and tries to negate all meta-theories except its own. See Eagleton, Foreword above.
4 R. D. Laing, *Knots* (London: Tavistock, 1970; reprinted London: Penguin, 1972), p. 83.
5 Samuel Beckett, *Watt* (Paris: Olympia Press, [1953] 1958), p. 87.
6 Martin Heidegger, *The Fundamental Concepts of Metaphysics*, trans. W. McNeill and N. Walker (Bloomington: Indiana University Press, 1995), p. 101.
7 Heidegger, *The Fundamental Concepts*, p. 103.
8 Beckett, *Watt*, p. 42.
9 Delivered on 24 July 1929. See Martin Heidegger, *Pathmarks*, trans. and ed. William McNeill (Cambridge: Cambridge University Press, 1998). On the role of nothing and Nothing in Heidegger in relation to Beckett see also Thomson, Chapter 4 above.
10 Pierre Thevenaz, *What Is Phenomenology?*, trans. J. M. Edie, C. Courtney and P. Brockelman (Chicago: Quadrangle, 1962), p. 57.
11 H. G. Maule, 'Industrial environment', in A. H. Bowley et al. (eds), *Psychology: The Study of Man's Mind* (London: Odhams Press, 1949), p. 259. Rose Adders, *The Bored @ Work Doodle Book* (London: Carlton, 2008).
12 E. H. Gombrich, 'Pleasures of boredom', in *The Uses of Images* (London: Phaidon, 1999), pp. 212–25. For another excellent example see David Maclagan, 'Solitude and communication: beyond the doodle', *Raw Vision* (Summer 1990), 33–8.
13 Gombrich, 'Pleasures of boredom', p. 225.
14 11 September – 9 October 1937.
15 Beckett also advises us 'to obliterate texts [rather] than to blacken margins, to fill in the holes of words', *Molloy* (London: Calder, 1959), p. 13.

16 Robert Riskin, 'Mr. Deeds Goes to Town', in P. McGilligan (ed.), *Six Screenplays by Robert Riskin* (Berkeley: University of California Press, 1997), p. 456.
17 W. S. Maclay, E. Guttmann and W. Mayer-Gross, 'Spontaneous drawings as an approach to some problems of psychopathology', *Proceedings of the Royal Society of Medicine*, XXXI (1938), 1337–50.
18 *Ibid.*, 1346.
19 Joseph Wright (ed.), *The English Dialect Dictionary*, vol. 2 (London: Frowde, 1900), p. 122.
20 Heidegger, *The Fundamental Concepts of Metaphysics*, p. 79.
21 *Ibid.*, p. 98.
22 Samuel Beckett, *Waiting for Godot* (London: Faber & Faber, [1956] 1957), p. 47.
23 Heidegger, *The Fundamental Concepts of Metaphysics*, p. 99.
24 *Ibid.*, p. 93.
25 Oliver Sacks, *An Anthropologist on Mars* (London: Picador, 1995), p. 79.
26 Samuel Beckett, *Disjecta: Miscellaneous Writings and a Dramatic Fragment*, ed. Ruby Cohn (London: Calder, 1983), p. 172.
27 R. Muller, 'Coffee without brandy', *Observer* (1 September 1996).
28 Adam Phillips, *On Kissing, Tickling and Being Bored* (London: Faber & Faber, 1993), p. 71.
29 Heidegger, *The Fundamental Concepts of Metaphysics*, p. 82.
30 Phillips, *On Kissing, Tickling and Being Bored*, pp. 72–3.
31 Stephen Simmer, 'The academy of the dead: on boredom, writer's block, footnotes and deadlines', *Spring 1981* (1981), 91.
32 A phrase used by Enrique Pardo in his 1987 experimental theatre seminar 'Academy of boredom'. See Enrique Pardo, 'The theatres of boredom and depression: two gateways to imagination', *Spring 1988* (1988), 166–76.
33 Held at The Harry Ransom Center, University of Texas.
34 University of Reading, MS 3458.
35 This is in fact a smudged blot, trailing elegantly behind him and ending in Beckett's inky fingerprint.
36 See Anton Ehrenzweig, *The Hidden Order of Art* (Berkeley: University of California Press, 1967).
37 See Donald Woods Winnicott, *Playing and Reality* (London: Tavistock, 1971).
38 Samuel Beckett, *Proust and Three Dialogues* (London: Calder, 1965; reprinted 1970), p. 124.
39 Susan Sontag, 'Against interpretation', in *A Susan Sontag Reader* (London: Penguin, 1983), pp. 95–104.
40 David Maclagan, 'Freud and the figurative', *Inscape* (October 1983), 10–12.

41 Sontag, 'Against interpretation', p. 103.
42 David Maclagan, 'Between the aesthetic and the psychological', *Inscape*, 2 (1994), 51. Maclagan gives examples such as Rilke on Cézanne and Artaud on van Gogh. Others might include John Berger comparing Francis Bacon with Walt Disney, and Adrian Searle on Jackson Pollock.
43 BBC Radio Three, *Nightwaves* (9 September 1999).

6

Unwords

Shane Weller

In a well-known letter of 14 June 1967 to the literary critic Sighle Kennedy, Beckett counters her proposed literary couple of Joyce and Proust with the philosophical one of Democritus and Geulincx as the two 'points of departure' for any critical analysis of his works. As Beckett puts it: 'I simply do not feel the presence in my writings as a whole of the Joyce & Proust situations you evoke. If I were in the unenviable position of having to study my work my points of departure would be the "Naught is more real . . ." and the "Ubi nihil vales . . ." both already in *Murphy* and neither very rational.'[1] Aside from its substitution of the philosophical for the literary, what is perhaps most striking about Beckett's response to Kennedy is that these two proposed points of departure share something – or, more precisely, they share the nothing: the Democritean 'naught' and the Geulincxian 'nihil'. On closer inspection, however, this apparently shared concern with the nothing proves to be an antinomy, since, as Beckett was aware (and, as we shall see, this knowledge is evidenced by his philosophy notes of the 1930s), Democritus and Geulincx take diametrically opposed positions on what may be termed the ontological nothing. Whereas for the former the nothing exists (as the 'void' separating the 'atoms'), for the latter the nothing (as 'vacuum') is quite simply 'impossible'.[2] In his dismissal – as 'an utterly silly opinion' – of the Scholastics' claim that space is nothing (*nihil, nihilum*), Geulincx follows Descartes and ultimately Parmenides.[3] That said, unlike the Democritean 'naught', the Geulincxian 'nihil' to which Beckett refers in his letter to Kennedy is not an ontological but rather an ethical nothing: 'Where you are worth nothing . . .' (*Ubi nihil vales . . .*). So it is, then, that Beckett's seemingly straightforward countering of the literary by the philosophical, and his emphasis upon the importance of the nothing, in fact points to both an antinomy at the ontological level and a distinction between the ontological and the ethical in his own literary treatment of the nothing.

Taking Beckett's response to Kennedy as my own point of departure, my aim in this chapter is to offer a philologically orientated analysis of Beckett's engagement with the nothing as conceived ontologically and ethically, which is to say an analysis that focuses principally on his deployment of the words 'nothing', 'naught', 'nihil' and 'void', and a consideration of some of the sources by way of which these words entered his literary vocabulary and came to serve as markers for an aporetic experience. Following his own theorisation of a 'literature of the unword' (*Literatur des Unworts*) in his 9 July 1937 letter to Axel Kaun, these words might themselves be thought of as among Beckett's most important 'unwords'; that is to say, words that work against what in the letter to Kaun he terms the 'veil' (*Schleier*) of language in order to disclose that which lies beyond language, 'be it something or nothing' (*sei es etwas oder nichts*).[4] Not least among the reasons for a philological approach to these particular 'unwords' is Beckett's own marked attention to the textual history of his engagement with philosophical reflections on the nothing. For instance, in opting for the words 'naught' and 'nihil' in his letter to Kennedy, Beckett indicates not only the precise *textual* nature of his encounters with philosophical writings on the nothing over three decades earlier but also the *order* in which these encounters took place.

Although his encounters with the thought of Democritus and Geulincx between 1933 and 1936 would prove to be critical for his literary treatment of the nothing from *Murphy* onwards, Beckett's preoccupation with the concept of, and figures for, the nothing in fact preceded those encounters. As early as *Proust* (written in the late summer of 1930), Beckett is already placing a form of the nothing at the heart of his conception of Proust's – and, by implication, all genuine – art when he claims that 'The artist is active, but negatively, shrinking from the nullity of extracircumferential phenomena, drawn in to the core of the eddy'.[5] This statement suggests that the artistic procedure moves in the direction of a 'core' that is in fact nothing, and that this movement is itself an act of negation, albeit the paradoxical negation of a 'nullity'.

In his first completed novel, *Dream of Fair to Middling Women* (written in 1931–32), Beckett tends for the most part to emphasise the explosive disintegration of the 'art surface' in order to make that surface correspond to what is taken to be an 'incoherent reality'.[6] However, the novel also testifies in various ways to that nascent concern for the nothing already expressed in *Proust*. Early in the text, for instance, Beckett writes of the 'violent voiding and blanking' of Belacqua's mind, and, anticipating one of the key phrases in *Godot* (written almost two decades later), the novel's narrator states on three occasions that there is 'nothing to be done'.[7] In addition to the repeated valorisation of absence by the narrator – 'the object that becomes invisible before your eyes is, so to speak, the brightest and best'; 'Absence makes the heart grow fonder is a true saying'[8] – the nothing as such is at once playfully valorised and, importantly, identified as the principal reason for the 'difficulties' faced by the artist: 'there are few things more bel than a niente, but considered as a premise, and be you Abbot himself, it presents certain difficulties in the manner of manipulation', the passage in which this remark occurs echoing the 'core of the eddy' image in *Proust*: 'you find when you come to the core and the kernel and the seat of the malady that behold it is a bel niente'.[9] As for the 'Abbot' to whom Beckett refers here, John Pilling has suggested that he is possibly either the 'Abbé Gabriel' mentioned earlier in the novel or the Abbé de Saint-Réal in Stendhal's *Le Rouge et le noir*, who is also named in Beckett's Trinity College lectures of 1930–31, as recorded by Rachel Burrows.[10] The first of the two statements on absence quoted above also includes a reference to Stendhal, and, given that the 'bel niente' is thought here in relation to the writing of a literary work, it is not unreasonable to see Beckett's reflections on art in its relation to the nothing as essentially Stendhalian at this point in his development. This conclusion is also supported by entries on Stendhal in Beckett's 'Dream' Notebook of 1931–32, especially the phrase 'folie pour rien',[11] which, two decades later, will be echoed in the title of one of Beckett's own works, *Textes pour rien* (written in 1950–51).

An important philosophico-theological source for both the 'voiding' and the 'nothing' in *Dream* is Augustine's *Confessions*, from the Pusey translation of which the phrase 'A void place, a spacious nothing' is entered into the 'Dream' Notebook and then inserted into *Dream* as part of a description of Belacqua's state of mind after a pleasurable sense of being 'disembodied':[12]

> This sudden strange sensation was of a piece with the ancient volatili-
> sation of his first communion, long forgot and never brought to mind
> in all the long years that had run out with him since and rolled over
> that delicious event. Alas! it was a short knock and went as it had
> come, like that, it vacated him like that, leaving him bereft and in his
> breast a void place and a spacious nothing.[13]

Further evidence that Beckett was already at this time preoccupied with conceptions of the nothing as 'void' within a range of
discourses is to be found in other entries in the 'Dream' Notebook,
including the phrase 'Emptiness of space' from Sir James Jeans's
The Universe Around Us (1929).[14]

Prior to his sustained reading in philosophy shortly after the
completion of *Dream*, however, it is arguably Schopenhauer whose
influence is the strongest on Beckett's early reflections on an art
that would take the nothing as its object or aim. In Schopenhauer,
whom he first read (in French) in the summer of 1930, Beckett
encountered a philosophy at the heart of which lies the theory
of a liberating negation (*Verneinung*) that is orientated towards
the experience of what, from the perspective of the world as
representation (*Vorstellung*), is taken to be nothing:

> we freely acknowledge that what remains after the complete abo-
> lition of the will is, for all who are still full of the will, assuredly
> nothing [*nichts*]. But also conversely, to those in whom the will has
> turned and denied itself, this very real world of ours with all its suns
> and galaxies, is – nothing [*nichts*].[15]

Three years later, when reading Windelband, Beckett came upon
the following account of Schopenhauer's conclusions:

> At the close of his work he intimates that what would remain after
> the annihilation of the will, and with that, of the world also, would be
> for all those who are still full of will, certainly *nothing*; but considera-
> tion of the life of the saints teaches, that while the world with all its
> suns and milky ways is nothing to them, they have attained blessed-
> ness and peace. 'In thy nothing I hope to find the all.'[16]

If the Schopenhauerian nothing remains impossible to represent –
precisely because it lies beyond the very distinction between will
and representation – *Dream* none the less contains images that
evoke it. Of these, the 'night firmament' is among the most important for Beckett's future development, not least because that image

anticipates the reliance upon music in his later formulations of an art orientated towards a liberating nothing: 'The night firmament is abstract density of music, symphony without end, illumination without end, yet emptier, more sparsely lit, than the most succinct constellations of genius.'[17] Crucially, too, Schopenhauer brings together what Beckett would later find separated in Democritus and Geulincx, namely the ontological nothing on the one hand and the ethical nothing on the other; for, according to Schopenhauer, the *Verneinung* of the will is the only properly ethical act, and what it produces is precisely that which ontologically goes by the name 'nothing'. In short, for Schopenhauer, to desire nothing – or, one might say, to desire *the* nothing – is the only mode of ethical being. That this mode of being does not necessarily exclude pleasure will be among the most radical elements in Beckett's works.

While the nothing conceived as absence or void is already present in *Dream*, that presence remains a relatively marginal one in comparison with the emphasis upon incoherence, disaggregation, or disintegration. By the time of Beckett's first published novel, *Murphy* (written in 1935–36), however, an explicitly named and capitalised 'Nothing' has come to occupy the very centre of the work, Beckett placing the description of an unmediated experience of this 'Nothing' between Murphy's failed attempt to communicate with Mr Endon on the chessboard and the former's death:

> little by little [Murphy's] eyes were captured by the brilliant swallow-tail of Mr Endon's arms and legs, purple, scarlet, black and glitter, till they saw nothing else, and that in a short time only as a vivid blur, Neary's big blooming buzzing confusion or ground, mercifully free of figure. Wearying soon of this he dropped his head on his arms in the midst of the chessmen, which scattered with a terrible noise. Mr Endon's finery persisted for a little in an after-image scarcely inferior to the original. Then this also faded and Murphy began to see nothing, that colourlessness which is such a rare postnatal treat, being the absence (to abuse a nice distinction) not of *percipere* but of *percipi*. His other senses also found themselves at peace, an unexpected pleasure. Not the numb peace of their own suspension, but the positive peace that comes when the somethings give way, or perhaps simply add up, to the Nothing, than which in the guffaw of the Abderite naught is more real. Time did not cease, that would be asking too much, but the wheel of rounds and pauses did, as Murphy with his head among the armies continued to suck in, through all the posterns of his withered soul, the accidentless One-and-Only, conveniently called Nothing.[18]

It is here that Beckett signals the principal philosophical sources for his own literary conception of the ontological nothing. On the basis of his philosophy notes (now held at Trinity College Dublin), it is possible to identify not only the texts in which Beckett encountered summaries of pre-Socratic atomism (especially Leucippus and Democritus) but also the precise source for the word 'naught' in the expression of the atomist paradox, namely Archibald Alexander's *Short History of Philosophy*, in which one finds the following statement (duly recorded by Beckett):

> Aristotle, in his account of the early philosophers, says, 'Leucippus and Democritus assume as elements the "full" and the "void". The former they term being and the latter non-being. Hence they assert that non-being exists as well as being.' And, according to Plutarch, Democritus himself is reported as saying, 'there is naught more real than nothing'.[19]

While Alexander's text may – as Everett Frost observes[20] – become less important as an intellectual resource in the course of Beckett's note-taking enterprise than either John Burnet's *Greek Philosophy, Part I: Thales to Plato* (1914) or Wilhelm Windelband's *History of Philosophy* (1893), it is arguably more important than either Burnet or Windelband in philological terms, since, half a century after transcribing it from Alexander, Beckett deploys the word 'naught', together with 'void', at key moments in one of his major late prose texts, *Worstward Ho* (1983). Indeed, while the word 'void' is that text's most prevalent 'unword' (occurring a remarkable 52 times in the published version), and also having occurred in decisive statements in *The Unnamable* (written in 1949–50) – 'only I and this black void have ever been'[21] – and *Ill Seen Ill Said* – 'Grace to breathe that void. Know happiness'[22] – the word 'naught' (which occurs 11 times in *Worstward Ho*) is no less decisive, not simply on account of the impossibility that it names (Beckett here echoing Geulincx's insistence on the impossibility of the vacuum) but also because of the word's material quality (on which Beckett draws in the key phrase 'gnawing to be naught'), a quality that disappears in French translation, since the 'naught' in *Murphy* is translated as 'rien'[23] and the 'naught' in *Worstward Ho* remains untranslated by him.[24] So important is this particular 'unword' that all instances of its deployment in *Worstward Ho* warrant quotation:

Naught best. Best worse. No. Not best worse. **Naught** not best worse. Less best worse. No. Least. Least best worse. Least never to be **naught**. Never to **naught** be brought. Never by **naught** be nulled.

Nohow over words again say what then when not preying. Each better worse for **naught**. No stilling preying. The shades. The dim. The void. All always faintly preying. Worse for **naught**. Worser for **naught**.

Same stoop for all. Same vasts apart. Such last state. Latest state. Till somehow less in vain. Worse in vain. All gnawing to be **naught**. Never to be **naught**.

Best worse no farther. Nohow less. Nohow worse. Nohow **naught**. Nohow on.[25]

It would be a mistake, however, simply to assume that, because Beckett refers explicitly to Democritus (as 'the Abderite') in *Murphy*, and because the word 'naught' is derived from a summary of his thought in Alexander, Democritus' theory of the nothing as what Alexander, Burnet and Windelband all term the 'void' is the only one that is operative in Beckett's works. The reference to the 'nice distinction' between *percipere* and *percipi* in *Murphy* directs the reader to another philosopher who will be important for Beckett, namely Bishop Berkeley, about whom Beckett encountered the following statement in Windelband: '*Body* is then nothing but a *complex of ideas*. If we abstract from a cherry all the qualities which can be perceived through any of the senses, what is left? Nothing.'[26] It is just such an abstraction of the qualities that is described in the above-quoted passage from *Murphy* on the experience of the 'Nothing'. And, like the 'naught', this conception of seeing the nothing also recurs half a century later in *Worstward Ho*: 'Old dim. When ever what else? Where all always to be seen. Of the nothing to be seen. Dimly seen. Nothing ever unseen. Of the nothing to be seen.'[27]

Furthermore, a pre-Socratic philosopher of the nothing who is arguably no less important to Beckett than Democritus – although much less often noted – is Gorgias of Leontini. Although Gorgias is not named in Beckett's published works, in a letter of 21 April 1958 to A. J. Leventhal he refers to the three fundamental propositions of what in Burnet is described as Gorgias' 'cosmological nihilism'.[28] In the letter to Leventhal, these three propositions are given as follows:

1. Nothing is.
2. If anything is, it cannot be known.
3. If anything is, and can be known, it cannot be expressed in speech.[29]

As with the Democritean 'Naught is more real', so here too the phrasing is strikingly close to that in Alexander, as noted down by Beckett in the early 1930s:

> In his chief work – *On Nature or the Non-existent*, which has been preserved by Sextus Empiricus – he [Gorgias] emphasises his three famous propositions: 1st, nothing exists; 2nd, even if anything did exist, it could not be known; 3rd, and even if it could be known, it would be incommunicable.[30]

As C. J. Ackerley has argued, Gorgias haunts *Watt* (written in 1941–45) in various ways, that novel being a crucial counterpoint to *Murphy* not least because it presents the nothing as that which disconcerts the mind seeking rationality in the real:

> What distressed Watt in this incident of the Galls father and son, and in subsequent similar incidents, was not so much that he did not know what had happened, for he did not care what had happened, as that nothing had happened, with the utmost formal distinctness, and that it continued to happen, in his mind, he supposed, though he did not know exactly what that meant.[31]

In his fine commentary on the novel and its genesis, Ackerley observes that Notebook 1 of the manuscript contains a chapter entitled 'The Nothingness', and he connects this with the 'soul-landscape' included in the Addenda of the published text, which he identifies as the novel's 'primal scene'.[32] The nothing in *Watt*, especially if one takes it (as so many commentators have done) as being figured in Mr Knott, may be related back not only to pre-Socratic thought on the 'void' but also to Kant's conception of the noumenon, about which Beckett read the following passage in Windelband: 'Noumena, or *things-in-themselves*, are therefore *thinkable in the negative sense as objects of a non-sensuous perception*, of which, to be sure, our knowledge can predicate absolutely nothing, – they are thinkable as *limiting conceptions* of experience.'[33]

Watt's inability to bear the thought of the nothing obviously sets him apart not only from Murphy (for whom the experience of the nothing is a 'positive peace') but also from the voices in texts such as *Ill Seen Ill Said* and *Worstward Ho*, and aligns him instead with the scientist or rationalist as defined by Heidegger in *Introduction to Metaphysics*, a text first published in 1953, the same year as *Watt*, and based on a lecture series delivered at the University of Freiburg in 1935:

> One cannot, in fact, talk about and deal with Nothing [*das Nichts*] as if it were a thing, such as the rain out there, or a mountain, or any object at all; Nothing remains in principle inaccessible to all science [*Wissenschaft*]. Whoever truly wants to talk of Nothing must necessarily become unscientific. But this is a great misfortune only if one believes that scientific thinking alone is the authentic, rigorous thinking, that it alone can and must be made the measure even of philosophical thinking.[34]

According to Heidegger, only the philosopher and the poet (*Dichter*) are in a position to 'talk about Nothing' (*vom Nichts zu reden*), and even they can proceed only by way of an indicating (*hinzeigen*) rather than direct presentation or representation.[35] For Beckett, too, the nothing will remain that towards which text after text indicates by way of those 'unwords' that increasingly dominate his works – with, as we have seen, the words 'void' and 'naught' being so central to the worsening that is enacted in *Worstward Ho*.

Not only do Beckett's various reading notes of the 1930s help us to identify key sources for his thinking (and indeed his indicative naming) of the nothing as 'void' and 'naught', they also clarify the nature of the aporia of the ontological nothing within which his works will come increasingly to locate themselves. On the one hand, first in Alexander, and then in Burnet and Windelband, Beckett encounters Parmenides' claim regarding the impossibility of non-being, a claim that will recur in different forms in both Descartes and Geulincx. In Burnet, for instance, Beckett records the following summary of Parmenides' argument on 'the consequences of saying that anything *is*':

> In the first place, it cannot have come into being. If it had, it must first have arisen from nothing or from something. It cannot have arisen from nothing; for there is no nothing. It cannot have arisen from something; for there is nothing else than what *is*. Nor can anything else besides itself come into being; for there can be no empty space in which it could do so. *Is it or is it not?* If it *is*, then it is now, all at once. In this way Parmenides refutes all accounts of the origin of the world. *Ex nihilo nihil fit*.[36]

On the other hand, as we have seen, Beckett also encounters the atomist theory of the 'void' that separates the atoms, a theory the way towards which was prepared by Melissus, who, according to Burnet, made it 'necessary for Leukippos to affirm the existence of the Void'.[37] In Windelband, Beckett notes the following atomist counter-argument to Parmenides:

> If [. . .] the plurality of things, and the mutations taking place among them as they come and go, were to be made intelligible, then instead of the single world-body, with no internal distinctions which Parmenides had taught, a plurality of such must be assumed, separated from one another, not by other Being, but by that which is not Being, Non-being: *i.e.* by the incorporeal, by *empty space*. This entity, then, which is Non-being [*i.e.* not Being in the true sense], must have in its turn a kind of Being, or of metaphysical reality ascribed to it, and Leucippus regarded it as the unlimited, the άπειρον, in contrast with the limitation which Being proper possesses, according to Parmenides.[38]

While the passage from *Murphy* quoted above clearly suggests that the nothing can, albeit fleetingly, become an object of experience, and indeed an object of pleasurable experience, the Parmenidean denial of the possibility of non-being will come to exert an increasingly important pressure in Beckett's later works, and this not least because that denial finds a later advocate in Geulincx, Beckett's second proposed 'point of departure' for any interpretation of his oeuvre.

In his 11 pages of notes on Geulincx's *Metaphysics*, taken in March 1936 when *Murphy* was only months from completion, Beckett records proposition 4 in Part Two ('Concerning Body, or Somatology'): 'A vacuum is impossible' (*Vacuum est impossibile*).[39] As proposition 5 makes clear, Geulincx means by this that space is not nothing (*nihil, nihilum*); rather, it is a body (*corpus*). Geulincx goes on to expose what he takes to be a contradiction at the heart of the philosophy that insists upon the existence of the nothing conceived spatially: 'They [the Scholastics] admit (as they must) that space has such and such dimensions, yet they also want to say that it is nothing. But a nothing with dimensions is just as absurd as a white nothing, a nothing wearing a coat, or a nothing walking down the street.'[40] While these 'absurd' images will arguably find their place in Beckett's oeuvre, Geulincx's denial of the very possibility of the nothing also finds expression there, above all in *Worstward Ho*: 'All gnawing to be naught. Never to be naught.'[41]

Of course, as noted at the outset of this chapter, when he proposes Geulincx as one of the two points of departure for an interpretation of his works, Beckett is referring not to the philosopher's denial of the possibility of the ontological *nihil* but rather to his thinking of the ethical *nihil*. In fact, Beckett encountered the key phrase '*Ubi nihil vales, ibi nihil velis*' prior to his first-hand reading of Geulincx in 1936, since it is quoted in a footnote in Windelband that was duly recorded by Beckett three years earlier:

> The 'autology', or *inspectio sui*, is, therefore, not only the epistemological starting-point of the system, but also its ethical conclusion. Man has nothing to do in the outer world. *Ubi nihil vales, ibi nihil velis*. The highest virtue is a modest contentment, submission to God's will – humility.[42]

By January 1936, Beckett was ready to acknowledge that such an ethics would have to occupy a central place in his own work, although not simply (as has often been assumed) as *the* ethics of that work. This complication of the Geulincxian ethics of humility (and of quietism more generally) is already made clear in a letter of 16 January 1936 to Thomas MacGreevy, in which Beckett declares: 'I suddenly see that Murphy is [a] break down between his: *Ubi nihil vales ibi nihil velis* (position) and Malraux's *Il est difficile à celui qui vit hors du monde de ne pas rechercher les siens* (negation).'[43] Just as the Democritean affirmation of the ontological nothing is part of a more general economy within Beckett's works, the other pole of which is the Parmenidean/Geulincxian denial of that nothing, so Geulincx's ethical nothing is part of a more general economy, the other pole of which is a desire for company (that is, for the world) that finds expression in the line from André Malraux's novel *La Condition humaine* (1933), which was to become the epigraph to chapter 9 of *Murphy*. This need for company will also remain present throughout Beckett's oeuvre, being figured, for instance, as the hand-in-hand of father and son in *Worstward Ho*.[44]

On the one hand, Beckett engages with the ethicalised nothing of negation in both Geulincx and Schopenhauer, or what in his *German Diaries* he terms the 'fundamental unheroic'.[45] Here, it is complete abandonment, or the reduction to nothing of power, that becomes the sole ethical mode of comportment. When reading Geulincx's *Ethics* in 1936, Beckett recorded the claim that 'The root of Ethics is humility, to withdraw from oneself', and also that

'we learn by inspecting ourselves that we can do nothing about
any part of the human condition, we have no power, and no right
over it; that it is all down to someone else's power'.[46] In the face of
such absolute powerlessness, the ethical imperative becomes self-
abandonment: 'Disregard of oneself, neglect and abandonment of
onself',[47] and this might reasonably be seen as precisely what the
figures in Beckett's postwar fiction attempt to do. But, of course,
Geulincx does not stop there, for he goes on to clarify that this self-
abandonment is also a giving of oneself *'entirely into God's hands'*.[48]
In Beckett, however, those hands are either absent – as is suggested
in *All That Fall* (written in 1956) – or unloving – as suggested by
the bitterly ironic use of 'merciful' as the epithet for God in *Not
I* (written in 1972). This leads us to return to what Alexander,
Burnet and Windelband all label the 'nihilism' of Gorgias, something that certainly haunts Beckett's works. As Alexander puts it:

> If Protagoras affirmed that every opinion was equally true, Gorgias
> declared that every opinion was equally false. Such thoroughgoing
> scepticism makes knowledge impossible. All is delusion. Gorgias has
> been called, with reason, a philosophical nihilist.[49]

This is not to say that Beckett's oeuvre constitutes the unambigu-
ous expression of either cosmological or ethical nihilism, even if his
interest in nihilism dates back at least as far as 1931, with the following entry from Jules de Gaultier's *De Kant à Nietzsche* occurring
towards the end of the 'Dream' Notebook: 'knowledge the Nihilist
founding the modes of a more solid illusion, nourishing the darkness in which Life prospers'.[50] Rather, through his deployment of
a series of 'unwords', Beckett explores the antinomies within the
thinking of both the ontological and the ethical nothing, and he
does so by drawing on a wide range of philosophical sources, some
of which are more evident that others, but all of which have to be
taken into account if one wishes to do justice to the complexities of
his literary treatment of the nothing.

If Beckett's works locate themselves within the aporias of both
the ontological and the ethical nothing, they do so also at the affective level. On the one hand, and in a decidedly Schopenhauerian
fashion, his narrators and *dramatis personae* state the nothing as
the supreme object of desire. Just as Schopenhauer, as quoted in
Windelband, declares: 'In thy nothing I hope to find the all', so
the Beckett of both *Murphy* and *Ill Seen Ill Said* makes the nothing

that which promises all, and in *Endgame* has Clov retort to Hamm: 'Better than nothing! Is it possible?'[51] On the other hand, and not just in *Watt*, the thought of the nothing is presented as anything but pleasurable. For instance, in the 'Whoroscope' Notebook Beckett records the phrase 'Sit stupid in the gloom of perpetual vacancy' from Johnson's *Rasselas*, and then in a letter of 9 July 1935 to Arland Ussher declares: 'I now sit stupid in the gloom of perpetual vacancy. The silence which refreshed you as respite from utterance, uninterrupted would oppress you.'[52] Similarly, at the end of the radio play *Embers* (1959), Henry consults his diary and says: 'Saturday . . . nothing. Sunday . . . Sunday . . . nothing all day. [*Pause.*] Nothing all day. [*Pause.*] All day all night nothing.'[53] The mood here is far indeed from that at the end of *Ill Seen Ill Said.* In short, then, just as the nothing is presented both as that which underlies all and as that which is impossible, so it is presented both as that which is most desired and as that which is most feared or resisted.

The aporetic logic governing both the ontological and the ethical nothing finds its first culminations in *The Unnamable* and *Texts for Nothing*, and by 1959, in a letter to A. J. Leventhal, Beckett can even characterise each of his texts as a 'next next to nothing'.[54] In order to grasp why Beckett's 'unwords' can be thought by him to result only in the production of a 'next to nothing' rather than opening on to the nothing as such, one has to consider not only the aporetic logic derived from the philosophers considered above but also Beckett's encounter with the critique of language theorised by Fritz Mauthner in his *Beiträge zu einer Kritik der Sprache*.

We have seen that, as early as *Proust*, Beckett is theorising an artistic procedure that is negative in nature and that takes as both its object and its aim a nothing figured there as the 'core of the eddy' and later as the 'void'. It is just such a conception of art that finds its first fully developed articulation in his 9 July 1937 letter to Axel Kaun, in which he declares that 'more and more my own language appears to me like a veil that must be torn apart in order to get at the things (or the nothingness) behind it [*an die dahinterliegenden Dinge (oder das dahinterliegende Nichts) zu kommen*]', and follows this with the assertion: 'To bore one hole after another in it [language], until what lurks behind it – be it something or nothing [*sei es etwas oder nichts*] – begins to seep through: I cannot imagine a higher goal for a writer today.'[55] Such a literature will,

Beckett asserts, be a literature of the 'unword' (*Unwort*). The description of language as a veil (*Schleier*) in this letter is significant not least because it builds on a passage in German on the 'veil of hope' (*Hoffnungsschleier*) in Beckett's 'Clare Street' Notebook, dating from August 1936. As Mark Nixon observes, this veil may be thought in relation to what Schopenhauer terms the 'veil of Maya'.[56]

What cannot be emphasised strongly enough, however, is that on both occasions on which he refers to the nothing (*das Nichts*) in the letter to Kaun, Beckett situates it within the frame of the 'perhaps' by way of an 'or' (*oder*). In short, in this letter Beckett refrains from simply identifying the nothing as the real that a literature of the unword would disclose. A decade later, in the essay 'Peintres de l'empêchement' (June 1948), he returns to the image of the veil, characterising genuine art as 'Un dévoilement sans fin, voile derrière voile, plan sur plan de transparences imparfaites, un dévoilement vers l'indévoilable, le rien, la chose à nouveau';[57] here, too, he retains the 'perhaps' by offering both 'le rien' *and* 'la chose à nouveau' as the two possibilities for that which lies behind the veil. Only if one ignores Beckett's use of the *oder* in the letter to Kaun or the splice comma in 'Peintres de l'empêchement' can one conclude – as does Richard Coe, for instance – that nothingness is the 'ultimate reality' in Beckett's works.[58]

Beckett's 1937 theorisation of a literature of the unword might seem to indicate that, to his reading of Schopenhauer and Geulincx, and about Democritus and Gorgias, he had by now added a close reading of Mauthner's *Beiträge*, in which the Austrian philosopher argues that the only way to overcome the kind of word superstition (*Wortaberglaube*) that leads us to mistake linguistic entities for non-linguistic ones is by turning language back against itself in an act of linguistic self-dissolution (*Selbstzersetzung*).[59] Such a conclusion appears all the more reasonable when one considers that, in his letter to Kaun, Beckett advocates 'some form of nominalist irony'[60] as a stage on the way towards a fully realised literature of the unword: not only does Mauthner (in one of the passages from volume II of the *Beiträge* on which Beckett took verbatim notes) assert that 'The nominalism of the Middle Ages is the first attempt at a genuine self-dissolution of metaphorical thinking',[61] but he also identifies Goethe's use of irony as that which enables him 'more than any other writer before or after him to rise above all possible linguistic limits'.[62] The evidence is, however, now strongly in favour of dating Beckett's substantial note-taking from Mauthner to 1938; which is to say, after the letter to Kaun, even if he had already encountered Mauthner's work indirectly on his 1936–37 trip to Germany, when reading Karl Ballmer's pamphlet *Aber Herr Heidegger!* (1933).[63] Beckett's sustained reading of Mauthner took place, then, between the completion of *Murphy* and the beginning of work on *Watt*; for, in striking contrast to *Murphy*, *Watt* is a work in which the status of language as such is placed in question, and this placing in question is explicitly related to the nothing in that novel: 'the only way one can speak of nothing is to speak of it as though it were something'.[64] *Watt* is the first of Beckett's major works in which a dissonantal art of the kind outlined in the letter to Kaun begins to emerge: language becomes a mode of *Selbstzersetzung*, and it does so in the interests of a nothing that resists articulation. In short, it is with *Watt* that Beckett moves decisively towards an apophatic art whose object will be a nothing that is at once impossible and unavoidable. The consummation of this art comes, however, almost forty years later, in the unprecedented deployment of the unwords 'void' and 'naught' in *Worstward Ho*, where the aporias of both the ontological and the ethical nothing are enacted in a literary language that remains unlike any other: 'Nohow over words again say what then when not preying. Each better worse for naught. No stilling preying. The shades. The dim. The void. All always faintly preying. Worse for naught. Worser for naught.'

Notes

1 Samuel Beckett, *Disjecta: Miscellaneous Writings and a Dramatic Fragment*, ed. Ruby Cohn (London: John Calder, 1983), p. 113.
2 Arnold Geulincx, *Metaphysics*, trans. Martin Wilson (Wisbech: Christoffel, 1999), p. 55. As Wilson observes, 'by *vacuum* Geulincx understands somewhere where there is literally nothing, not even space', *ibid.*, p. 56, n. 1.
3 *Ibid.*, p. 57.
4 Beckett, *Disjecta*, p. 172.
5 Samuel Beckett, *Proust and Three Dialogues* (London: Calder & Boyars, 1970), p. 65.
6 Samuel Beckett, *Dream of Fair to Middling Women*, ed. Eoin O'Brien and Edith Fournier (Dublin: Black Cat, 1992), p. 102.

7 *Ibid.*, pp. 4, 5, 89, 190.
8 *Ibid.*, pp. 12, 40.
9 *Ibid.*, p. 161.
10 See John Pilling, *A Companion to 'Dream of Fair to Middling Women'* (Tallahassee, FL: Journal of Beckett Studies Books, 2004), p. 274.
11 John Pilling (ed.), *Beckett's 'Dream' Notebook* (Reading: Beckett International Foundation, 1999), entry 919.
12 *Ibid.*, entry 125.
13 Beckett, *Dream*, p. 185.
14 Pilling (ed.), *Beckett's 'Dream' Notebook*, entry 1067.
15 Arthur Schopenhauer, *The World as Will and Representation*, trans. E. F. J. Payne, 2 vols (New York: Dover, 1966), vol. 1, pp. 411–12.
16 W. Windelband, *A History of Philosophy, with Especial Reference to the Formation and Development of Its Problems and Conceptions*, trans. James H. Tufts (London: Macmillan, 1893), p. 621.
17 Beckett, *Dream*, p. 16.
18 Samuel Beckett, *Murphy* (London: George Routledge & Sons, 1938), p. 246.
19 Archibald B. D. Alexander, *A Short History of Philosophy*, 3rd edn (Glasgow: Maclehose, Jackson & Co., 1922), pp. 38–9; cf. Trinity College Dublin (TCD) MS 10967/75.
20 See *Samuel Beckett Today / Aujourd'hui: Notes diverse holo*, eds Matthijs Engelberts, Everett Frost, and Jane Maxwell, 16 (2006), 67–8.
21 Samuel Beckett, *Trilogy: Molloy, Malone Dies, The Unnamable* (London: John Calder, 1959), pp. 305–6.
22 Samuel Beckett, *Ill Seen Ill Said* (London: John Calder, 1982), p. 59.
23 Samuel Beckett, *Murphy* (Paris: Les Éditions de Minuit, 1965), p. 176.
24 After Beckett's death, *Worstward Ho* was translated into French by Edith Fournier, the word 'naught' being rendered as 'rien'.
25 Samuel Beckett, *Worstward Ho* (London: John Calder, 1983), pp. 31–2, 41, 46–7.
26 Windelband, *History of Philosophy*, p. 470; cf. TCD MS 10967/206–10.
27 Beckett, *Worstward Ho*, p. 24.
28 John Burnet, *Greek Philosophy, Part I: Thales to Plato* (London: Macmillan, 1914), p. 122.
29 Quoted in Matthew Feldman, *Beckett's Books: A Cultural History of Samuel Beckett's 'Interwar Notes'* (London: Continuum, 2006), p. 76.
30 Alexander, *Short History of Philosophy*, p. 51; cf. TCD MS 10967/48.
31 Samuel Beckett, *Watt* (London: John Calder, 1976), p. 73.
32 C. J. Ackerley, *Obscure Locks, Simple Keys: The Annotated* Watt (Tallahassee, FL: Journal of Beckett Studies Books, 2005), pp. 210–12.

33 Windelband, *History of Philosophy*, p. 547; cf. TCD MS 10967/223ff.

34 Martin Heidegger, *Introduction to Metaphysics*, trans. Gregory Fried and Richard Polt (New Haven, CT: Yale University Press, 2000), p. 27.

35 *Ibid.*, p. 28.

36 Burnet, *Greek Philosophy*, pp. 67–8; cf. TCD MS 10967/12.

37 *Ibid.*, p. 86; cf. TCD MS 10967/13.

38 Windelband, *History of Philosophy*, pp. 42–3; cf. TCD MS 10967/32.

39 Geulincx, *Metaphysics*, p. 55; cf. TCD MS 10971/6/4.

40 *Ibid.*, p. 57.

41 Beckett, *Worstward Ho*, p. 46.

42 Windelband, *History of Philosophy*, p. 417, n. 2; cf. TCD MS 10967/189v.

43 Quoted in James Knowlson, *Damned to Fame: The Life of Samuel Beckett* (London: Bloomsbury, 1996), p. 219.

44 Beckett, *Worstward Ho*, p. 32. For an analysis of the Beckettian hand-in-hand, see my 'The politics of body language: the Beckett embrace', in Thomas Baldwin, James Fowler and Shane Weller (eds), *The Flesh in the Text* (Oxford: Peter Lang, 2007), pp. 141–59.

45 Samuel Beckett, *German Diaries 4*, entry of 18 January 1937.

46 'Samuel Beckett's notes to his reading of the *Ethics* by Arnold Geulincx', in Arnold Geulincx, *Ethics*, trans. Martin Wilson, eds Han Van Ruler, Anthony Uhlmann and Martin Wilson (Leiden and Boston: Brill, 2006), pp. 315, 327.

47 *Ibid.*, p. 352.

48 *Ibid.*, p. 344.

49 Alexander, *Short History of Philosophy*, p. 51; cf. TCD MS 10967/48.

50 Pilling (ed.), *Beckett's 'Dream' Notebook*, entry 1146. See also Shane Weller, *A Taste for the Negative: Beckett and Nihilism* (Oxford: Legenda, 2005) and '"Gnawing to be naught": Beckett and Pre-Socratic nihilism', *Samuel Beckett Today/Aujourd'hui: Des éléments aux Traces/ Elements and Traces*, 20 (2008), 307–19.

51 Samuel Beckett, *The Complete Dramatic Works* (London: Faber & Faber, 1986, 1990, 2006), p. 121.

52 Quoted in John Pilling, '"For interpolation": Beckett and English literature', *Samuel Beckett Today / Aujourd'hui: Notes diverse holo*, eds Matthijs Engelberts, Everett Frost and Jane Maxwell, 16 (2006), 220–1.

53 Beckett, *Complete Dramatic Works*, p. 264.

54 Samuel Beckett to A. J. Leventhal, 3 February 1959; quoted in Dirk van Hulle, '"Nichtsnichtsundnichts": Beckett's and Joyce's transtextual undoings', in Colleen Jaurretche (ed.), *Beckett, Joyce and the Art of the Negative* (Amsterdam and New York: Rodopi, 2005), p. 49.

55 Beckett, *Disjecta*, pp. 171–2 (translation slightly modified).
56 UoR MS 5003. On this important passage in the 'Clare Street' Notebook, see Mark Nixon, '"What a Tourist I Must Have Been": The German Diaries of Samuel Beckett' (Ph.D. thesis, University of Reading, 2005), pp. 178–81.
57 Beckett, *Disjecta*, p. 136.
58 Richard Coe, *Beckett* (London: Oliver & Boyd, 1964), p. 13.
59 Fritz Mauthner, *Beiträge zu einer Kritik der Sprache* (Leipzig: Felix Meiner, 1923), vol. 2, p. 476; cf. TCD MS 10971/5/1. (All translations from Mauthner's *Beiträge* are my own.)
60 Beckett, *Disjecta*, p. 173.
61 Mauthner, *Beiträge*, vol. 2, p. 474; cf. TCD MS 10971/5/1.
62 *Ibid.*, vol. 2, p. 506; cf. UoR MS 3000.
63 See Karl Ballmer, *Aber Herr Heidegger!* (Basel: Rudolf Geering, 1933), p. 19. I would like to express my gratitude to Matthew Feldman for having alerted me to this reference and for having supplied me with a copy of Ballmer's pamphlet.
64 Beckett, *Watt*, p. 74.

7

Into the void: Beckett's television plays and the idea of broadcasting

Jonathan Bignell

In the context of a tradition of critical discussion that characterises Beckett's plays for television (and his other work) as attempts to engage with nothingness, absence and death, this chapter argues that the television plays are critical explorations of the problematics of presence and absence inherent in the conceptions and histories of broadcasting.[1] Television as a medium and a physical apparatus sets up spatial and temporal relationships between programmes and their viewers, relationships with which Beckett's television plays are in dialogue. Broadcasting necessarily entails an incomplete encounter between viewer and programme, and a certain risk that the audience will not engage with what is offered to it. Here too, Beckett's television plays stage and explore the potentials of broadcasting and its attendant possibilities of failure. By taking account of the medium's historical and cultural roles, Beckett's television plays can be shown to engage with debates about the operation, social function and aesthetic possibilities of broadcasting.

Television and temporality

There is a long-standing assumption that the television medium's 'essence' is determined by its possibility to relay events and performances live, or to recreate an experience for the viewer that simulates a live broadcast. This essentialism is perpetuated by television's customary broadcast of news, sports events or national occasions at or close to the time of their occurrence, and the concomitant aim for the medium to connect with the lived temporality of its audience. In theoretical terms, this emphasis on liveness corresponds to an inclination to consider television semiotically as a medium of denotation: a medium that presents, shows and witnesses, rather than re-presents, tells or narrates.[2] However, at the same time, the use of such semiotic methodologies has directed attention away from features of the media that are specific to them because of these methodologies' principle of comparing visual representations with verbal language. For example, the notion that tense in television is always present (because the image is present on the screen to the spectator), whatever the narrative temporality being represented, is based on the denotation that derives from the photographic basis of the television (and film) media. Temporality in Beckett's plays is very often significant, since they deal with experiences that are remembered, retold or re-enacted, often inaccurately or with differences between each version, and they stage the characters' attempts to reinvoke or resurrect something lost and desired. In this respect, they exploit the tensions between tenses in television as a broadcast medium and the assumed temporality of its programming. This argument is the basis of Graley Herren's recent study of Beckett's screen work,[3] which suggests that the dramas work with Henri Bergson's theory of perception.[4] As Herren notes, Bergson argued that 'the present is always already memory, the past masquerading as the present. Thus, in exploiting television's capacity to make the dead seem "live," Beckett is only reiterating the function of perception itself, which always already serves as a memory machine.'[5] As a broadcast medium, television produces an assumption of its collective simultaneous presence to each of a programme's viewers, whether the programme was recorded live or not, but what television shows is necessarily something that is elsewhere, and which has already taken place. Its metaphysics of presence is predicated on absence.

Newly invented electronic media have been consistently associated with paranormal or spiritual phenomena in which absent or dead people are revivified.[6] Electronic presence generated anxiety and enthusiasm with the advent of telegraphy, radio broadcasting, television and, more recently, computer communication and virtual reality. Jeffrey Sconce's study of this history shows how spiritualism can be read as a utopian response to the power of electrical telegraphy, and maintains that radio was seized on as a way of communicating with the afterlife, for example. Television, he argues, 'was another technology for conjuring the dead, the alien, the interdimensional, the uncanny'.[7] The medium could be understood in this way because of its

> paradox of visible, seemingly material worlds trapped in a box in the living room and yet conjured out of nothing more than electricity and air. Whereas radio and telegraphy had always provided indexical evidence of distant places and invisible interlocutors (occult or otherwise), television appeared at once visibly and materially 'real' even as viewers realized it was wholly electrical and absent. [. . .] Its ghosts were truly ghosts – entities with visible form but without material substance.[8]

The invocation of versions of a past in *Eh Joe* (1966) and . . . *but the clouds* . . . (1977), and of absent beloveds in those two plays and in *Ghost Trio* (1977), seems to match the history that Sconce describes, and to operate as a commentary on it as well as a staging of its paradoxes of communication.

But it is important to separate the representation of absence that is so central to Beckett's plays from the negative theology which attributes a Romantic and transcendental presence to this absence. It is certainly the case that there is an absent beloved in *Ghost Trio*, and another absent beloved and an ungraspable past for M in . . . *but the clouds* . . . , an illusory representation of grace in *Nacht und Träume* (1983), a dead and absent beloved in *Eh Joe* and an empty centre in *Quad* (1981). The personae of the plays constitute themselves in relation to these absences, but this does not posit the absences as the origins or centres of meaning. Instead, the personae are constituted as subjects in relation to these absent objects of desire, and both subject and object are constitutive of each other. The plays are the drama of this mutually interdependent relationship, and the plays move towards the recognition of this relationship for their personae and thus, ideally, for the audience. Within some of the plays, present figures draw attention to their performance status and the possibility of conjuring up an image of the absent other (visually presented, for example, in the image of the woman M1 desires in . . . *but the clouds* . . . as a superimposed television image). Drawing attention to absence becomes equivalent to drawing attention to presence, in the context of the simultaneous presence and absence of the signified in television.

There is an ambivalent temporality produced in the relationship between image and voice in Beckett's television plays, since there is potentially a temporal separation between the two. A voice implies the presence of a speaker, and easily if not definitively establishes a temporal moment of enunciation in relation to which a past and a future may be constructed in the discourse that is enounced. Although the visual image on screen may be present to the viewer, it can be difficult or impossible to establish whether the image represents a past, a present or a future in narrative terms. The voice in *Ghost Trio* is able to predict the movements of the male Figure, so that the action of the drama seems to be brought into existence in a virtual space. The voice in *Eh Joe* may be the product of Joe's consciousness, or Joe may be the product of the consciousness of the voice. W and M2 in . . . *but the clouds* . . . are summoned into existence by M1. . . . *but the clouds* . . . uses repetition, ambiguity and the absence of dialogue, and the ventriloquism by M1 of W's recitation of Yeats's poem 'The tower', to retain a ghostly and fluid quality in the image, at the same time as drawing attention to the mechanical reproduction and apparent fixity provided by the television technology. Both M2 and W appear or reappear as if they were ghosts. The evocation of phantom-like figures summoned up by memory is especially significant in . . . *but the clouds* . . . and in *Ghost Trio*, where their simultaneous presence but ambiguous status as present or past is enforced by the use of superimposition and their presentation in central lighted areas of the screen frame, surrounded by indefinite dark shadows. The dreamt self B in *Nacht und Träume* is represented in a way which allows him to seem to be the projection of the dreamer A's mind, since the technical effect of a 'wipe' is used to expand the space occupied by B in the frame until it takes over the whole of the screen. The image of the B sequence seems to grow out of A's space while he sleeps. However the repetition of A's actions by the identical figure of B, once this new image has taken up the whole of the screen space, suggests a *mise en abyme* in which either, both or neither the A and B sequences might be dreams. The effect of this is to displace the activity of witnessing all of the images on to the 'dreaming' of their creator, the agency of the television apparatus that delivers them or even the television viewer.[9]

At the start of *Ghost Trio*, Voice draws attention to the fact that the visual images are all in shades of grey, thus remarking implicitly on the unusual fact that the play was recorded in monochrome at a time when television programmes were made in colour. The title of *Ghost Trio* clearly alludes to the notion of death, and the paradoxical life after death that a ghost represents, offering an internal significance for the greyness inasmuch as it might connote ghostliness. *Ghost Trio*'s single character, Figure, holds a cassette player in his hands and at intervals the soundtrack introduces phrases from Beethoven's 'Ghost' Trio, one of the intertexts that might explain the play's title. But with further relation to television specifically, the phenomenon of shadowed edges around the edges of shapes within a picture (caused by inaccurate aerial positioning or weather effects) is called 'ghosting' and is particularly noticeable in monochrome pictures and in images with strong contrasts of dark and light, like those in *Ghost Trio*. The grey that is used for all of the images in the play is also the colour that a television screen takes on when it is switched off. As well as the multiple connotations of greys and monochrome as signifiers within Voice's monologue and the play's visible action, setting up relays and patterns of connotation around death, ghostliness and a forlorn and exhausted tone, monochrome has material significance in relation to the choices of television *mise en scène* and the meaning of monochrome for producers and audiences at the time of production. Colour television in Britain was first broadcast in 1967, on the BBC2 channel. By 1977, much of the viewing audience was watching television in colour habitually, and the use of monochrome was most common in repeated programmes from the past, and occasional news footage. Their lack of colour distinguishes Beckett's television plays after *Eh Joe* from the programmes surrounding them in the schedules of the time, and has connotations of the past. This in itself produces another kind of ghostliness, whereby the productions are dislocated from the temporality of television's present at the time of their broadcast, and offer frameworks for interpretation that link them to earlier 'dead' modes of television production that they seem to revivify.

Across Beckett's plays for television, audio-visual forms and narrative temporalities adopt and implicitly comment upon the cultural histories of television as an apparatus that plays on hesitations between substantial and insubstantial, present and absent, living and dead. Television broadcasting technology operates by sending audio-visual signals that arrive almost instantaneously on the screen of their viewer, constructing a present moment that

has been important to the promotion of the medium as a window
on the world, live and direct. But each moment of a broadcast is
evanescent, vanishing as the scanning beam of the cathode ray
tube moves on to shape the next visual frame. While programmes
may be broadcast live, the images they show necessarily represent
somewhere other than the viewer's space, and while appearing in
the present of viewing time they may be images that have been
recorded and reshown. The insistently present television image is
thus always haunted by the possibility that what is conjured up is
an image of something that is no longer there, that is always about
to vanish or may already have gone. In this respect television and
radio are unlike theatre, where performers and audience share
the same space and time, and where no transmission technologies
intervene to introduce a delay between the time of performance
and its reception. Television is also unlike cinema, in which films
must always have been made at a previous time and can never be
'live'. Beckett's television plays draw on these hesitations in which
the television image is a something apparently conjured out of
nothing, the present moment of the play is hedged on either side
by what has disappeared or not yet been transmitted, and the here
and now of the performance is a representation of a there and then.
Memory, loss, dreams and absences in the plays are neither trium-
phantly recuperated into an achieved presence nor mourned as
definitively irretrievable, thus matching the involutions of nothing
into something and something into nothing that broadcasting has
worked through.

The presence and absence of the audience

The conceptions of medium and audience that Beckett's television
plays suggest can be understood in terms of the contrasting implications of broadcasting as dissemination. The original meaning of
'broadcasting' was the scattering of seed over the soil, an activity
assimilated as a metaphor and then an accepted designator for the
transmission of radio and television signals. Thus broadcasting as
dissemination retains the connotations of fertility, growth, renewal
and promise. At the same time, both broadcasting and dissemination also signify the control of the process by a single agent, the
indiscriminate nature of the distributive act, the necessary delay
between casting the seed (or sending the signal) and its arrival at

its destination, and the impossibility of knowing whether the seed or message will take hold and lead to a desired result. Like the discussion of the television image's absence and presence in the preceding section of this chapter, broadcasting as a concept holds together contrasting and mutually implicated notions.

Until the advent of interactive television at the end of the twentieth century, the apparatus of television transmission and reception had a single form. This consisted of centrally generated broadcast signals received by a mass audience that was situated in a different physical space from the space of transmission. The audience was imagined as a large public group, so that John Durham Peters can describe the ideal of broadcasting as 'an idealized configuration among speakers and audiences. It conjures visions of the agora, the town meeting, or the "public sphere".'[10] But the audience was nevertheless atomised by its separation into single viewers or small groups watching their television sets or listening to their radios. The spatial distinction between transmission and reception entailed the necessary non-response of the audience to whom a broadcast was addressed, situating a gap, delay or absence as a constitutive fact of communication. In this broadcast model, the viewer or listener is posited as a destination or receiver, but cannot be present as an interlocutor. The absence of the viewer in this model of broadcasting haunts it, and is remedied by attempts to provide channels of response from the audience back to the broadcaster, such as audience surveys, letter-writing to producers, or 'right to reply' programmes where individual viewers' concerns could be debated. Within programmes, acknowledgement of the audience is carried out by the viewer's solicitation or delegation via representatives. Viewer delegates in television include representations of internal auditors or addressees, and visible or audible audiences within programmes. In television programmes other than Beckett's drama, such as chat shows or situation comedy, audience groups are seen and heard in programmes with the function of standing in for the television audience. They applaud, laugh, groan or otherwise comment on the programme in the ways that home viewers are imagined to do. By contrast, television drama almost never uses this address to the viewer, since the positioning of the audience for the programme is different, and closer to the notion of spectatorship deployed in cinema. In the case of television drama or cinema, the codes of camera point of view, editing and sound work to hollow out a provisional space or position for the viewer to occupy, a place from where the diverse components of the narrative can make sense and to which they are directed.

In Beckett's work for television, there are figures who act as delegates for the viewer, inasmuch as they are addressees within the fictional world. These figures are not straightforwardly images of a television viewer, but their function as addressees situates them structurally in a parallel role. They include Joe in *Eh Joe*, who is the addressee of Voice. Later, Figure in *Ghost Trio* seems at least some of the time to be addressed by Voice, and Voice explicitly addresses the television viewer at the start of the play by introducing him or her to the *mise en scène* and the schema of reception she expects. She orders the viewer to 'tune accordingly' and to 'keep that sound down', for example. In . . . *but the clouds* . . . , M1 addresses his voice to the viewer and tells his own story, accompanied by visual representations of aspects of that story such as M2's departures 'to walk the roads'. Beckett's television plays work within a tradition of hollowing out the place of the viewer or listener, directing an address to him or her, and including figures within the text who may stand in for the television viewer as a destination for communication. However, Beckett's plays also undercut or complicate the achievement of a communicative relation between sender and receiver, both within the diegesis of the plays and in their address to their viewer. What is at stake here is whether communicative address and interaction can establish a substantial relation between two figures, or whether it is evidence of an absence of relation, a something that is actually a nothing. Most obviously, in *Eh Joe* the accusation and questioning by Voice produces no reply from Joe, and in *Ghost Trio* the instructions to the viewer from Voice might not be obeyed and there are some mismatches between Voice's statements about what Figure will do and what he visibly does. In . . . *but the clouds* . . . , M1 repeatedly revises the narrative he tells about himself, and M2 re-enacts a simple sequence of movements so that M1, and thus the camera, and the play itself, can 'make sure we have got it right'. These stagings of communication within the plays, and between the plays and their viewers, can be understood as working through the non-communication inherent in the nature of broadcasting itself, where messages may not arrive, may not be understood or may fail to produce a desired effect.

In a European broadcasting context, the relationship of sender and addressee takes a specific form. The notion of broadcasting as the casting of seed that may fruitfully grow in the soil of the audience community is evident in the British concept of Public Service Broadcasting, where the universally available broadcast of material considered socially valuable, like Beckett's work, aims for its future productivity for its audience. Beckett's British television plays following *Eh Joe* were all presented under the auspices of *Arena*, BBC2's flagship arts programme, and this is highly significant for their institutional status and their address to their audience. For the majority of television viewers, arts television programmes are their primary access to the arts.[11] This has the effect of ensuring continuity of television coverage of the arts, but it also reinforces the ghettoisation of arts programmes and the divisions between an assumed minority audience of informed viewers and an ignorant majority. The bridge between the audience and the art is most often the personality, whether a television personality acting as presenter or the personality of the artist proposed as the source and explanatory context for the work. For example, Melvyn Bragg led the presentation of *The Lively Arts: Shades* (1977) and interviewed Martin Esslin about Beckett's life and work in the programme. Beckett's *Ghost Trio*, . . . *but the clouds* . . . and *Not I* (1975) appeared in *Shades* as artworks that were felt to need intermediary figures between them and the audience. Bragg brought an already distinguished reputation as a cultural commentator and public intellectual that suited both the presumed difficulty and prestige of Beckett's work, and also promised that he would be an accessible and reliable conduit for its understanding by the audience. The commissioning of original dramas by Beckett as a writer associated with theatre, and also the presentations of his theatre plays on television, functioned as advertisements for theatre as art, and could be justified by broadcasters as a means of supporting theatre as a national cultural institution. For the producers of Beckett's plays for television, an interest in audience reception and the need to engage the audience co-existed with the opportunity to dismiss negative audience responses and small numbers of viewers on the basis of the public service remit of the BBC in Britain and SDR in Germany, which was to present 'the best' of arts culture as defined by professional television personnel and an informed reviewing culture in the press.[12] Beckett's work was admired by a cultural elite who shared interests in a common European legacy

of knowledge, taste and experience. He was a totem for a cultur-
ally powerful group with links to arts production and television
broadcasting, and this made possible the formation of networks of
personnel and financial support for television programmes about
Beckett and programmes that would broadcast his theatrical and
literary work.

Historically, in Britain there has been a long-standing assumption that television in itself is not valuable, but becomes so when
it transmits something valuable in a democratic and socially useful
way.[13] Beckett's work benefited from this ideology inasmuch as it
was conjoined with aims to bring high culture, such as literature,
theatre or music, to a wider audience. But Beckett's plays could
not be assimilated into the other means for television to acquire
value by making use of its supposed privileged relationship to
reality, exemplified by broadcasting public events, or connecting with public sphere concerns via news or current affairs programmes. Television broadcasts of Beckett's work are not 'popular'
or 'commercial' television, but, inasmuch as television is regarded
as a bad object, it functions as the other against which valuable
forms of culture or cultural viewing practice are constructed.
Since the viewing practices of television have been understood
as variable, distracted, domestic and private, the identification of
aesthetic value in programmes by assuming an attentive, concentrated, public and socially extended viewing of them, such as is
given to art cinema, serious theatre or painting, poses problems
for television producers and academic evaluation. The mode of
viewing required for sensitive aesthetic judgement seems alien
to the medium. It is in this context that criticism has addressed
Beckett's television work as valuable because of its difference from
the programmes surrounding it, and its requirement of a different mode of viewing engagement from that which is assumed for
those other surrounding programmes. In other words, Beckett's
television work has been praised for not being like television. The
disparagement of television in general as a trivial medium works
as the pre-established negative against which Beckett's plays are
set, redeeming television from itself. If television is nothing, it is
argued, Beckett's plays can be something valuable.

This hope for the medium acts as an antidote to prevalent views
(emerging in the 1950s and 1960s) among intellectual commentators that television was a cultural void. As Jeffrey Sconce explains,

'the medium's distinctive "electronic elsewhere" became instead an "electronic nowhere". Rather than portray television as a magic means of teleportation, these more ominous portraits of the medium saw television as a zone of suspended animation, a form of oblivion from which viewers might not ever escape.'[14] Critics have valued Beckett's television plays as ways for viewers to understand and explore problems of identity, death, love and meaning in general, countering assumptions about television's role in cultural dumbing-down. Jonathan Kalb, for example, claims that 'television has been dominated by the narrowly circumscribed formats of commercial programming since its birth, and those formats have contributed to egregious, worldwide psychological changes: shrinking attention spans, discouraging reading and encouraging passive, narcotized habits of viewing art of all kinds'.[15] Linda Ben-Zvi has argued that Beckett's plays for television and radio educate the audience about their means of production: 'Beckett foregrounds the devices – radio sound effects, film and video camera positions – and forces the audience to acknowledge the presence of these usually hidden shapers of texts.'[16] Thus the plays are argued to empower the audience by requiring attention to the conventions of signification in the medium, and redressing its more usual tendency towards cultural 'oblivion'.

This quasi-religious and hopeful vision of broadcasting as communication is evident in Beckett's television work, not only in the historical circumstances of its production in Britain and Germany but also in the risk, hope or belief in communicative effectivity that the plays' dialogic scenarios depend on. The pedagogic functions of Voice in *Ghost Trio* and her relation to the viewer, which include the authority of Voice's tone and her instructions as to how to view, could be interpreted in relation to the ideology accompanying the BBC's public service functions. Although Part I of the play introduces the audience to the space, and Part II to the movement of the figure, the third Part of the play has no voice-over. The dynamics of the audience's relationship to the play therefore change, with the implication that by Part III the viewer will have learned to find his or her place as the audience shaped by the play's discourse, and thus a communicative relationship will have been achieved. Since the television set is likely to be placed in a room, among the domestic objects of the household, the plays' focus on domestic interiors that is most striking in Voice's attention to the layout and space of the room setting both makes a link with the viewer's own environment and also establishes the difference and distance between the represented room and the viewer's own space. It is particularly striking that Voice not only describes the set, the colours and shapes of the items in it and the disposition of the Figure, but also remarks on the technical and material means of the viewer's perception of this information. Voice's command that the viewer should not raise the volume on the television set, for example, is not simply a recognition that the drama is conveyed by means of the camera and sound recording equipment, but also that it is being received on domestic television apparatus in the home of the viewing audience. Again, this not only draws attention to the means of representation in a self-conscious way but also affects the inclusion and exclusion of the audience from the drama. As a conduit for images and sounds, the television apparatus both provides access to those images and sounds, and mirrors the represented room with the viewer's, but also announces the viewer's separation from the moment of image and sound recording and excludes the viewer from the room supposedly matching the one in which he or she sits.

Jonathan Kalb has adopted a version of this argument and argues that, like paintings by Caravaggio, the television plays are like 'windows looking inward on particular souls', and represent 'Man existing on his own in a kind of nothingness'.[17] He also maintains that inasmuch as parallels between the plays' characters and the viewer are established spatially and by narration, that 'nothingness' carries over into the viewing situation. In Kalb's view, Beckett's plays have something to offer, which is an insight into the 'soul' of equivalent value to the insight offered by an Old Master such as Caravaggio. But the soul thus revealed is isolated and surrounded by 'nothingness', a situation that parallels the isolation of the television viewer. The something that Beckett's plays offer is in fact a nothing, or more precisely a revelation of the nothingness that haunts humankind in general. But it is reductive to turn a something into a nothing and to argue that the something communicated by Beckett's drama has a nothing as its content. The result of the argument is that nothing becomes the fundamental ground of existence, and the communicative relationship between television and its viewer is something that acts as a vehicle for staging non-communication and nothingness. It is an argument characterised by pathos and melancholy.

Arguments for the productive and educative functions of Beckett's television dramas match the values of public service broadcasting, and have been made on the basis of critical analyses of the plays' audio-visual forms. Eckart Voigts-Virchow asks: 'How does this formal examination of Beckett's camera plays, then, position their reductive, repetitive, static, monochrome, interior closeness in the TV environment?', and answers that it sidelines them as outdated and rarefied (both rarely seen and aimed at an elite audience).[18] The plays themselves were seen only by a tiny sector of the British population, and the arts programmes that broadcast them or discussed them were predominantly on niche services like the BBC's Third Programme on radio, or arts programmes and late-evening discussion programmes on the BBC2 television channel. Beckett's plays for television and adaptations for television of his theatre work were marginal to the schedules, so that their effectivity in constructing and communicating with their audience was undercut to some extent by their relationship with the broadcast programming surrounding them.

British broadcasters' policy has been to mix programmes together in the schedule so that audiences might come across them by chance and be stimulated by relatively demanding fare that they might not consciously choose to view. The audience was conceived as a citizenry whose cultural knowledge and involvement could be gently raised by insinuating 'quality' material amongst popular entertainment. Beckett's plays for television need to be understood in relation to British television culture, and the institutional culture of the BBC in particular. The linkage between Beckett's television dramas and the modernist aesthetic that Beckett was perceived to represent functioned through the value of Beckett's name and associations, which played an important role in legitimating the educative and conservational values underlying Public Service Broadcasting. The formal experimentation, theatrical background and admitted complexity of Beckett's television plays supported the claims of the BBC to present the best of contemporary arts practice despite, or even because of, the distance between such practice and the mainstream forms of television dramatic entertainment. For many of the production staff who worked on the realisation of Beckett's television plays, and for many of the Beckett critics who have analysed them, the plays are valuable for two contrasting reasons. They are 'not like television' and thus have a positive value in redressing the medium's supposed tendency towards dumbing-down its audience. But they are also valuable because they appear to offer a metacritique of what the television medium is as a communication apparatus. The plays are thus understood in a dual role, at once inside television as an inoculation against its more usual triviality, and also outside it at a critical distance from where the plays offer a critique of the television medium that broadcasts them. Again these formulations demonstrate the precarious separations between inclusion and exclusion, and participation and negation, that have appeared consistently in this chapter and which consistently threaten to slip into each other.

Ekart Voigts-Virchow points to the titles of the plays as indications that they refer to the questioning of being through the questioning of television: 'Significantly, his titles address three metaphors which may be related to precisely the ontological destabilization of TV: images as *ghosts*, as *clouds*, and as *dreams*.'[19] Ghosts, clouds and dreams are not produced under the conscious agency of a subject, and are immaterial and intangible. In *Ghost Trio*, Figure thinks he hears an indication of the presence of a woman who does not appear. In . . . *but the clouds* . . . , memory and voice seem to conjure up the ghostly presence of a lover. In *Nacht und Träume*, the play seems to dramatise the experience of a dream or vision. The means of realising these ideas in television form are themselves in dialogue with the assumptions of iconic representation in the medium, supporting those critical interpretations which focus on the plays as metadiscourses about the medium. Inasmuch as the self communicates and stages relations with an other outside itself, it must also be recognisable to itself as an other that another self might communicate with. Similarly, the other must be posed as a potential self with whom the communicating self can establish a relation. Self and other invert and double themselves in the process of communication, and as a precondition for staging that communication.[20] The verb 'staging' is useful for understanding how this works in the plays, because communication is a process in which spatial position and temporal extension provide the perceptible ground for relations between selves to be proposed. Communication in the television plays 'takes place' even if the act of communication and the significance of what may be communicated are undercut and incomplete. Place and stage demonstrate the specific concrete materiality of the communicative relation in Beckett's television plays, in contrast to the idealisation and abstraction of language and personae that are so often remarked on in Beckett's work.

Beckett and the ethics of broadcasting

The persistent motif of interpreting Beckett's work in relation to philosophical concerns with identity, language and otherness can be recast as a meditation on the communicative relations which are at stake in broadcasting. Beckett's television dramas frequently divide their personae into two; voice and body, present and past, internal and external. One of the consequences of this is that the personae lack a sense of their own identity as comprising a unity between these two parts. Figure's look at himself in the mirror in *Ghost Trio*, and his failure to realise in the present his desire for the absent loved one signified by Beethoven's music, is an example of this. In a similar way, Joe seems unable to recognise Voice as a part of himself. In . . . *but the clouds* . . . , M cannot reconcile himself with M1 and complete a satisfactory narrative connecting his present to the past. Within these terms, there is no necessity for Romantic nostalgia and negative theology. For the interdependent relation between self and other, inner and outer, representation and the real, object and concept, are constitutive of meaning and do not in themselves possess an ethical or moral value. This also explains the divide in Beckett's plays between image and sound, and between body and voice, for this separation works with the possibility that there can be a correspondence between these media of representation, yet also denies their equivalence and translation into each other. Symbolisation, whether in image or language, can be regarded as a form of 'writing' that establishes a constitutive relationship between the real and its representation. Yet this relationship can never be one of equivalence or adequacy. Furthermore, each system of symbolisation has its own particularity as a signifying system, and is necessarily untranslatable into another. The apparent parallels between Beckett's drama and these debates in Western metaphysics emerge from the specific forms of symbolisation and communicative relation that broadcasting depends on, inasmuch as it constructs both a necessary relationship and a necessary non-correspondence between the broadcast and its viewer.

Theoretical discourses about television audiences regard the audience either as an object constructed by television or as a subject empowered to interact actively with it. Audiences are either considered as passive, positioned and interpolated by television or on the other hand regarded as active appropriators of meaning amid a complex social and cultural context. Beckett critics have argued that his television work is important because it is radically different from the mass culture that surrounds it on television, and has a productive role in turning the audience from passive to active viewers, and recognising the homogeneity of the majority of television broadcasting. This is a noble aim, but historical evidence shows that it repeatedly failed and that it was support from institutionally powerful television producers and cultural opinion-formers that brought Beckett's dramas to the screen. Yet Beckett's television plays cannot be dismissed because of this, since broadcasting as a concept and social practice is always predicated on transmission without the assurance of reception or response.[21]

Beckett's backward-looking investigation of what the medium could do and could be drew inevitably on discourses about television that were developed and contested before his first media productions were conceived. These discourses were inherited from discourses about radio in particular, which shaped the concept of broadcast communication as the summoning up of absence into presence, and a reliance on the audience as a public that was constituted by and for programmes but which could not be fully known. Television's inauguration as a programme medium from the early 1930s, its institutionalisation and the development of scheduling, audience address and a requirement to work for the public good, each offer contexts in which norms were negotiated that could then be experimented with by later programmes such as those that Beckett originated. Beckett criticism has repeatedly taken its bearings from his declarations that speaking, writing and communicating are impossible but inescapable, and his screen dramas stage this communicative relation as a structure, theme and formal template for the audio-visual texts he produced. Television as broadcast communication, and television as a medium for self-consciously performing communication and its failures aesthetically, are historically specific potentialities which Beckett's work takes up. As the centre-periphery model of broadcasting wanes with the rise of technologies of media convergence, interactivity and narrowcasting, and as the ideology of public service is threatened by the marketisation and privatisation of the media, Beckett's television dramas acquire new kinds of significance. They point to the tensions and paradoxes inherent in broadcasting, where 'something' and 'nothing', presence and absence, living and dead, and sending and receiving have shaped the public being of social-democratic societies. Broadcasting is dissemination in good faith, despite its haunting by the prospect that some of what is broadcast will turn out to be a dead letter sent into the void.

Notes

1 Some of the ideas advanced here are developed more fully in Jonathan Bignell, *Beckett on Screen: The Television Plays* (Manchester: Manchester University Press, 2009). The dates given are for the first broadcast of each television play.
2 Stephen Heath and Gillian Skirrow, 'Television: a world in action' *Screen*, 18:2 (1977), 7–59.
3 Graley Herren, *Samuel Beckett's Plays on Film and Television* (New York and Basingstoke: Palgrave Macmillan, 2007).
4 Henri Bergson, *Matter and Memory*, trans. N. Paul and W. Palmer (New York: Macmillan, 1912).
5 Herren, *Samuel Beckett's Plays*, p. 13.
6 Jeffrey Sconce, *Haunted Media: Electronic Presence from Telegraphy to Television* (Durham, NC: Duke University Press, 2000).
7 *Ibid.*, p. 126.
8 *Ibid.*
9 See Graley Herren, 'Splitting images: Samuel Beckett's *Nacht und Träume*', *Modern Drama*, 43 (2000), 182–91; and Graley Herren, '*Nacht und Träume* as Beckett's *agony in the garden*', *Journal of Beckett Studies*, 11:1 (2001), 54–70.
10 J. D. Peters, *Speaking into the Air: A History of the Idea of Communication* (Chicago: University of Chicago Press, 1999), pp. 210–11.
11 J. A. Walker, *Arts TV: A History of Arts Television in Britain* (London: John Libbey, 1993).
12 Jonathan Bignell, 'Beckett at the BBC: the production and reception of Samuel Beckett's plays for television', in L. Ben-Zvi (ed.), *Drawing on Beckett: Portraits, Performances, and Cultural Contexts* (Tel Aviv: Assaph, 2003), pp. 165–82. See also Bignell, *Beckett on Screen*.
13 Charlotte Brundson, 'Problems with quality', *Screen*, 31:1 (1990), 67–90.
14 Sconce, *Haunted Media*, p. 131.

15 Jonathan Kalb, 'The mediated Quixote: the radio and television plays, and *Film*', in J. Pilling (ed.), *The Cambridge Companion to Beckett* (Cambridge: Cambridge University Press, 1994), pp. 124–44, p. 137.

16 Linda Ben-Zvi, 'Samuel Beckett's media plays', *Modern Drama*, 28:1 (1985), 22–37, p. 24.

17 Jonathan Kalb, *Beckett in Performance* (Cambridge: Cambridge University Press, 1989), p. 99.

18 Ekart Voigts-Virchow, 'Exhausted cameras: Beckett in the TV-zoo', in J. Jeffers (ed.), *Samuel Beckett: A Casebook* (New York: Garland, 1998), pp. 225–49, p. 235.

19 Ekart Voigts-Virchow, 'Face values: Beckett Inc., the camera plays and cultural liminality', *Journal of Beckett Studies*, 10:1/2 (2000–1), 119–35, p. 124.

20 Herren, *Samuel Beckett's Plays*, p. 16.

21 Paddy Scannell, 'Love and communication: a review essay', *Westminster Papers in Communication and Culture*, 1:1 (2004), 93–102.

8

Beckett, Feldman, Salcedo . . . *Neither*

Derval Tubridy

Writing to Thomas MacGreevy in 1936, Beckett describes his novel *Murphy* in terms of negation and estrangement:

> I suddenly see that *Murphy* is break down [sic] between his *ubi nihil vales ibi nihil velis* (positive) & Malraux's *Il est difficile à celui qui vit hors du monde de ne pas rechercher les siens* (negation).[1]

Positioning his writing between the seventeenth-century occasionalist philosophy of Arnold Geulincx, and the twentieth-century existential writing of André Malraux, Beckett gives us two visions of nothing from which to proceed. The first, from Geulincx's *Ethica* (1675), argues that 'where you are worth nothing, may you also wish for nothing',[2] proposing an approach to life that balances value and desire in an ethics of negation based on what Anthony Uhlmann aptly describes as the *cogito nescio*.[3] The second, from Malraux's novel *La Condition humaine* (1933), contends that 'it is difficult for one who lives isolated from the everyday world not to seek others like himself'.[4]

This chapter situates its enquiry between these poles of negation, exploring the interstices between both by way of *neither*. Drawing together prose, music and sculpture, I investigate the role of nothing through three works called *neither* and *Neither*: Beckett's short text (1976), Morton Feldman's opera (1977), and Doris Salcedo's sculptural installation (2004).[5] The Columbian artist Doris Salcedo's work explores the politics of absence, particularly in works such as *Unland: Irreversible Witness* (1995–98), which acts as a sculptural witness to the disappeared victims of war. Her installation *Neither* draws on both Feldman's music and Beckett's text, creating a sculpture that has much in common with the negative spaces of Beckett's theatre. The American composer Morton Feldman's *Neither* has been called an 'anti-opera', a stripped down, minimalist monodrama. Described as 'shockingly beautiful as it is disorienting and distancing' the music of *Neither* echoes the movement of Beckett's text in an oscillation between two poles of impossibility.[6]

Samuel Beckett's brief and evocative text was written for Morton Feldman in a collaboration initiated by Feldman. Commissioned by the Teatro dell'Opera in Rome to work on a composition, Feldman approached Beckett through a mutual friend and was offered some existing material. His response to the texts was that 'they were pregnable, they didn't need music'.[7] Preferring to work with something else, Feldman met Beckett in 1976 at the Schiller Theatre in Berlin where Beckett was rehearsing *Footfalls* and *That Time*. Over lunch the writer and composer discussed the project. Just as with Beckett's work with Jasper Johns on the artist's book *Foirades/Fizzles*, the coming together of Beckett and Feldman was more a meeting of minds than an intimate collaboration. Feldman describes his discussion with Beckett, emphasising that there did not need to be any compromise on the part of either one of them since they were both in complete agreement about many things:

> For example – he was very embarrassed – he said to me, after a while, 'Mr Feldman, I don't like opera.' I said to him, 'I don't blame you!' Then he said to me, 'I don't like my words being set to music,' and I said, 'I'm in complete agreement. In fact it's very seldom that I've used words. I've written a lot of pieces with voice, and they're wordless.' Then he looked at me again and said, 'But what do you want?' And I said, 'I have no idea!'[8]

Feldman showed Beckett the score of a piece that he had written using lines from Beckett's script for *Film*.[9] Beckett, an assured musician himself, took a keen interest in the score and, as John Dwyer recalls, responded by saying that there was only one theme in his life:

> 'May I write it down? [asked Feldman]. (Beckett himself takes Feldman's music paper and writes down the theme . . . It reads 'To and fro in shadow, from outer shadow to inner shadow. To and fro, between unattainable self and unattainable non-self.') . . . 'It would need a bit of work, wouldn't it? Well, if I get any further ideas on it, I'll send them on to you.'[10]

This was the beginning of the libretto for *Neither*. At the end of the month, while Beckett was still rehearsing in Berlin, a card arrived in Buffalo, New York, where Feldman was Professor of Music. On it was a brief note from Beckett: 'Dear Morton Feldman. Verso the piece I promised. It was good meeting you. Best, Samuel Beckett.'[11] On the back of the card was the handwritten text *neither*: 'To and fro in shadow from inner to outershadow from impenetrable self to impenetrable unself by way of neither'.[12]

Beckett's ten-line text opens with a movement of gentle undulation between two boundaries ghosted by darkness, a reflexive motion between a self and its negation. It is this movement within the space of negation that I would like to focus on in my readings of Beckett's text, Feldman's opera and Salcedo's installation. Both Feldman and Salcedo respond to the structure of Beckett's text which traces its lines of enquiry between indeterminate points of arrival and departure. The text focuses on the movement between these points which are characterised in terms of locus ('inner to outershadow', 'two lit refuges'); subjectivity ('impenetrable self to unpenetrable unself'); and agency ('beckoned back and forth').

Writing on *Worstward Ho*, Carla Locatelli examines 'the implication of a *movement* of meaning' in Beckett's work, arguing that 'we can find a precise, pervasive orientation which even then emphasized the temporal (diachronic and dynamic) dimension of the work of art'.[13] Locatelli supports her argument by drawing on Beckett's critical writing on the painters Bram and Geer van Velde, 'La peinture des van Velde ou le Monde et le Pantalon', in which he argues that 'the work considered as pure creation, and whose function stops with its genesis, is destined to nothingness'.[14] The nothingness that Beckett refers to in this piece is neither here nor there in Beckett's 1976 text, echoing the movement of *Footfalls* with which Beckett was rehearsing at the time he wrote *neither*. The ethereal, insubstantial figure of May – 'dishevelled grey hair, worn grey wrap hiding feet, trailing'[15] – in *Footfalls* prefigures the attenuated self of *neither* whose 'unheard footfalls only sound' leave minimal trace as they move toward 'unspeakable home'. These 'unheard footfalls' of *neither* contrast with the importance of sound in *Footfalls* emphasised by May's insistence on hearing her steps: 'May: I mean, Mother, that I must hear the feet, however faint they fall. The mother: The motion alone is not enough? May: No, Mother, the motion alone is not enough, I must hear the feet, however faint they fall.'[16] Beckett directs that the steps in *Footfalls* are a 'clearly audible rhythmic tread', a rhythm picked up in *neither* by the rhythmic 'back and forth' of the text's lines which gradually diminish to stasis and silence: 'till at last halt for good, absent for good from self and other / then no sound'. The progressive reduction of sound in *neither* echoes the 'Sequel' of *Footfalls* in which the ghostly figure of Amy paces unheard: 'But many also were the nights when she paced without pause, up and down, up and down, before vanishing the way she came. [*Pause.*] No sound. [*Pause.*] None at least to be heard.'[17]

The paradox at the heart of *Footfalls* in which Amy denies her presence in church even as her mother, Mrs W, insists that she heard her voice: 'Amy: [. . .] I saw nothing, heard nothing, of any kind. I was not there. Mrs W: Not there? Amy: Not there. Mrs W: But I heard you respond. [*Pause.*] I heard you say Amen' is reconfigured in Beckett's *neither* in terms of a subject whose assertion – 'self' – and negation – 'unself' – are both 'impenetrable'.[18] The lighting of Beckett's play, with its emphasis on shadow – 'dim, strongest at floor level, less on body, least on head' and again 'fade up to dim on strip. Rest in darkness'[19] – underlines the tenuous position of the protagonist of *Footfalls*, just as the self of *neither* is 'intent on the one gleam or the other' as she or he moves between the 'two lit refuges' which withdraw their sanctuary as they are approached: 'as between two lit refuges whose doors once neared gently close, once turned away from gently part again'.

The staging of Feldman's opera *Neither* at the Teatro dell'Opera in Rome in May 1977, with a set designed by Michelangelo Pistoletto, has much in common with the aesthetics of Beckett's theatre. Centre stage is the Soprano, Martha Hanneman, sheathed in a dress which extends beyond the limits of her body to encompass the stage, ending only where shadow encroaches. The image she creates is a visual parallel to the sense of continuity in Feldman's composition. Feldman explains: 'What I'm trying to do is hold the moment. [. . .] I'm trying to hold the moment with the slightest compositional methodology. The thing is how do you sustain it, how do you keep it going?'[20] Keeping going is a key Beckettian trope. The protagonist of *The Unnamable* agonises over the impossibility, yet necessity, of going on: 'it will be I, it will be the silence, where I am, I don't know, I'll never know, in the silence you don't know, you must go on, I can't go on, I'll go on.[21] Much later Beckett himself reiterates this position in conversation with Charles Juliet, claiming 'I have to go on [. . .] I am up against a cliff wall yet I have to go forward. It's impossible isn't it? All the same, you can go forward. Advance a few more miserable millimetres.'[22] At another point in the opera Martha Hanneman is shrouded in black holding two lights, each a point of illumination in the penumbra of the stage across which groups of men wander. William Weaver, writing for the *International Herald Tribune*, was underwhelmed by Pistoletto's set, describing it as 'not very arresting or enhancing: some thumbprints of light on an off-white background and an aimless crowd that wandered on and off the stage'.[23] Brian Northcott of *The Sunday Telegraph* was more engaged, noting the ways in which the set complemented Feldman's music:

> At the same time it was the old Feldman, the timelessness and hush (there are only six loud bars in the same score), that Michelangelo Pistoletto chose to emphasise in his staging: placing the young American soprano, Martha Hanneman, motionless downstage and faintly illuminating the gloom behind her with pools of light fluctuating in counterpoint with the slow breathing – as of some sleeping giant – that Feldman's muted grindings and suspirations sometimes suggest, through which wandered lost groups of male figures like Giacometti statues vaguely come to life.[24]

Northcott describes Feldman's music in terms that remind us of Beckett. It is slow and quiet, little concerned with drama or self-expression 'or anything except pure, contemplative sound'.[25] The voice of the soprano traces a taught line through the orchestration, her pitch rendering the articulation of Beckett's words almost impossible: 'and the voice? At the beginning, while the cellos maintain a pulsating figure to convey "a feeling of quickness" characteristic of Beckett, the voice floats gently, unobtrusively, through the shifting orchestral texture, a fixed point within a changing context.'[26]

Feldman's initial response to Beckett's text was formal. He began to scan the sentences to get a sense of their position and their relation to each other: 'First of all, like a conventional composer, I began to scan the first sentence: *To and fro in shadow from inner to outer shadow*; it seemed to me as one long period of time.'[27] The key moment when text and composition came together for Feldman is when he 'noticed that it fell into a grid'. The pattern of the grid as a repetition of movement between points of intersection and empty space is critical to Feldman's and Salcedo's *Neither*. Writing about Beckett as a librettist, Howard Skempton remarks that 'the "grid" is a notable feature of *Neither*' describing the structure of Feldman's opera as 'a regular arrangement of bars within the system, each system containing half a line of text'.[28] Catherine Laws, however, suggests that Skempton's examination of Feldman's score is not fully comprehensive. In an astute analysis of the structure inherent in Feldman's *Neither*, Laws agrees with Skempton that the 'grid starts from the basis of subdivisions lasting for twelve bars, and each of these covers the breadth of one page of score' but argues that this 'division of the text into half a line per twelve bars is not always strictly adhered to'.[29]

Laws understands Feldman's approach to Beckett's text as an 'attempt to render in musical terms the pendular motion of a single insubstantial idea, viewed in varying contexts'.[30] However, Feldman had already begun writing the music for his collaboration with Beckett before he received Beckett's text. That is why, as Feldman explains with some humour, 'the piece begins textless. I was waiting for the text. I discovered what an overture is: waiting for the text!'[31] Reading Beckett's *neither* Feldman focuses on the movement 'to and fro' between the 'self' and 'unself' (N). As the composer explains:

> The poem is called *Neither* and if I may paraphrase it has to do with the fact – it's not a narrative, it becomes like a narrative – that there is no understanding of the self or the unself nor is there a synthesis. They're both on the outer shadows. We go back and forth between them. It became a narrative in defining a musical proximity to this thought.[32]

Feldman's approach to finding this 'musical proximity' to Beckett's thought lies in his analysis of the 'unself' in impersonal, mechanical terms. He describes his compositional strategy thus: 'I saw the "unself" as a very detached, impersonal, perfect type of machinery. What I did was to superimpose this perfect machinery in a polyrhythmic situation. So there's a new element here, a periodic element, which eventually emerges.'[33] The pulsing nature of the orchestration underlines this periodic element while also unsettling the grid-like nature of the piece. There is a tension, then, between the role of the grid which, in Laws's view, 'would seem to derive more importance from its value to the composer as a sequence of frames within which to arrange his material' and the acoustic experience itself:

> Given the constantly changing bar lengths, the varying pulses used within and against the metres, and the apparently arbitrary allocation of words or syllables within the sections, it has to be admitted that the regularity of many areas of the grid are not aurally perceptible.[34]

At the close of his 'Darmstadt Lecture' given in 1984, Feldman describes his work in terms of two aspects that he sees as characteristic of art in the twentieth century: 'One is change, variation. I prefer the word change. The other is reiteration, repetition. I prefer the word reiteration'.[35] Feldman's destabilisation of the grid structure which provided the impetus for his composition can be understood in terms of Derrida's notion of a difference that is necessarily contained within repetition. Writing on form and meaning in the context of Husserlian phenomenology, Derrida argues for 'the production of some *elliptical* change of site, within the difference involved in repetition'.[36] He qualifies this difference as a kind of displacement, one which is 'no doubt deficient, but with a deficiency that is not yet, or is already no longer, absence, negativity, nonbeing, lack, silence'.[37]

Beckett's writing is characterised by repetitions that range from the ebullient permutations of his novel *Watt* which seek to pin down signification even as the repeated phrases undermine the possibility of fully grasping what is being said:

> Then he took it into his head to invert [the order] of the words in the sentence, now that of the letters in the word, now that of the sentences in the period, now simultaneously that of the words in the sentence and that of the letters in the word, now simultaneously that of the words in the sentence and that of the sentences in the period, now simultaneously that of the letters in the word and that of the sentences in the period, and now simultaneously that of the letters in the word and that of the words in the sentence and that of the sentences in the period[38]

to the incremental changes characteristic of the late short pieces such as 'What is the word':

> afar –
> afar away over there –

afaint –
afaint afar away over there what –
what –
what is the word – [39]

in which the repetition builds up a resonance and pressure that
supports and strengthens our understanding of the text. Feldman
describes his response to Beckett's *neither* in terms of a reiteration
that gradually reveals the thinking behind the work: 'I'm reading
it. There's something peculiar. I can't catch it. Finally I see that
every line is really the same thought said in another way. And
yet the continuity acts as if something else is happening. Nothing
else is happening.'[40] Feldman uses repetition effectively in *Neither*
through the single note that the Soprano sings in the opening
minutes of the opera, rendering the enunciation of Beckett's words
secondary to the sound itself. Later, as Beckett's text speaks of
the figure 'beckoned back and forth' 'between two lit refuges', the
orchestra plays a series of brisk notes that ascend and descend as
if on steps of a stair going nowhere, an urgent advance and retreat
that prefaces the resignation of Beckett's 'till at last halt for good'.
As the piece closes, Feldman plays more freely with Beckett's text,
repeating the word 'neither' nine times and the phrase 'unspeakable home' eight times.[41] The ebb and flow of Feldman's text
echoes Beckett's 'to and fro' in a movement of 'rhythmic, dynamic,
and textural flux back and forth' which is:

> matched by the linear and chordal expansion and contraction of pitch
> areas around points which are themselves unable to be fixed. Thus,
> even the audibility of the compositional procedures and the interde-
> pendencies of the material are subjected to the process of 'coming
> and going'.[42]

Feldman was very taken with Beckett's practice of translating his
own work, and understood it as part of the creative process, as a
way of thinking through the work. He drew an immediate parallel with his own composition practice, describing it as a kind of
translation between different situations:

> What I do then is, I translate, say something, into a pitchy situation.
> And then I do it where it's more intervallic, and I take the suggestions
> of that back into another kind of pitchiness – not the original pitchi-
> ness, and so forth, and so on. Always retranslating and then saying,
> now let's do it with another kind of focus.[43]

We can think of translation as a kind of repetition that incorporates difference, drawing a parallel between Beckett's practice of translating his own work between English and French, and translating a thought from one medium to another – from writing to music, from writing to sculpture – rethinking it 'with another kind of focus'.[44]

Doris Salcedo rethinks the focus of Beckett's *neither* and Feldman's *Neither* in sculptural form for her installation at the White Cube Gallery in London, 2004.[45] In her proposal, Salcedo poses a question about the possibility of expression and articulation in the face of inhumanity. Echoing W. G. Sebald's concern about 'how to form a language in which terrible experiences, experiences capable of paralysing the power of articulation, could be expressed in art', Salcedo formulates the question that animates her installation: 'How to address the intolerable?'[46] 'Since I found no definitive answer to this question,' she continues, 'I titled this piece *Neither*'.[47] The context of Salcedo's enquiry is the space of the concentration camp, both historical and contemporary. The form of her enquiry is the grid.

In *Neither* Salcedo transforms the white cube of the gallery into a cage. She reconfigures the walls of the gallery by embedding wire mesh fencing into the sides of the space, distorting and extending the structure to disorient the viewer. At times the mesh is almost buried in the white plasterboard that secures it, at other times it pushes out from the wall to create a double boundary, the pattern of grid upon grid creating an optical dissonance that disturbs our spatial sense. The dark grey of the wire and the off-white of the plaster create a palette of semitones that shadow the space, darkening where the mesh is doubled, brightening where the mesh merges with the wall. At the entrance to the installation the mesh extends beyond the wall to limit our movement, the ragged edges of the wire a threatening boundary between exhibition and foyer. Yet the formal abstraction of the grid has a beauty in the intensity of its repetition as our eye moves 'to and fro in shadow from inner to outershadow'.

The indeterminacy of Beckett's lines is echoed by Salcedo's work, described in her proposal as 'an indeterminate space, located beyond [her] powers to articulate, to understand and measure the political structure in which we live'.[48] Beckett's *Endgame* (1957) is conceived in similar terms by Theodor Adorno who argues that the play 'takes place in a neutral zone between the inner and the outer, between the materials without which no subjectivity could express itself or even exist and an animation which causes the materials to dissolve and blend as though it had breathed on the mirror in which they are seen'.[49] Though written in 1958 and published in 1961 – predating Beckett's *neither* by eighteen years – Adorno's comments are a remarkably apt description of the 1976 text, drawing together the aesthetic and ethical concerns that link Salcedo's and Beckett's work, particularly in the context of Adorno's deep unease about the possibility of subjectivity and artistic expression after the Shoah: 'Cultural criticism finds itself faced with the final stage of the dialectic of culture and barbarism. To write poetry after Auschwitz is barbaric, and this corrodes even the knowledge of why it has become impossible to write poetry today.'[50]

The negations in *neither* allude to the kind of impossibility that Adorno writes about which, as Elaine Martin argues, concerns the annihilation of the very concept of the individual. Beckett's 'impenetrable self' gives way to an 'impenetrable unself', but neither position is tenable. Subjectivity is conceived of as a 'refuge', but one which is unreachable. The absolute solitude of the non-self is emphasised by 'unheard footfalls only sound', yet there are intimations of another agency in the doors that gently part and close, and the gleam of light that beckons 'back and forth'. As Beckett's text draws to a close the movement to and fro diminishes, finding stasis between 'self and other' in an indeterminate space that is neither one place nor another. This space exists beyond representation or expression: it is 'unspeakable home'.

Salcedo's transformation of the space of the gallery has an immediate and direct political charge. Her layering of mesh upon mesh in *Neither* is a visual counterpoint to Beckett's movement 'from impenetrable self to impenetrable unself' as if the wire itself provides the 'way of neither'. The space of her installation is 'an interior space that negates the possibility of interiority, of intimacy and remembrance'.[51] As an interior it evokes the idea of a refuge, but with walls fused with fencing asylum is refused: 'as between two lit refuges whose doors once neared gently close, once turned away from gently part again'. The negation of Beckett's text is made manifest in Salcedo's use of wire fencing and plasterboard: materials that create a space that 'juxtaposes interiority with exteriority'.[52] This confounding of inside and outside, of the private and the public, defines a politics of space in which the individual and the community intersect. Salcedo underlines the connection between ethics and aesthetics in her work when she says: 'I don't believe that space can be neutral. The history of wars, and perhaps even history in general, is but an endless struggle to conquer space. Space is not simply a setting, it is what makes life possible. It is space that makes encounters possible. It is the site of proximity, where everything crosses over.'[53]

The 'site of proximity' that Salcedo creates in *Neither* enables us to rethink the space of neither in Beckett's text which, with an almost syllogistic precision, occupies a place between two modes of negation. Salcedo worked for a short time in theatre, designing stage sets, and it was 'in the Colombian theatre of that time, with its political overtones, that [her] interests in art and politics came together'.[54] Salcedo's installation *Neither* echoes the grey light and bare interior of *Endgame* in which life is almost extinguished and outside of which all is corpsed. It recalls the space of *Ghost Trio* (written a year before Beckett's *neither*) in which the light is 'faint, omnipresent, no visible source', and colour is absent: 'Colour: none. All grey. Shades of grey.'[55] As Beckett directs:

> Now look closer. Floor.
>   3. *Cut to close-up of floor. Smooth grey rectangle 0.70 m. x 1.50 m. 5 seconds.*
>   4. v: Dust. [*Pause.*] Having seen that specimen of floor you have seen it all. Wall.
>   5. *Cut to close-up of wall. Smooth grey rectangle 0.70 m. x 1.50 m. 5 seconds.*[56]

Beckett's prose describes a similar territory. *Lessness* (1969) suggests the simplicity of the cell, a 'refuge' that is 'four square all light sheer white blank planes all gone from mind'.[57] The closed space of Salcedo's *Neither* gains resonance with a reading of Beckett's fizzle *Closed Space* (1973–75) in which 'All needed to be known for say is known. There is nothing but what is said. Beyond what is said there is nothing. What goes on in the arena is not said. Did it need to be known it would be. No interest. Not for imagining.'[58]

Discussing Salcedo's series of works called *Atrabiliarios* (1991–96), Carlos Basualdo describes the artist's interest in space as a 'point of intersection' between the public and the private spheres. He understands Salcedo's space as 'less a space for communication than for community, for sharing something akin to a secret, and therefore to silence'.[59] The role of silence in Salcedo's *Neither* operates on two levels. It bears witness to the undoing of the individual subject for whom silence is the closest possible refuge to an 'unspeakable home'; and it bears witness to the silence of a community in the face of the unspeakable, a silence that carries ethical implications. Jean-François Lyotard argues for a concept of silence that is dynamic and engaged even in the face of an impossible, incommensurable situation, one that he terms a *differend*:

> Why these encounters between phrases of heterogeneous regimen? Differends are born, you say, from these encounters. Can't all of these contacts be avoided? – That's impossible, contact is necessary. First of all it is necessary to link onto a phrase that happens (be it by a silence, which is a phrase), there is no possibility of not linking onto it. Second, to link is necessary; how to link is contingent.[60]

Lyotard's image of a phrase linking on to another is visually encapsulated by the overlapping wire that forms the structure of Salcedo's *Neither*. The artist's use of chain-link fencing is both beautiful and chilling: the even repetition of the diamond pattern has a meditative quality akin to Beckett's *neither*, and the movement of pattern upon pattern at the points when the fencing overlap convey an optical illusion not dissimilar to Bridget Riley's *Descending* (1965). Yet the material denotes barriers and exclusion. It has, as Rod Mengham explains, 'been seen increasingly on our television screens, as a means of confinement in concentration camps in Bosnia and Guantanamo Bay, and in various parts of the world in the form of holding pens for illegal immigrants'.[61]

In *Shibboleth*, commissioned by Tate Modern as part of the Unilever Series (2007–8) Salcedo once again uses chain-link fence, this time embedded in the fissure that intersects the floor of the Turbine Hall. The mesh supports the sides of the crack that Salcedo has inscribed in the concrete entrance ramp of the hall, at times visible, at other times obscured. Like the wire mesh of *Neither*, *Shibboleth* forms a boundary, here inverted in a 'negative space' that describes the radical objectification of the other in the 'history of racism' which, as Salcedo explains, 'runs parallel to the history of modernity': 'Its appearance disturbs the Turbine Hall in the same way the appearance of immigrants disturbs the consensus and homogeneity of European societies.'[62] *Shibboleth* underscores the silence of these 'others' against which a community defines itself. Its title refers to a turn of phrase or a social custom that acts as a test of, or impediment to, acceptance in a particular social group. The story from which the term gets its meaning describes the massacre of the Ephraimites by the Gileadites as recounted in chapter 12 of the Old Testament Book of Judges:

> The Gileadites, having defeated the Ephraimites in battle, challenged any survivors seeking to cross the river Jordan to enunciate the word 'shibboleth'. The Ephraimites, unable to form the 'sh' sound of the victor's language, pronounced the word 'sibboleth' instead, and in so doing spelt their own death sentence: forty-two thousand of them were killed.[63]

Salcedo describes *Neither* as 'a piece about uncertainty and ambiguity'.[64] *Neither* and *Shibboleth* can be understood in terms of the 'countermonument', a memorial that addresses 'the radical discontinuity between the event and its experiencing, a form that bears witness to that which cannot be accounted for'.[65] Charles Merewether's idea of the countermonument is part of what Rosalind Krauss the 'negative condition' of sculpture in the twentieth century. She describes it as 'a kind of sitelessness, or homelessness, an absolute loss of place.'[66]

For Gabriele Schwab, Beckett's politics are 'an issue of territory, interpellation, and otherness'.[67] Reread in the context of Salcedo's art, Beckett's *neither* gains particular relevance in the context of incarceration, asylum and immigration, as a text which explores the loss of identity, the refusal of sanctuary, the lack of another with whom to connect: of people 'unheard' and 'unheeded', silenced in this 'unspeakable home'. Morton Feldman's *Neither* explores the edges of this silence, the voice of the soprano pushed to the limits of her capacity in order to express what Feldman understands as the subject of Beckett's text: 'whether you're in the shadows of understanding or non-understanding, I mean, finally you're in the shadows. You're not going to arrive at any understanding at all.'[68]

Feldman's and Salcedo's formal responses to Beckett's text, each work echoing and reiterating the gridlike structure of his prose, provide a way to think about the negation inherent in these works. They contextualise the response that Lyotard urges us to make – even if that response is silence – and the responsibility we must take, particularly in the face of silence. In conversation with Charles Juliet, Beckett makes an uncharacteristically specific analysis of the relationship between ethics and aesthetics, arguing that 'moral values are not accessible and not open to definition':

> To define them, you would have to make value judgements, and you can't do that. [. . .] You can't even talk about truth. That is part of the general distress. Paradoxically, it's through form that the artist can find a kind of solution – by giving form to what has none. It is perhaps only at that level that there may be an underlying affirmation.[69]

Beckett, Feldman, Salcedo are each concerned with our response to silence, and the ways in which we can make audible, or visible that which cannot be expressed.

Through two works called *Neither*, each of them poised between alternatives about which a negative statement is made, Feldman and Salcedo respond to the challenge of a Beckettian aesthetic that situates itself between Malrauxian estrangement and Geulincxian negation. Feldman's opera makes manifest the sounds of Beckett's 'unself' in a music that evokes Malraux's 'solitude dernière'.[70] Salcedo's installation rethinks Geulincx's principle that allies human want to worth, creating a space in which ethics and aesthetics conjoin. Each of these works called *neither / Neither* is 'more and less, neither more nor less'[71] and each brings us closer to that 'unspeakable home' at the heart of Beckett's writing.

Notes

1 Samuel Beckett to Thomas MacGreevy, 16 January 1936, in Martha Dow Fehsenfeld and Lois More Overbeck (eds), *The Letters of Samuel Beckett 1929–1940* (Cambridge: Cambridge University Press, 2009), p. 299. He changed his name from McGreevy (the spelling used in the Beckett *Letters*) to MacGreevy to approximate more likely the Irish spelling of the name.

2 Trans. George Craig, in Fehsenfeld and Overbeck (eds), *The Letters of Samuel Beckett*, p. 302, n. 5.

3 Anthony Uhlmann, *Samuel Beckett and the Philosophical Image* (Cambridge: Cambridge University Press, 2006), pp. 86–113.

4 André Malraux, *Man's Fate*, trans. Stuart Gilbert (New York: Random House, 1961), p. 246.

5 Samuel Beckett's title is not capitalised, unlike Feldman's and Salcedo's.

6 Raymond Tuttle, 'Neither' (Review), *Classical Net* 2001, http://www.

classical.net/music/recs/reviews/c/col20081a.php. Accessed January 2009.

7 Howard Skempton, 'Beckett as librettist', in Chris Villars (ed.), *Morton Feldman Says: Selected Interviews and Lectures 1964–1987* (London: Hyphen Press, 2006), p. 75.

8 *Ibid.*

9 James Knowlson, *Damned to Fame: The Life of Samuel Beckett* (London: Bloomsbury, 1996), p. 631.

10 John Dwyer, 'In the shadows with Feldman and Beckett', *Lively Arts, Buffalo News*, 27 (November 1976). Quoted in James Knowlson, *Damned to Fame*, p. 631.

11 Knowlson, *Damned to Fame*, p. 631.

12 Samuel Beckett, *neither*, in *The Complete Short Prose 1929–1989*, ed. S. E. Gontarski (New York: Grove, 1995), p. 258. All subsequent quotations from Beckett's *neither* are from this edition.

13 Carla Locatelli, *Unwording the World: Samuel Beckett Prose Works after the Nobel Prize* (Philadelphia: University of Pennsylvania Press, 1990), p. 246.

14 'L'oeuvre considérée comme création pure, et dont la fonction s'arrête avec la genèse, est vouée au néant'. Samuel Beckett, 'La peinture des van Velde ou le Monde et le Pantalon', in *Disjecta*, ed. Ruby Cohn (London: John Calder, 1983), pp. 119–20. Quoted and translated by Locatelli, *Unwording the World*, p. 246.

15 Samuel Beckett, *The Complete Dramatic Works* (London: Faber & Faber, 1986), p. 399.

16 *Ibid.*, p. 401.

17 *Ibid.*, p. 402.

18 *Ibid.*, p. 403.

19 *Ibid.*, p. 399.

20 Morton Feldman quoted by Skempton, 'Beckett as librettist', p. 76.

21 Samuel Beckett, *The Unnamable* (London: Calder & Boyars, 1975), p. 132. See also John Pilling Chapter.

22 Samuel Beckett in Charles Juliet, *Conversations with Samuel Beckett and Bram van Velde,* trans. Janey Tucker (Leiden: Academic Press Leiden, 1995), p. 141.

23 William Weaver, *International Herald Tribune* (14 June 1977).

24 Bayan Northcott, 'Review of Morton Feldman's *Neither*', *The Sunday Telegraph* (26 June 1977).

25 *Ibid.*

26 Skempton, 'Beckett as librettist', p. 76.

27 Feldman quoted by Skempton, 'Beckett as librettist', p. 75.

28 *Ibid.*, pp. 75–6.

29 Catherine Laws, 'Morton Feldman's *Neither*: a musical translation

of Beckett's text', in Mary Bryden (ed.), *Samuel Beckett and Music* (Oxford: Clarendon Press, 1998), p. 63.

30 Laws, 'Morton Feldman's *Neither*', p. 61.

31 Feldman quoted by Skempton, 'Beckett as librettist', p. 75.

32 Feldman quoted by Stuart Morgan in 'Pie-slicing and small moves: Morton Feldman in conversation with Stuart Morgan', *Morton Feldman Says*, p. 83.

33 Feldman quoted by Skempton, 'Beckett as librettist', p. 76.

34 Laws, 'Morton Feldman's *Neither*', p. 63.

35 Feldman, 'Darmstadt Lecture', in *Morton Feldman Says*, p. 208.

36 Jacques Derrida, *Speech and Phenomena*, trans. David B. Allison (Evanston: Northwestern University Press, 1973), p. 128.

37 *Ibid.*

38 Beckett, *Watt* (London: John Calder, 1981), pp. 166–7.

39 Beckett, 'What is the Word', *Grand Street*, 9:2 (1990), 17–18.

40 Feldman, 'Darmstadt Lecture', p. 194.

41 Morton Feldman, *Neither: An Opera in One Act on a Text by Samuel Beckett for Soprano and Orchestra* (London: Universal Edition, 1977).

42 Laws, 'Morton Feldman's *Neither*', p. 76.

43 Feldman, 'Darmstadt Lecture', p. 194.

44 *Ibid.*, p. 194.

45 White Cube Gallery Press release for *Neither* by Doris Salcedo, 10 September–18 October, 2004: 'Neither also refers in part to an opera by American avant-garde composer Morton Feldman from 1977, which incorporates a libretto written by Samuel Beckett, whose sparse, nihilistic poetry conveys the weight of human existence.'

46 Doris Salcedo, 'Proposal for a project for White Cube, London, 2004', in Achim Borchardt-Hume (ed.), *Doris Salcedo: Shibboleth* (London: Tate, 2007), p. 109.

47 *Ibid.*

48 *Ibid.*

49 Theodor W. Adorno, 'Trying to Understand *Endgame*', in Jennifer Birkett and Kate Ince (eds), *Samuel Beckett: Longman Critical Reader* (London: Longman, 2000), p. 48.

50 'Kulturkritik findet sich der letzten Stufe der Dialektik von Kultur und Barberei gegenüber: nach Auschwitz ein Gedicht zu schreiben, ist barbarisch, und das frißt auch die Erkenntnis an, die ausspricht, warum es unmöglich ward, heute Gedichte zu schreiben.' Theodor Adorno, *Gesammelte Schriften*, ed. Rolf Tiedemann (Frankfurt am Main: Suhrkamp, 1997), 10.1:30, trans. Elaine Martin, 'Re-reading Adorno: the "after-Auschwitz" aporia', *Forum*, 2 (2006), 1–13, 3. http://forum.llc.ed.ac.uk. Accessed January 2009.

51 Salcedo, 'Proposal for a project for White Cube', p. 109.

52 *Ibid.*
53 Salcedo, 'Carlos Basualdo in conversation with Doris Salcedo', trans. Dominic Curran, in Nancy Princenthal, Carlos Basualdo and Andreas Huyssen (eds), *Doris Salcedo* (London: Phaidon, 2000), p. 12.
54 *Ibid.*, p. 8.
55 Beckett, *Ghost Trio*, in *The Complete Dramatic Works*, p. 408.
56 *Ibid.*
57 Beckett, *Lessness*, in *The Complete Short Prose*, p. 197.
58 Beckett, *Fizzle 5: Closed Place*, in *The Complete Short Prose*, p. 236.
59 Salcedo, 'Carlos Basualdo in conversation with Doris Salcedo', p. 12.
60 Jean-François Lyotard, *The Differend*, trans. Georges Van Den Abbeele (Manchester: Manchester University Press, 1988), p. 29.
61 Rod Mengham, '"Failing better": Salcedo's trajectory', *Doris Salcedo: Neither* (London: Jay Jopling White Cube, 2004), pp. 9–11, p. 11.
62 Doris Salcedo, 'Proposal for a project for the Turbine Hall, Tate Modern, London 2007', in *Doris Salcedo: Shibboleth*, p. 65.
63 Achim Borchardt-Hume, 'Sculpting Critical Space', in *Doris Salcedo: Shibboleth*, pp. 15–16.
64 Doris Salcedo, 'Proposal for a project for White Cube, London, 2004', p. 109.
65 Charles Merewether, 'To bear witness', in Dan Cameron and Charles Merewether (eds), *Doris Salcedo* (New York: New Museum of Contemporary Art, 1998), p. 17.
66 Rosalind Krauss, 'Sculpture in the expanded field', *The Originality of the Avant-Garde and Other Modernist Myths* (Cambridge, MA: The MIT Press, 1986), p. 279.
67 Gabriele Schwab, 'The politics of small differences: Beckett's *The Unnamable*', in Henry Sussman and Christopher Devenney (eds), *Engagement and Indifference: Beckett and the Political* (Albany: State University of New York Press, 2001), p. 56.
68 Feldman, 'The note man on the word man: interview with Everett Frost', *Morton Feldman Says*, p. 232.
69 Charles Juliet, *Conversations*, p. 149.
70 André Malraux, *La Condition humaine*, in *Romans*, Bibliothèque de la Pléiade (Paris: Gallimard, 1947), p. 353.
71 Derrida, *Speech and Phenomena*, p. 128.

9

From *Film* to literature: theoretical debates and the critical erasure of Beckett's cinema

Matthijs Engelberts

In an age in which belief in metanarratives and the stark oppositions upon which they tend to rely is thought to be dwindling in
postmodern societies, and identities are increasingly perceived as
constructed, heterogeneous and porous, it is no wonder that contemporary theory no longer forcefully opposes word and image as
two radically distinct entities. The study of the relations between
literature and film, for instance, no longer seeks to find new ways
of contrasting these two media, but rather to 'rethink' the interrela-
tion and to highlight the 'complex word and image engagements
both within and between the two media'.[1] Another token of the
evolution is the credo coined by W. J. T. Mitchell that 'all media
are mixed media'.[2] It is clear, however, that this way of envisag-
ing the relations between word and image is inscribed against and
feeds upon a weighty and age-old tradition of opposing words and
images that still exerts its influence. The separation and opposition
of artistic media, a strong tendency in the modernist era, was particularly marked in the literature–film debate. Cinema indeed often
sought to define itself as an artistic medium of the moving image
governed by principles seen as being radically different from those
of verbal language, a constant refrain from Arnheim to certain
strands of *Cahiers du Cinéma*, while literature often reacted to this
new medium by considering it as at most ancillary to its own art.
In an analysis of this mutual animosity, Kristeva's concept of the
abject may prove useful: when they chose to distance themselves
from the 'opposing' field, filmmakers, writers and theoreticians
tended to present the 'other' as so radically different that any
contact and mingling would lead to the deformation or extinction
of the art they championed.

Beckett's *Film* was written (1963, Paris) and filmed (1964, New York) at what is often considered to be the tail end of the modernist period, yet it draws on the idea of cinema as an art that is not verbal, and, as I will attempt to show, its fate has been largely determined by the strained relations between film and literature. Manifestly envisaged as a cinematic work by its scriptwriter, it was nevertheless often fiercely rejected by the field of cinema, and would subsequently be appropriated by the literary camp. As cinema, *Film* came to nothing; from its very first screenings, and for a long time afterwards, it was excoriated for occupying that zone in which cinema perishes owing to the fatal influence of the word and of literature. In the history of cinema, many films have of course been criticised for embodying a supposed literary ascendancy or affiliation; *Film,* however, seems to be an extreme case because of the apparent success of concurrent attempts to annihilate the project as a piece of cinema, in spite of the vigorous efforts it makes to avoid any exclusive affiliation to the literary field.

Film is a provocative title for an established literary author and playwright to choose on entering the minefield of cinema/literature relations, since it suggests a strong cinematic orientation. Indeed, the script contains no speech and it thematises the act of looking as much as the image itself; it moreover seems to enter into a very pointed dialogue with a particular strand of cinema criticism.[3] *Film* can be regarded as engaging with elements of early cinema theory (which Beckett had read in the 1930s), referring to the debate surrounding silent film, colour and, to some extent, close-ups. *Film* thus plays on the oppositions created between the verbal and the visual, which both the script and the film help to revive. Yet, as will be shown, it was subsequently rejected by the world of cinema, barred from the halls of film as a result of this same antagonism between word and image.

Newspapers and magazines: Venice and *Cahiers du Cinéma*

First we will consider the way in which cinema critics approached *Film* in newspapers and magazines (some of them specialist).[4] The critics who wrote these reviews had not necessarily seen the script of the film, and in some cases it had simply not yet been published. This corpus of articles, although international in scope, is not very large, since *Film* was only rarely screened in (commercial) theatres. However, it was shown at various international festivals in the two years following its production. The Venice film festival of 1965 was one of the first – and the critics from *Cahiers du Cinéma* were on hand.

Although it was more than ten years since the first article-manifestos of the *nouvelle vague* had appeared in *Cahiers du Cinéma*, it was to be expected that the idea of commissioning a literary author to produce a script would be viewed with scepticism in a publication which had led a ferocious campaign for the independence of film from the written word and literature. Yet its treatment of *Film* is revealing. In a seven-page supplement covering the 1965 Venice festival, Jean-André Fieschi and André Téchiné comment upon the films shown that year and (briefly) discuss the short film shot in New York. 'Beckett is a scribbler who never goes to the cinema' ('Beckett est un littérateur qui ne va jamais au cinéma'),[5] is the programmatic opening sentence of these few lines, which were amongst the first to be written on *Film* following its release. The dense text which follows this first sentence is not especially easy to grasp, not least because the authors, who clearly possess a very good knowledge of Beckett's oeuvre, embark upon a rapid comparison of the working processes of literature and cinema. Indeed, somewhat begrudgingly perhaps, the authors do appreciate that *Film* possesses a 'real effectiveness' ('efficacité réelle') that the article does not take the time to explore further. It is stated, however, that this cinematic effectiveness 'can only be acknowledged through reference to a previously defined, circumscribed, familiar approach, on the basis of semiological relationships that are radically foreign, external, other'. The foreign, external, 'other' entity that the critic rejects in this rhythmic tricolon is literature. Beckett's general literary approach, as the author remarks perspicaciously, is to aim at the self-desctruction of discourse: 'Beckett does not speak in order to break silence but rather to deliver it to us intact, and in all his novels, up until *Comment c'est*, every sentence contains the negation of the statement which follows it.' Here, then, is an argument which would much later be propounded in literary Beckett studies, already being sketched out in cinema criticism. However, in order to transpose this literary process, which the article calls a 'mechanism for disintegrating the sign that is specific to the literary system' into the 'autonomous language' of the cinema, one must, according to *Cahiers du Cinéma*, be a filmmaker. Yet the authors of the article announce from the outset that *Film* has been made 'in the absence of any conscious knowledge of the methods it employs' and concludes his short review by returning to the alleged ignorance of the cinema shown by *Film*: 'cinema is a form of expression rooted in resistance, a form entirely foreign to Beckett, who no more controls it than he ever really discovers it'.

Thus, for *Cahiers du Cinéma*, cinema resists this attempt by literature to colonise its autonomous space. It should be noted that not one shot from *Film* is discussed in the article, nor is any mention whatsoever made of the participation of such personalities from the film world as Buster Keaton or Boris Kaufman,[6] who directed the cinematography, or of the short film's particular cinematic features, such as the absence of colour and, more particularly, sound. In these critics' view, then, *Film* – that is to say, the film of that name – is a work of literature. By 1965, auteur theory was already well established in European cinema, and Beckett, as a literary figure, was not exactly the sort of auteur that those who called for directors who 'wrote with a camera' (as Alexandre Astuc, one of the first defenders of auteur theory, put it evocatively but also somewhat ambiguously) had in mind.

Newspapers and magazines: the man with a movie camera, a pen or a hat?

When one considers the corpus of articles in its entirety, it becomes apparent that the critics seem to skirt around the issue of authorship. Who actually made *Film*? In one of the first references in the press to *Film* after its shooting, the magazine *Movie* mentioned in its April 1965 edition (thus prior to the film's release) that 'There was some publicity recently concerning a Becket [*sic*] film starring Buster Keaton'.[7] 'A Beckett film': clearly, then, the film was not presented as the work of its director, as one would expect in a cinema review, following usual practice, but as that of the writer of its script. The same thing happens in *Sight & Sound*, whose critic briefly mentions Barney Rosset's project,[8] before adding that 'So far, only the Beckett section is completed'.[9] In the world of cinema, then, *Film* is referred to primarily as the work of its scriptwriter: the man with a pen.

While this manner of presenting the short film would change somewhat following its release, it would continue to diverge from normal practice. The section in *Cahiers du Cinéma* on the 1965 Venice festival presents a number of films, but Schneider's is the only one to receive a subtitle featuring two names instead of one: '*Film* de Samuel Beckett et Alan Schneider (U.S.A.)'.[10] Almost one year later, the same journal would publish, in an article on the Tours festival, a few short remarks on '*Film* d'Alan Schneider et Samuel Beckett'.[11] In the meantime, this habit had begun to catch on in the United States, with the *New York Times* publishing a review of the short film 'which Alan Schneider has directed and for which Samuel Beckett, the absurdist, wrote the script'.[12] And, when the same newspaper would comment almost three years later upon the brief reappearance of *Film* on the big screen in New York, Alan Schneider's short is the only one out of the six on the programme where the author of the script is given a separate credit: 'written by Samuel Beckett, directed by Alan Schneider'.[13] Oddly, the listing also adds, again only for *Film*, the names of the editor and the director of cinematography, as if it were necessary to insist upon the fact that this really was a work of cinema. The difficulty of situating *Film* aesthetically thus seems to have given rise to a certain uneasiness which is expressed in this divergence from usual practices.

The presentation of the film in these publications is of course less striking when one considers that Beckett was more famous than Schneider, who was himself better known as a theatre director, that the author of the script was present on the set and that Schneider himself later wrote, in 1969, that Beckett was 'the real director'.[14] However, this uncertainty surrounding authorial attribution is never stated explicitly and becomes apparent only in this unusual manner of referring to the work: *Film*, then, was generally presented when it first appeared as a *written* film. It may therefore be said that it was seen from the very outset as a literary work, even down to the manner in which basic information relating to it was presented in film reviews. With hindsight, the few lines on *Film* which appeared, in April 1965, in the aptly titled *Movie*, seem to prefigure the destiny of the short film in what thus becomes a rather striking metaphor: 'As far as production is concerned, the New York scene is zero. There was some publicity recently concerning a Becket film starring Buster Keaton. Some footage was taken, but there is no trace of a finished film.'[15] Nothing is happening in New York, and *Film* has categorically not become a film – it seems to have been doomed to come to naught in the universe of cinema.

The uncertainty surrounding the film's attribution not only concerns the director and the author of the script but also extends to the lead actor. This can be seen in American reviews from the very moment that *Film* was first shown publicly in a cinema theatre. At the third New York film festival, on 14 September 1965, a special evening was dedicated to the films of two actors, Buster Keaton and Bette Davis. *Film* was shown 'sandwiched in between two Keaton shorts, a standard one he'd made some years earlier and a new railroad commercial he'd just completed',[16] complained Schneider of the evening's screenings. The review of the evening published in the *New York Times* rated the other two shorts favourably in comparison to *Film*, which was, according to the critic, 'a miserable and morbid exercise' and 'a cruel bit of obvious symbolism'.[17] Cruel no doubt because the hero and the film's theme did not correspond to the expectations of the critic, who notes almost with horror that the character 'even rejects himself'; yet cruel too, according to the *New York Times*, because poor Keaton is not treated with the respect due to him. Indeed, Keaton is spoken of by the author of the review as if the actor had been dragged into a venture unworthy of this hero of the cinema: 'It is a cruel bit of obvious symbolism in which to involve an old star who has given a lot of pleasure to millions of people, and who has since admitted that he didn't know what "Film" was all about.'[18] According to Schneider, another American critic told the director 'how stupid we were to keep Keaton's back to the camera until the end'.[19] It is clear, then, that script and film are appropriated through the iconic personality of the artistic field in question. If, for lovers of literature, as we shall see, *Film* is a Beckett, for film-lovers, *Film* was often, from the moment it was released, a Keaton movie – bearing the stamp of the man with a hat.

Or at least it should have been. Schneider is indeed not entirely wrong, but unfortunately not entirely right, either, when he states that 'already the film was becoming Keaton's and not Beckett's'.[20] This remark is valid only if it is taken to refer to the fact that, in the field of cinema, the film is often perceived in relation to its lead actor and not, as Schneider would have preferred, to the author of the script. Nevertheless, the review in the *New York Times* and other pieces of criticism show the extent to which *Film* is regarded not as a film by the 'real' Keaton but as a film by a Keaton exploited by a literary author ('Beckett, the absurdist') who does not know enough about the world of cinema, and whose lack of knowledge is supposedly apparent in the way that the short film misuses one of the stars of the golden age of silent cinema. *Film* is thus often featured as a failed Keaton, spoiled by a literary author.

By 1984, when *Film* was finally released in France, the critics' tone has changed, but they do not seem to have changed their tune. To be sure, now certain critics were unrestrained in their praise; the short was released in France twenty years after it was made, when Beckett's stature and renown were even greater than they had been in 1965. 'This is one of the most beautiful night-mares that the seventh art has ever given us' declared *Télérama* without a hint of irony, before proceeding to invoke Bergman and Fellini.[21] However, for the French critics of 1984 too, the cin-ematic aspect of *Film* is often reduced to the on-screen presence of Buster Keaton. Critics might admire both Keaton and Beckett – despite the fact that this is a 'film d'amateur', as *L'Humanité* put it.[22] Yet even when both are praised, it is Keaton who nevertheless comes out on top, playing a role which, according to the critic in *L'Humanité*, 'draws all its power from the autobiographical ele-ments which it may be seen to contain' – elements from Keaton's, not Beckett's, autobiography. This surprising reading of the film as an autobiographical document on Keaton (to my knowledge this is the only example of such an interpretation) shows the extent to which *Film* is seen in relation to its lead actor, even if the author of the script is lauded in the same breath in this article. More often, however, it is a case of Keaton taking the limelight *in spite of* Beckett. '[Keaton] wrests the script from its author's hands, just like that, by being there, seen. That is what cinema is' wrote *Le Quotidien de Paris*.[23] This, it would seem, was the price paid by *Film* to become a work of cinema: by wresting its script from the grasp of the literary field.

In *Le Monde*, the review of *Film* describes the short as an 'invol-untary homage to the director-star of *The General*'.[24] Once again, then, it is Keaton who turns *Film* into a work of cinema, in spite of Beckett; the critic from *Le Monde* goes on to pay highly ambigu-ous tribute to the script, 'a specimen of an "experimental" cinema *avant la lettre* which seems to have preserved the notion of *mise en scène*, of the transformation of literary material'.[25] Beckett the film-maker, then, but also (too much so, perhaps?) the man of the theatre and man of letters.

The locus of *Film* in research databases

Let us now consider some figures regarding the further reception of *Film*. As of the end of 2008, a search of the most widely used bibliographic databases yielded a total of around fifty articles dealing specifically with the script of *Film* or on the film itself in at least one of its two versions. Forty-two of these texts feature on the literature-oriented MLA database; seven short texts, some of them very short, have been logged on the International Film Archive Database (FIAF),[26] two of which were published in the journal *Literature/Film Quarterly* and so also feature in the MLA bibliography, as this journal – sometimes criticised for this reason in cinema research – focuses on the links between literature and cinema. Some of the remaining five articles on the FIAF database are simply reviews rather than research articles, such as the article discussing the remake by David Clark commissioned in 1979 by the British Film Institute (BFI). It can therefore quite confidently be stated that around 10 percent of the total number of commentaries on *Film* featuring in the major research bibliographies belong to a category other than literary studies. In terms of the number of pages, the percentage is even lower, given that the reviews logged on the FIAF database are very short in comparison to literary research articles. It should also be noted that the bibliographies consulted returned only a very small proportion of the monographs or collections of texts which contain paragraphs or chapters on *Film*. These are quite numerous and in general belong to the category of studies on Beckett aimed at a 'literary' audience.[27] Without delving further into bibliometric matters, it can be fairly safely stated that fewer than 5 per cent of the pages written on *Film* are to be found in sources that are not literary in orientation. This is surely a rather low score for a work of cinema.

Yet, one might object, is this not a fate reserved for all scripts published by authors with a literary reputation, even when the texts in question have made their way on to celluloid, as is the case for *Film*? And is this not due, among other reasons, to the fact that literature departments (English, French, general, comparative) are at present, in the research institution that is the university, more numerous than cinema departments? Let us attempt to reply to these objections by briefly citing some comparable examples of 'literary' films from the same period. For *India Song* (1973), there

are around 35 entries on the MLA bibliography and about the same
number in the FIAF database. This is a far more equitable distribu-
tion for a work which is none the less explicitly situated in the literary and theatrical domain in addition to that of cinema, given that
its genre identity is defined in the subtitle to Duras's text as 'texte
théâtre film'.

The reason for this difference does not seem to lie in the fact that
Duras made a considerable number of films, or that *India Song* is
a full-length feature, as the following example demonstrates. The
only film written and directed by Jean Genet, *Un chant d'amour*,
was similarly made by a literary author with no standing in cinema
circles, with a team of collaborators generally lacking experience
in this field. The result, a remarkable short produced in 1950, for
decades had a very restricted circulation, featuring neither on the
festival circuit nor on commercial screens. However, the number
of entries for *Un chant d'amour* in the FIAF bibliography is higher
than for *Film*. Beckett's, Schneider's and Keaton's *Film* thus appears
to be an extreme case: from an institutional point of view (or in
any case from the point of view of university research), it is to a
very great extent a 'literary' work.

Editions

It is interesting to note that editorial policy has tended to validate
this approach. The French version of *Film* features in a collection
of theatre texts entitled *Comédie et actes divers*, which also contains
two radio plays and a television play. This diversity of media is
not in any way hinted at either on the book's cover or in its list of
contents, where the accent is placed rather on 'comédie' and 'actes'
– French terms which evoke the theatre even more unequivocally
than the English words 'comedy' and 'acts'. In English-language
editions the situation is not much different. The text was published in Britain for the first time in 1967, three years after the
film was shot and two years after it was shown at the New York
and Venice film festivals (the French edition came eight years after
Schneider had filmed his version in 1964).[28] As with the French
edition, it appeared in a collection of texts written for different
media: theatre, television and cinema. *Eh Joe and Other Writings*
is the somewhat uninformative title of this collection, published in
London, which none the less insists on the 'written' aspect of these

texts, thereby situating them primarily in the sphere of literary art rather than that of the moving image which, while it clearly makes wide use of writing, only rarely brings its contribution into prominence, and sometimes openly rejects it. There is no mention on the book's title page of such terms as screenplay, script or scenario.[29] In New York, a year after its London publication, *Film* was presented not as a 'writing' but simply a 'dramatic' text featuring in the collection *Cascando and Other Short Dramatic Pieces*. It should be pointed out, then, that the script and the film became separate entities in the public domain only some time after the screenings of *Film* at international festivals. There was an interval between screening and publication of two years in the United Kingdom, three in the United States and seven in France: when the first critical reviews of the work appeared, *Film* was available only on celluloid. *Film* thus only became a printed text once it had already been forcibly excluded from the cinematic field.

After first being published in collections of texts which to some extent erase its cinematic orientation, *Film* was published separately, and this time identified as cinema script, in an edition which also featured stills from Schneider's film. This edition was published in 1969 by Grove Press, whose director, Barney Rosset, had been behind the cinema project, having commissioned the script which was then filmed by his own production company, Evergreen Theatre. It is therefore hardly surprising that this edition presents *Film* very clearly as being a cinematic work, the title page reading 'Complete Scenario / Illustrations / Productions Shots'. This presentation of the text of *Film* would, however, remain an exception. The standard edition of the script has, since 1986, been the one found in the *Complete Dramatic Works*, which would quickly establish itself as the text's most widely available and commonly cited edition. *Film*, then, has been positioned first and foremost as a theatre text, both in French and English. It thus tends to be presented as a work of literature, in accordance with the traditional view of the literary triad (narrative, poetry, drama).

The text of the script

Let us now consider for a moment the actual wording of the literary text that *Film* has become. It is striking, in this context, to note that *Film* is not a work in which words occupy a privileged position, in terms either of form or of content. *Film* is, after all, the script to a 'silent' film. The text of *Film* describes a sequence of moving images, with almost no sound, in which the act of looking is the principal theme, alongside the image itself. This is already being emphasised in the simple scene where the central character looks at photographs taken over the course of his life – photographs he then destroys after contemplating them, just as the camera will later destroy this same character as it focuses upon him as a double of itself. We have already noted, moreover, that *Film* enters into a dialogue with cinema theory. Overall, the text turns towards the cinematic sphere and does not seem particularly geared towards engaging with the art of language.

This distance in relation to literature becomes visible also when one considers the difference, in terms of aesthetic effect, between the text of the script and the majority of Beckett's other texts that are usually taken to constitute his fictional body of work, whether narrative or dramatic texts in the widest sense. As a sample, two brief passages from the script are transcribed below.

> The film is divided into three parts. 1. The street (about eight minutes). 2. The stairs (about five minutes). 3. The room (about seventeen minutes).

> 3. The room
> Here we assume problem of dual perception solved and enter O's perception (8).[30]

It must be said that it would be difficult to pick out these sentences, as they stand here, as being in any way particularly Beckettian, and they are equally unlikely to be identified as especially literary. They obviously constitute 'stage' directions, but it should be noted that these often possess their own linguistic aesthetic in Beckett's work. In comparable texts, such as the stage directions in Beckett's television plays, the repetitive and drily technical character of these indications is often quite striking as a linguistic phenomenon in its own right such as, for example, in *Nacht und Träume*. In the script of *Film*, however, the words themselves are not in any way foregrounded and seem devoid of any aesthetic function. The function of the sentences quoted above and others like them is not to produce a literary effect, such as defamiliarisation (the ostranenie, 'distancing' of the formalists). Instead, it is the *images* described in these terms which must fulfil an aesthetic function on the screen: the five-minute sequence in the stairwell, or the double perception of O ('object') and E ('eye'). Beckett's first text for the screen, then, is aesthetically not comparable in every respect with his other texts which consist only of directions (without dialogue), whether these were written for the stage (*Actes sans paroles*) or for the screen. These other texts without dialogue are formulated in a more terse and striking manner and seem to be addressed less exclusively to theatre and cinema practitioners.

Another element which brings out the distance between the fictional texts published by Beckett and his only published cinematic text is the presence of a first-person entity which manifestly corresponds to the author himself. *Film* is thus something of a *hapax legomenon* within the Beckettian oeuvre: a unique and remarkable exception in a body of work where the 'I' is constantly brought into question, constantly denied – *Pas Moi* – both in the author's novels and in his plays. In *Film* the 'I' occurs in passing, is used without comment, unproblematically and, so to speak, spontaneously, as if in everyday conversation. This unquestioned 'I' does moreover appear to refer to the actual person who wrote the text, the author of the script, Samuel Beckett, who asks the production team to find a technical solution to the problem of the double perception of O and E: 'This poses a problem of images which I cannot solve without technical help. See below, note 8'.[31] *Film* is thus, to my knowledge, the only text in the body of fictional work published under Beckett's name in which an 'I' clearly indicates, without any comment or obviously intended literary effect, the author of the text. It should be noted that neither *Actes sans paroles* nor the texts of Beckett's television plays, with or without dialogue, feature this appearance of the authorial 'I'.

Interestingly, it has been contended that all Beckett's plays from *Play* onwards are 'extraliterary'. This argument is presented in an article on *Ghost Trio*, a screenplay for television which, according to the author of the article, 'is among S[amuel] B[eckett]'s "unreadable" late works, part of a postliterary phenomenon that began with *Play* in 1963'.[32] 'Postliterary' perhaps offers little improvement over 'extraliterary' (which is used as a synonym two sentences later) in this context; but, if the contention were to be examined, it would become clear that not all the 'late works' can be called 'extraliterary' in the same sense. If the 'late' works are taken to mean only the (late) texts for stage and screen, it would seem that *A Piece of Monologue* or *That Time* cannot be said extraliterary in the same sense as *Film*, which goes much further in this sense than the other late plays. In fact, it may no longer seem pertinent, in the case of *Film*, to call the script 'extra*literary*', except perhaps if one were seeking exclusively to highlight its special status with regard to the majority of Beckett's work. It is indeed rather uncommon to define cinema scripts as 'extraliterary', since that designation manifestly rests on an assumed centrality of literature in the cultural field and by the same token presupposes that the absence of scripts from the literary domain needs to be underlined, commented upon or perhaps even contested.

As far as both the formal characteristics of the text of the script and its content are concerned, then, *Film* is not inscribed primarily within the literary sphere; it was not conceived of in terms of the production of an aesthetic effect through its specific features as a linguistic artefact. The text itself is not the aesthetic medium targeted here; the script was clearly written as a 'semifinished product' to be used in the elaboration of a final artefact belonging to the aesthetic sphere of cinema. Yet the text's currency has become limited almost exclusively to the literary 'market'. A strange fate, then, for this cinema script written by an author who would become a Nobel literature laureate; a script which would see its cinematic nature erased through a sort of undeclared act of literary irredentism and through an excommunication on the part of the cinema which, in contrast, was sometimes loudly declared as such.

Film's slide towards literature (along with its erasure as a work of cinema) is a result on the one hand of conditions that are particular to this work but undoubtedly also, on the other, of the rivalry and protectionism that have often marked relations between the moving image and literature. Beckett was obviously a well-known literary author before his text was filmed or the script of *Film* was published, and his reputation following *Film* remained that of a literary author. Nor did he ever, unlike other French authors of the time who wrote cinema scripts, such as Duras or Robbe-Grillet, officially direct a film for the big screen. *Film* is also a short, and as such belongs to a relatively obscure sector of the cinematic sphere. The script was, furthermore, filmed by a director from a theatre background who had little experience behind the camera, and made by an inexperienced production company whose origins lay in the literary world. These factors undeniably go some way to explaining the 'literaturisation' of *Film*. However, they can by no means account entirely for what became of the script and the first film which was made from it. When one concentrates solely on the material quoted here, other elements are obliterated which might be argued to mark out a very different trajectory for *Film* – if only the fact that it was shot by a veteran director of cinematography, Boris Kaufman, the brother of Dziga Vertov, famous Soviet filmmaker and theoretician and director of *A Man with a Movie Camera*. It took the tense and complicated relations between literature – that art of the word which none the less frequently engages in complex ways with images – and cinema – that art of the moving image which none the less frequently engages so closely with words – and it took a perception of Beckett as an iconical 'literary' author (and authority), and therefore a divisive figure in these now simmering, now open hostilities, to situate *Film* to such an overwhelming degree in the literary field, and to so irrevocably expel it from the field of cinema. *Film*, then, will always simply 'have gone on giving up [. . .], not being there' as the *Texts for Nothing* have it,[33] and as such it throws an exceptionally revealing light on the difficult nature of the relations between literature and emerging media in the twentieth century.

Notes

1 Kamilla Elliott, *Rethinking the Novel/Film Debate* (Cambridge: Cambridge University Press, 2003), p. 17.
2 See for instance W. J. T. Mitchell, 'Showing seeing: a critique of visual culture', in Mirzoeff, Nicholas (ed.), *The Visual Culture Reader*, 2nd edn (London: Routledge, 2002), p. 91.
3 See Matthijs Engelberts, '*Film* and *Film*: Beckett and early film theory', in Linda Ben-Zvi and Angela Moorjani (eds), *Beckett at 100: Revolving It All* (New York: Oxford University Press, 2008), pp. 152–76, and, for a French version, '*Film et Film*: Beckett et les premières théories cinématographiques', in *Samuel Beckett Today / Aujourd'hui: Présence de Samuel Beckett / Presence of Samuel Beckett*, ed. Sjef Houppermans, 17 (2006), 331–50.
4 These reviews in newspapers and magazines do not usually feature on the databases referred to in the section on research databases in the present chapter.
5 Jean-André Fieschi and André Téchiné, '*Film* de Samuel Beckett et

Alan Schneider (U.S.A.)', *Cahiers du Cinéma* (Dossier 'Venise 65'), 171 (October 1965), 48–9.

6 Boris Kaufman had previously worked with, among others, Jean Vigo and Elia Kazan and had won an Oscar ('best cinematography') in 1955 for *On the Waterfront*. The cameraman on *Film* was Joe Coffey.

7 Andrew Sarris, 'New York', *Movie*, 12 (April 1965), 41.

8 A project consisting of three films, with scripts commissioned from Beckett, Ionesco and Pinter.

9 'Project One', *Sight & Sound*, 34:2 (Spring 1965), 61–2.

10 Fieschi and Téchiné, '*Film* de Samuel Beckett', 49.

11 J.-L. C. [unsigned review], 'Retour à Tours ou Vanité du portrait', *Cahiers du Cinéma*, 177 (April 1965), 17–19.

12 Bosley Crowther, 'Bette Davis and Keaton Movies Are Shown', *New York Times* (15 September 1965), 41:1.

13 A. H. Weiler, 'Now cinema!', *New York Times* (9 April 1968), 56:1.

14 Alan Schneider, 'On directing *Film*', in Samuel Beckett, *Film* (New York: Grove, 1969), p. 63.

15 Sarris, 'New York', 41.

16 Schneider, 'On directing *Film*', pp. 90–3. The first Keaton short of the evening was in fact made forty years before the festival, *Seven Chances* (1925).

17 Crowther 'Bette Davis and Keaton movies are shown', 41.

18 *Ibid.*

19 Schneider, 'On directing *Film*', p. 93.

20 *Ibid.*, p. 90. See also Jonathan Bignell (ed), *Writing and Cinema* (Harlow: Longman, 1999)

21 B.G. [unsigned review], '*Film*: Godot ne viendra plus', *Télérama*, 1782 (7 March 1984).

22 Jean Roy, '*Film*', *L'Humanité* (14 March 1984).

23 A.H. [unsigned review], '*Film*: Keaton joue Beckett', in *Le Quotidien de Paris* (7 March 1984).

24 L.M. [unsigned review], '*Film*, d'Alan Schneider et *L'Enfant invisible* d'André Lindon', *Le Monde* (21 March 1984).

25 *Ibid.*

26 Databases last accessed on 31 December 2008. Only those articles dealing with *Film* have been included (articles on the series 'Beckett on film' (2000), for instance, have been left out). For the MLA count, only articles and books published by literary journals and publishers have been included (since some entries in MLA pertain to film or media studies).

27 The fact that the vast majority of commentaries on *Film* have appeared in journals, reviews and books with a literary orientation does not imply that none of these texts addresses its cinematic or media aspects.

Scholars such as Enoch Brater and Linda Ben-Zvi, and more recently Eckart Voigts-Virchow and especially Jonathan Bignell, have written on *Film* and on Beckett's television plays from the point of view of media or cinema studies; however, these texts remain closely linked to the literary arena, owing in part to the circulation of the books and journals in which they have been published (this is of course also true of the present chapter).

28 Samuel Beckett, *Comédie et actes divers* (Paris: Les Éditions de Minuit, 1966). This edition does not yet include *Film*, which had not yet appeared in English; the French translation of the script would feature in the revised 1972 edition.

29 Two notes, one of them at the beginning of the book, none the less refer to the text as the project for a cinematic work. Samuel Beckett, *Eh Joe and Other Writings* (London: Faber, 1966), pp. 7 and 30.

30 Samuel Beckett, *The Complete Dramatic Works* (London: Faber & Faber, 1986, 1990, 2006), pp. 323 and 326. The parenthetical '8' refers to one of the explanatory (and uncharacteristic) notes at the end of the text that also appears in the next quote from Beckett's film script.

31 Beckett, *The Complete Dramatic Works*, p. 323.

32 C.J. Ackerley and S.E. Gontarski, *The Grove Companion to Samuel Beckett* (New York: Grove Press, 2004), p. 225.

33 See also John Pilling, Chapter 1 above.

10

Beckett and unheard sound

Catherine Laws

The prospect of silence

Beckett's work has often been perceived as pushing towards its own obliteration, ever closer to the silencing of the voice. His 'characters' – though hardly that – with decaying, almost useless bodies, situated in barren environments, steadily insist that there is nothing to say and no possibility of knowledge or understanding, while (and by) fizzling on with their increasingly broken, empty, repetitive, hopeless – and often very funny – narratives of their very attempts to tell meaningful stories. In the process, the language fragments and fissures even as it pours forth; whether truncated and percussive, or accumulative and spieling, the effect is equally one of impending exhaustion – of the voice on the brink of silence. Furthermore, this notion of a trajectory ever towards, but never quite achieving, a final annihilation of the voice would seem to be validated by the author, who described his writing as 'an unnecessary stain on the silence'.[1]

As Mary Bryden points out, running alongside this is 'an extraordinarily acute attunement to sound: not just to noise, but to intimate, ambient sound'.[2] An encroaching silence beyond this threatens, oxymoronically, 'to drown all the faint breathings put together'.[3] Nevertheless, Beckett's work is always alive to the buzzings and hummings of apparently insignificant sound – extraneous environmental noise, but also the clamour of the mind's endless dialogue with itself. This is often a curse or, at best, a false distraction from the painful experience of being, but its silencing is feared as much as it is craved.

The overarching critical narrative of the drive towards silence encompasses its own implicit paradoxes; the impossibility of the absolute cessation of the voice, the inaccessibility of silence as an experiential reality, and the simultaneous desiring and fear of that experience, born of uncertainty as to what 'real silence' might mean: death? the void? some other purgatorial form of nothingness? Hélène Baldwin focuses on the Unnamable's incessant revolving of this ambivalent yearning and its inexpressibility: 'that's not the real silence, it says that's not the real silence, what can be said of the real silence, I don't know'.[4] This dilemma forms a central preoccupation of Beckett's work – in the *Trilogy*, especially, but also in those other texts of the 1950s and 1960s that recircle the same inaccessible absence, rewording the unsayable: *Texts for Nothing* is a good example, or *Enough*. Again, Beckett's own rhetoric, as reported by Charles Juliet, underlines the irony: 'Writing has led me to silence. . . .. However, I have to go on'.[5]

The dialectic of inner and outer silence, encompassing the sounds that point to its absence, becomes a marker of the broader interrogation of interiority and exteriority, self and other, being and non-being. However, Beckett doesn't stay entirely trapped within this loop. As his texts twist and turn, the opposition of sound and silence – and especially of voice and silence – starts to come undone. The shadowy, partial figures glimpsed through the torn language of the later work – creatures of ambiguous identity, location, even existence – lie beyond formulations rooted in a linear trajectory, whether towards silence, the void or death. The endpoint always hovers as an absent presence, but is never reached. Instead, there emerges an attempt to articulate an existential 'betweenness' – neither 'there' or ever quite 'not there' – and the approach to sound and the possibility of its absence is part of this.

Silence is usually defined only negatively, as an absence,[6] and particularly in Western culture specifically as an absence of or abstention from language. Beckett's earlier work appears to rehearse this, with silence mostly conceived in intentional terms only, articulated by and through the cessation of sounds. This entails a vacillation between the positive and negative characteristics of silence as opposed to sound, linked to uncertainty surrounding the distinction between apparently self-produced and external sound: 'Only the words break the silence, all other sounds have ceased. If I were silent I'd hear nothing. But if I were silent the other sounds would start again, those to which the words have made me deaf, or which have really ceased. But I am silent, it sometimes happens, no, never, not one second.'[7]

However, as Carla Locatelli perceives, silence becomes integral to Beckett's radical interrogation of language. His voices move beyond the Western cultural and philosophical positing of silence only as a lack, breaking through 'this farrago of silence and words of silence that is not silence'.[8] Furthermore, Beckett's texts of the mid-1970s and beyond perform the attempt to find a discourse that can express the difference between silence and 'no sound' as part of the wider destabilising of the coupling of language and representation, suggesting a more complex relationship between sound, silence and the perceiving self. As Locatelli suggests, by attempting an understanding of silence from a perspective other than that of language, 'we can see how the alternative saying/not saying does not necessarily translate into the logocentric dichotomy language/silence'.[9]

Music and silence in early Beckett

To my mind, Beckett's later conception of sound and silence is implicit in his earlier notions and uses of music. The critical reading of Beckett's work as a gradual extinguishing of the voice is often accompanied by a related and yet seemingly contradictory one: increasing musicalisation. These two narratives would seem incompatible; how can an impulse towards silence parallel or encompass an aspiration towards a state of music? As an art of sound, music is galvanised and provoked, even threatened and antagonised, by silence. Nevertheless, discussion of Beckett's work often includes reference to an increasing musicality not simply alongside but as part of the drive towards silence. The stutters, sputters, gaps and repetitions that express the impossibilities of language and its prevarications on the threshold of its own ending draw attention to the sounding qualities and patterns of repetition and difference, leaving a sense of meaningfulness without coherence of narrative or connotation.

On one level, this reveals that both music and silence are, ironically, positioned by Beckett as others – sometimes ideal others – of sound in general and language in particular. These are fairly typical modernist strategies. Numerous twentieth-century writers venerated music's apparent vagueness of meaning yet fullness of expression, perceiving in this a means to rejuvenate tired language. At the same time (and often in the same work), there develops a parallel desire for silence, exposing a dream of obliteration in the face of the post-Freudian crisis of the subject and representation. Beckett is central to Susan Sontag's 1967 depiction of a prevalent 'aesthetics of silence', where the persistence of the myth of art's absoluteness in the face of God's absence leads to 'a craving for the cloud of unknowing beyond knowledge and for the silence beyond speech, so art must tend to anti-art, the elimination of the "subject" (the "object", the "image"), [. . .] and the pursuit of silence'.[10] However, Beckett's later work both draws on and gradually subverts these oppositions in quite particular ways. In this there might seem something of a parallel with John Cage's rejection of the opposition of music and silence. However, while the two share a sense of the impossibilities of absolute silence these are of a very different kind, and the tensions between sound and its absence are dissimilar in quality. Cage aspires to an almost egoless contemplation and appreciation of sound events as and when they appear,[11] but this fascinated openness is not replicated in Beckett; the agency, even tyranny, of the listening self is inescapable, and there emerges a focus on the *perception*, or non-perception, of sound and music as indicative of a state of not-quite-being but not-quite-not-being in the world.

A brief consideration of some of the shifts in Beckett's use of music, and the relationship to silence, is helpful. As Nicky Losseff and Jenny Doctor point out, music often functions within literature or philosophy as a metaphor for what cannot be said.[12] While contemporary ('new') musicology has become increasingly concerned with elucidating the contextual and cultural meanings embodied by musical sound and form, and while late twentieth-century linguistics and semiotics emphasise the arbitrariness of linguistic designation, the literary and philosophic conception of music as the 'beyond' of language persists from its nineteenth-century idealist envisioning.

To an extent this is reflected in Beckett's work, with music sometimes idealised as a model for what literature might be or do if freed from the banalities of language, and sometimes providing a refuge from the very struggle with meaning. However, this is not straightforward; music is by no means a singular entity in

Beckett. It is manifested in different ways: thematised as an 'idea', or a formal and/or expressive model (perhaps most obviously in the early novel *Dream of Fair to Middling Women*, and in the radio plays *Words and Music* and *Cascando*); as actual music in the plays, whether pre-recorded (as in *All That Fall*, *Ghost Trio* and *Nacht und Träume*, for example) or sung by characters (often in the 'old style', as with Winnie in *Happy Days*); as references to music and musicians (from Pythagoras to vaudeville); and through the musicalising of language effected by attention to qualities of sound and rhythm and increasing use of forms of structural variation and motivic development (a process that becomes more apparent, in different ways and at different levels, in Beckett's writing from the *Trilogy* on).

Moreover, I will argue that the intertwining of ideas of silence within the evocation of music in the early prose leads to the undoing of the apparent oppositions of language–music and language–silence manifested as linear trajectories. If the impossibility of the coincidence of these processes is never explicitly considered, its attempt engenders Beckett's later, more complex envisioning of the relationship between sound, its perception, and the self.

In the early novel *Dream of Fair to Middling Women* (completed in 1932), music plays a small but significant role. Beckett's substantial reading and note-taking for *Dream* included ideas and phrases from *La Musique chinoise*, by the French musicologist Louis Laloy.[13] These are not extensive, but are used to articulate ideas about what a novel should (or shouldn't) be or do. *Dream* self-consciously grapples with its own development, calling novelistic conventions into question: character, situation, action, causality. In order to explain the recalcitrance of his materials, the narrator draws on the myth of the origins of the Chinese musical scale. If only his characters could act like the twelve different Chinese liŭ and liŭ sung by the male and female phoenix of the myth, 'we could write a little book that would be purely melodic, think how nice that would be, linear, a lovely Pythagorean chain-chant solo of cause and effect, a one-figured teleophony that would be a pleasure to hear'.[14]

Through the Chinese metaphor (and the consequent, idiosyncratic elaboration of analogies with melodic and harmonic structures, intonation and Pythagorean tuning),[15] music is presented as an idealised model of what this novel might aspire towards but cannot achieve. However, while early narrative interventions imply that the desire for a unified structure of cause and effect persists despite the failure to force the characters into line, later remarks suggest that to produce a rounded novel, with characters conforming neatly to meaningful, complementary roles, would, in the end, be unsatisfactory. Instead, the very obduracy and complexity of these characters develops into an implicit sign of the novel's potential faithfulness to experience.

As this goes on, the protagonist, Belacqua, outlines his own literary ideals: 'The experience of my reader shall be between the phrases, in the silence, communicated by the intervals, not the terms of the statement [. . .]. I think of Beethofen [*sic*], [. . .] I think of his earlier compositions where into the body of the music he incorporates a punctuation of dehiscence, flottements, the coherence gone to pieces, the continuity bitched to hell'.[16] This language echoes that earlier in the book, where the narrator bemoans the structural problems caused by the unruliness of his characters. Both employ the idea of music as a model, but while the narrator's depiction of music is of a linear, unified model of cause and effect, Belacqua here evokes a more complex and sophisticated music that he sees as transcending the limits of language and somehow able to reflect the disintegrated nature of experience; one that favours discontinuity, fragmentation, unpredictability – and silence.

This is apparently exemplified by Beethoven (one of Beckett's favourite composers). Belacqua refers to Beethoven's music as an 'incoherent continuum', wherein artistic utterance serves primarily to articulate a position at the edge of a void of meaning, and Beethoven and Rimbaud are artists who 'delimit the reality of insane areas of silence, whose audibilities are no more than punctuation in a statement of silences'.[17] Beethoven is, in some respects, a strange choice; the idea that his works reject cohesion and unity is hardly credible musicologically, especially today. Beethoven's more fragmentary treatment of often quite simple motives, relative to his predecessors and contemporaries, perhaps explains Beckett's choice,[18] but the influence of Schopenhauer is also evident.[19] For Schopenhauer, like Belacqua, Beethoven's music reveals the true chaos of things and suggests the void beyond: 'a true and complete picture of the world, which rolls on in the boundless confusion of innumerable forms, and maintains itself by constant destruction'.[20]

Schopenhauer invokes Pythagorean ideas of tuning in his idealist
vision of music as both the highest art form and yet revealing of
the impossibility of ultimate knowledge, and Beckett's allusions
to ideas of melody, harmony and intonation, and specifically to
Beethoven's 'dire stroms [*sic*] of silence',[21] exhibit a distinctly
Schopenhauerian tinge. For Schopenhauer, music becomes the
perfect pessimistic symbol, and his identification of Beethoven as
the consummate exemplar coincided nicely with Beckett's musical
tastes and his own aesthetics of failure.

In *Dream*, two snippets of musical notation appear in the text,
both slight adaptations of a phrase from the first movement of
Beethoven's *Seventh Symphony*. The extract comes from the end
of the climax that develops after the exuberant *tutti* statement of
the *vivace* main theme; it interrupts with a sudden *sforzando* low C
sharp held by strings alone. Overall, the sense of propulsion is by
no means diverted – the interruption is brief – but something of the
previous certainty is lost: the apparently unassailable impulsion of
the music has for an instant been arrested, its unreflecting momen-
tum called to attention. Through the association of Beethoven with
Belacqua's literary aspirations, this musical pause comes to represent Belacqua's attempt to capture the ineffable experience that
lies 'between the terms' of language.

Dream, then, does not retain music as an undifferentiated
idea, but instead admits different conceptions into play. While
the Chinese musical metaphor appears to set music against literature as able to transcend the limits of language, the move
towards a more complex view, incorporating silence, destabilises
that simple opposition, undoing the reduction of meaning to the
'sayable' and the positioning of music as its sensual and expressive but irrational and meaningless other. Beckett's Beethovenian
model here begins to undermine the striving for knowledge and
certainty, for art as a means to enlightenment, clarity and understanding, shifting instead towards uncertainty of meaning and
identity. The two others of language, music and silence, become
entwined in this early attempt to find a form that can 'accommo-
date the mess' (as Beckett later put it).[22] In this lies an intimation
of Beckett's later language of disintegrated surface and shade-like
states of being.

The musical references in *Dream* form just one part of a network
of allusion and quotation that infuses the text at every level.

Nevertheless, the particular recourse to Beethoven resurfaces. In a letter to his friend Axel Kaun, written in 1937 (a few years after the completion of *Dream*), Beckett asked:

> Is there any reason why that terrible materiality of the word surface should not be capable of being dissolved, like for example the sound surface, torn by enormous pauses, of Beethoven's Seventh Symphony, so that through whole pages we can perceive nothing but a path of sounds suspended in giddy heights, linking unfathomable abysses of silence?[23]

Here, silence is again, paradoxically, intertwined with music as others of language. In some respects, this is unsurprising. For musicians, silence is often a compositionally meaningful presence between phrases or even individual notes, indicative of a meditative pause in the sonic narrative, or forming a communicative point of reference for performers.[24] Beyond this can lie the conceptual sense of silence as ever-present beneath the musical surface, a backdrop from which sounds emerge and finally disappear; this idea is apparent in a wide range of twentieth-century compositions.[25] As Jenny Doctor observes, 'in this conception, silence thus shifts from being something that stops action – a silencer, a structural articulator or frame – to being the main canvas'.[26] In any of these manifestations, however, silence is, as Losseff and Doctor point out, cognitive in its deepest sense,[27] demanding acknowledgement as an intentional object of perception. Similarly, in Beckett's early positing of Beethoven's ruptured music as a possible model for his own work, but equally in his increasingly musical, fragmented language that apparently keeps the underlying silence at bay, silence is *composed in*, defined still in terms of the cessation of sound, objectified for cognition, and evoked only by the act of listening *for* it. In these manifestations, as Sontag says, '"Silence" never ceases to imply its opposite and to depend on its presence [. . .]. Silence remains inescapably a form of speech [. . .] and an element in a dialogue.'[28]

'that unheeded neither': unheard sound

In some of Beckett's later texts, however, the picking away at the relationship between sound and silence leads to an alternative proposition: unheard sound. This is apparent in his rather different

use of Beethoven in the television play *Ghost Trio*, completed in
1976.[29] An unidentified male figure inhabits a bare room, await-
ing the arrival of a woman who never appears. He holds a tape
recorder, and intermittently we hear extracts from the 'Largo' of
Beethoven's Piano Trio Opus 70 No. 1 in D minor, nicknamed 'The
Ghost'. In each case Beckett specifies the exact passages to be heard,
indicating the relevant bar numbers of the score. The drama is one
of waiting and listening; a simple, formalised and abstracted visual
scene with repetitive sequences of minimal action, contrasted with
the evocative but ambiguous expectation of a tryst, articulated by
the music. Throughout, the camera, directed by a voice-over from
an unidentified woman, interrogates the space and its minimal
contents, zooming in and out between three viewing positions as if
scrutiny of the scene might reveal its meaning.

The music seems to be used to suggest an idea of elsewhere – or
at least of 'not here': the beyond of the room, real or imagined – the
space in which the longed-for woman presumably exists. However,
Beckett's use of the Beethoven is not that straightforward. The
excerpts we hear are not simply Beethoven's 'Largo' played through
a tape machine so as to symbolise the absent presence of the
woman, drawing on its Romantic spirit for emotional sustenance.
The status and origins of the music remain subtly equivocal; it
comes and goes, but not always in exact or obvious coincidence
with the operation of the tape player. Sometimes it instead seems
to be provoked by the camera moving closer to the door, as if sym-
bolising the outside of the room. But not always. Even more subtly,
Beckett manipulates the excerpts from the Beethoven, introducing
them in an order that could not occur through the ordinary process
of listening to a tape recording, and carefully omitting the second
subject of the movement – that which would in conventional,
old-fashioned musicological terminology be designated female in
character. In this way Beckett again undermines the assumed link
between the music and the tape recorder, and in so doing suggests
a possible trace, however insubstantial, of imaginative agency in
the summoning of the music.

Beckett does not simply present a scene of hopeless waiting;
a post-human world drained of colour, with music figuring the
absent love, controlled by the eye of the viewer moving in and out
across the space, searching for meaning. This is apparent on one
level, but the uncertainty of the origin, location and status of the

music, and its recomposed structure offer a counter-balancing; the faintest suggestion that the figure might be *using* the music to conjure thoughts of the woman. Suddenly, the apparent powers of production in this play are called into question: the figure is no longer necessarily a simple object of scrutiny, mastered by the camera and its controlling voice (and, implicitly, by us as viewers). The 'betweenness' of the music – we cannot be certain if it is 'really' reproduced by the tape player or entirely imagined – articulates the figure's potential resistance to subjection, the possibility of residual creative agency in the face of the technological interrogation of the scene.

The figure in *Ghost Trio* does not speak. To say that the Beethoven fills his silence, articulating his expectations – standing in for his voice, even – borders on the crass and banal, implying that the music is used in a manner conventional to television and film. However, the visual presence of the source of the music along with its self-conscious invocation but uncertain status transform this notion into something more complex. The ambiguities are such that the Beethoven we hear in *Ghost Trio* exists in a strange limbo as a perceptual object, neither within nor without either the scene or the figure. In this sense, the figure neither speaks nor is silent; the music is both exterior and interior, heard and yet curiously unheard.

The manuscripts of *Ghost Trio* reveal that Beckett did not simply select the extracts of the Beethoven to be heard in the play, as one might expect. Instead, he listed a larger number of passages and then decided which should be audible and which should remain 'unheard'. Effectively (and strangely), then, Beckett divided the Beethoven in three: the music that had no role in the play, the music to be heard, and music that stays 'unheard' and even unperceived.[30] The latter poses a phenomenological and philosophical conundrum in the context of a play: in what sense does it exist – or at least exist differently from the omitted music – if it cannot be heard? While this aspect of Beckett's precompositional thinking is undetectable in the final play, the ambiguities of the production of the music create an implicit counterpart to this third realm beyond the included and excluded music.

More concretely, this instance of unheard sound is not unique: the idea emerges elsewhere, especially in other texts of the mid-1970s, often linked to footsteps. The manuscripts show that Beckett vacillated over whether the steps of the Figure in *Ghost*

Trio should be audible; it was clearly a significant decision. In the end he made them soundless, whereas, in *Footfalls* (1975), V describes her daughter's need to hear her own pacing: 'No, Mother, the motion is not enough, I must hear the feet, however faint they fall.' However, when May takes up the story and describes the nights when 'she' paced without pause, there is a moment when the figure vanishes and there is suddenly 'No sound. [*Pause.*] None at least to be heard.'[31]

Beckett spoke to Charles Juliet of the significance of constant pacing to and fro and of counting his footsteps;[32] these ideas resurface time and again in this period. In the poem 'Roundelay' (1976), steps, and the ability to hear them, seem to act as an indicator of the persistence of perception, even if minimal and ever-fading ('steps sole sound . . . then no sound . . . steps sole sound . . . at end of day').[33] As Elizabeth Drew comments, the contrast between existence and non-existence is mediated by that between stasis and movement,[34] but the oppositions are undermined by uncertainty as to whether presence or absence (of sound, of perception, of the self) is willed or actual.

'écoute-les' (from the *Mirlitonnades* of 1976–81) demands that we listen to the gradual and difficult accumulation of words, equated with the placing of one foot in front of another ('écoute-les / s'ajouter / les mots / aux mots / sans mots / les pas / aux pas / un à / un').[35] However, both *Company* (1980) and 'pas à pas' (also from the *Mirlitonnades*) suggest that the taking of steps does not necessarily indicate progression or even location in time or space (one can 'plod on from nought' and end up there too: 'pas à pas / nulle part'),[36] and that perceiving footfalls is no guarantee of their presence or absence: 'You do not count your steps any more. You do not hear your footfalls any more. Unhearing unseeing you go your way.'[37] As Drew says, 'The journey, which is the active union of space and time, becomes a key to the inner realm where time and space are obliterated'.[38]

This shadowy state of 'betweenness' is expressed in *neither* (1976).[39] The sense is of continual wandering to and fro, coming and going between different gradations of shadow, between self and 'unself', achieving stasis only by abandoning such distinctions and even then only in the negative, inexpressible terms of the final words: 'unspeakable home'. Halfway through this short text comes the line, 'unheard footfalls only sound'. The positive presence of the sound of steps that nevertheless cannot be heard – or perhaps even the sound of not hearing the footfalls – suggests an undoing of the opposition of sound and silence. The impossible neither of this auditory state, and the concomitant ambiguity of the relationship between the existence of sound and its perception, parallel the ghostly limbo of the text, where some kind of residual agency seems to persist but without the substance of identified self or 'unself'.

In Beckett's later work there emerges a particular focus on the conscious act of listening in and for itself (as opposed to listening to music as an escape from language and the everyday). The image of the listener, usually with head in hand, recurs, often accompanied by vacillation between the idea that things might eventually be 'still' in that 'same soundless place'[40] and the persistent sense, in contrast, that there will 'still' always be stirrings: 'all quite still or try listening to the sounds all quite still head in hand listening for a sound'.[41] In *Sounds* (1978), a contrast is set up between straining to hear even the tiniest sounds of a still night ('never quite for nothing even stillest night') and the possibility that complete stillness might allow the listener to 'let himself be dreamt away to where none at any time [. . .] where no such thing no more than ghosts make nothing to listen for no such thing as a sound'.[42] *Sounds* also lists sounds present by their absence, while in *A Piece of Monologue* (1977) the idea of sound truly disappearing is posited but immediately corrected: 'Nothing stirring [. . .] Nothing to be heard anywhere. [. . .] No. No such things as none.'[43]

Silence, conventionally conceived as non-utterance and non-perception, consequently signifies the obliteration of the self and hence an ultimate state of nothingness, both terrifying and transcendent. In this way silence becomes a force for redemption through its very rejection of meaning: salvation and relief achieved by means of a sonic void. In these late Beckett texts, though, silence is neither produced or banished intentionally; 'no sound' is not necessarily indicative of silence and meaninglessness, and the relationship between the presence of sound and its perception is uncertain. Sound can persist but unheard, stirrings can be still. Both sound and its possible absence seem to be posed as questions, provocations to the still fizzling, unresolved predicament of subjectivity.

Beckett commented more than once that as he grew older the sense of hearing was becoming more important,[44] adding 'There is always something to listen to'.[45] The meaning is unclear though: is it ambient sound to which Beckett refers, or sounds in the head? Juliet describes Beckett sitting still for hours, listening to his 'inner voice',[46] but even if this is accurate we have no idea what he listened for or heard, and whether actively or passively. Beckett's late texts induce precisely this auditory ambiguity and its ambivalent relationship to consciousness, evoking the sounds and not-quite-sounds that balance on the tympanum, between interior and exterior, between moments of significant auditory cognition and the continuous soundings beyond perception.

Simon Critchley argues that silence, the void and meaninglessness are not the goal of Beckett's work, for this would proffer release and salvation, however negative (and as Beckett said, 'Negation is no more possible than affirmation').[47] Instead, 'it is a question of meaninglessness becoming an achievement rather than a fact, meaninglessness becoming the work of Beckett's work', and, within this, 'writing is the necessary *desacration* and *desacralization* of silence'.[48] Silence and music might seem to offer salvation from words, but implicit in Beckett's early entwining of ideas of the two lie both the impossibility of stopping speaking and the persistent possibility of finding a means of meaning that does not falsify the transient, contingent, uncertain experience of perception. This entails the unpicking of both music and silence as transcendent, ideal others of language, and the imaginative re-production of sound, music and silence, heard and unheard, as markers of the blurring of interior and exterior, self and unself, being and non-being, and of the uncertain, ghostly perseverance of imaginative agency even in the face of death.

In this respect, the apparent persistence of a desire for silence is less significant than the insistent, if shadowy, presence of unheard sound. Beckett seems here to focus not on silence or absent sound but on a kind of leastness of sound; the traces of sound that emerge when listening can come and go (as in *Stirrings Still* (1983–87), when 'in the end he ceased if not to hear to listen'),[49] or perhaps an ideal and probably unattainable kind of hearing that is released from the anguish of self-perception.

Notes

1 John Gruen, 'Samuel Beckett talks about Beckett', *Vogue*, 127:2 (February 1970), 108.

2 Mary Bryden, 'Beckett and the sound of silence', in Mary Bryden (ed.), *Samuel Beckett and Music* (Oxford: Clarendon, 1998), p. 24.

3 Samuel Beckett, *The Lost Ones*, in *The Complete Short Prose 1929–1989*, ed. S. E. Gontarski (New York: Grove, 1995), p. 223.

4 Samuel Beckett, *Trilogy* (London: Picador, 1979), p. 376. See the discussion in Hélène L. Baldwin, *Samuel Beckett's Real Silence* (University Park and London: Pennsylvania University Press, 1981), p. 83.

5 Charles Juliet, *Conversations with Samuel Beckett and Bram van Velde*, trans. Janey Tucker (The Hague: Academic Press Leiden, 1995), p. 141.

6 This is the case with all recent *OED* definitions, for example.

7 Samuel Beckett, *Texts for Nothing*, in *The Complete Short Prose 1929–1989*, p. 131.

8 *Ibid.*, p. 125.

9 Carla Locatelli, 'Delogocentering silence: Beckett's ultimate unwording', in Enoch Brater (ed.), *The Theatrical Gamut: Notes for a Post-Beckettian Stage* (Ann Arbor: University of Michigan Press, 2005), p. 70.

10 Susan Sontag, 'The aesthetics of silence', in *Styles of Radical Will* (New York: Picador, 2002), p. 5.

11 See Cage's comments in *Empty Words* (London: Marion Boyars, 1980) and *Silence* (London: Marion Boyars, 1978).

12 Nicky Losseff and Jenny Doctor, 'Introduction', in Nicky Losseff and Jenny Doctor (eds), *Silence, Music, Silent Music* (Aldershot: Ashgate, 2007), p. 1.

13 This source was discovered by Sean Lawlor, and subsequently incorporated into John Pilling's edition of *Beckett's 'Dream' Notebook* (Reading: Beckett International Foundation, 1999) and his annotated companion to the novel issued as volume 12 of the *Journal of Beckett Studies* (2003).

14 Samuel Beckett, *Dream of Fair to Middling Women*, eds Eoin O'Brien and Edith Fournier (Dublin: Black Cat, 1992), p. 10.

15 A more detailed discussion of ideas of music in *Dream*, including the significance of Beethoven and the influences of Schopenhauer and Pythagoras alluded to below, forms part of my forthcoming book *'Headaches Among the Overtones': Music in Beckett, Beckett in Music* (New York and Amsterdam: Rodopi, 2010).

16 Beckett, *Dream of Fair to Middling Women*, pp. 137–8.

17 Beckett, *Dream*, p. 102.

18 Tia Denora shows that in its own time Beethoven's music was perceived as harmonically adventurous, structurally ambiguous, thickly orchestrated and volatile in dynamic range. Tia Denora, *Beethoven and the Construction of Genius* (Berkeley, Loss Angeles and London: University of California Press, 1995), p. 129.

19 Beckett's reading of Schopenhauer fed directly into his monograph on Proust (1931), and the influence certainly persisted into the late 1930s; Matthew Feldman comments on the evidence for this in the 'Philosophy Notes'. Traces are less obvious but still present in *Dream*, including the terms of the musical discussion. In particular, John Wall argues for the influence of Schopenhauer's conception of the relationship between consciousness and the body here (as opposed to the Cartesian dualism more commonly referenced). See Matthew Feldman, *Beckett's Books: A Cultural History of Samuel Beckett's 'Interwar Notes'* (London: Continuum, 2006), pp. 48–9; John Wall, 'Murphy, Belacqua, Schopenhauer and Descartes: metaphysical reflections on the body', *Journal of Beckett Studies*, 9:2 (Spring 2000), 21–61. For wider consideration of Schopenhauer's influence on Beckett, see: Terence McQueeny, 'Samuel Beckett as critic of Proust and Joyce' (Ph.D. thesis, University of North Carolina, 1977); J. D. O'Hara, 'Beckett's Schopenhauerian reading of Proust: the will as whirled in re-presentation', in Eric van der Luft (ed.), *Schopenhauer: New Essays in Honor of His 200th Birthday* (Lewiston, Queenston and Lampeter: The Edwin Mellon Press, 1988), pp. 273–92; Nicholas Zurbrugg, *Beckett and Proust* (Gerrards Cross: Colin Smythe, 1988).

20 Arthur Schopenhauer, *The World as Will and Representation*, 2 vols., trans. E. F. J. Payne (New York: Dover, 1969), II, p. 450.

21 Beckett, *Dream*, p. 139.

22 Beckett quoted in Tom Driver, 'Beckett by the Madeleine', *Columbia University Forum*, 4:3 (1961), 24.

23 Samuel Beckett, 'German letter of 1937', in *Disjecta: Miscellaneous Writings and a Dramatic Fragment*, ed. Ruby Cohn (London: John Calder, 1983), p. 172.

24 See Losseff and Doctor, *Silence, Music, Silent Music*, p. 1.

25 In 'The texture of silence', Jenny Doctor focuses on this idea as exemplified in the music of Webern, drawing also on a range of parallel instances (including Beckett's radio plays). Jenny Doctor, 'The texture of silence', in Losseff and Doctor (eds), *Silence, Music, Silent Music*, pp. 15–36. In addition, though, it is worth noting that similar conceptions are manifested in music of very different styles; more recently, for example, in the work of composers as diverse as György Kurtág and Arvo Pärt.

26 Doctor, 'The texture of silence', pp. 27–8.

27 Losseff and Doctor, *Silence, Music, Silent Music*, p. 1.

28 Sontag, 'The aesthetics of silence', p. 11.

29 Samuel Beckett, *Ghost Trio*, in *Collected Shorter Plays* (London: Faber and Faber, 1984), pp. 245–54.

30 For a more detailed discussion of the music in *Ghost Trio*, see Michael Maier, '*Geistertrio*: Beethoven's music in Samuel Beckett's *Ghost Trio*: part one', in *Samuel Beckett Today / Aujourd-hui: Endlessness in the Year 2000*, eds Angela Moorjani and Carola Veit, 11 (2001), pp. 267–78; Catherine Laws, 'Beethoven's Haunting of Beckett's *Ghost Trio*', in Linda Ben-Zvi (ed.), *Drawing on Beckett: Portraits, Performances, and Cultural Contexts* (Tel Aviv: Assaph, 2003), pp. 197–214.

31 Samuel Beckett, *Footfalls*, in *Collected Shorter Plays*, pp. 241–42.

32 Charles Juliet, *Conversations*, pp. 162 and 163–4.

33 Samuel Beckett, 'Roundelay', in *Collected Poems in English and French* (New York: Grove, 1977), p. 35.

34 Elizabeth Drew, 'Head to footsteps: "fundamental sounds" in "dread nay" and "Roundelay"', in *Samuel Beckett Today / Aujourd-hui*, eds Angela Moorjani and Carola Veit, 11, pp. 295–6.

35 Samuel Beckett, 'écoute-les', in *Collected Poems 1930–1978* (London: John Calder, 1986), p. 71.

36 Samuel Beckett, *Company* (New York: Grove, 1980), p. 37; 'pas à pas' in *Collected Poems 1930–1978*, p. 86.

37 Beckett, *Company*, pp. 36–7.

38 Drew, 'Head to footsteps', 296.

39 Samuel Beckett, *neither*, in *The Complete Short Prose 1929–1989*, p. 258.

40 Samuel Beckett, *Still 3*, in *The Complete Short Prose 1929–1989*, p. 269.

41 Samuel Beckett, *Fizzle 7: Still*, in *The Complete Short Prose 1929–1989*, p. 242.

42 Samuel Beckett, *Sounds*, in *The Complete Short Prose 1929–1989*, pp. 267–8.

43 Samuel Beckett, *A Piece of Monologue*, in *Collected Shorter Plays*, p. 266.

44 Charles Juliet, *Conversations*, pp. 147 and 152.

45 *Ibid.*, p. 155.

46 *Ibid.*, p. 152.

47 *Ibid.*, p. 165.

48 Simon Critchley, *Very Little . . . Almost Nothing: Death, Philosophy, Literature* (London: Routledge, 1997), p. 152.

49 Samuel Beckett, *Stirrings Still*, in *The Complete Short Prose 1929–1989*, p. 263.

11

It's nothing: Beckett and anxiety

Russell Smith

On 11 August 1936, Samuel Beckett wrote the following passage –
in German – in his notebook:

> How translucent this mechanism seems to me now, the principle of
> which is: better to be afraid of <u>something</u> than of <u>nothing</u>. In the
> first case only a part, in the second the whole is threatened, not to
> mention the monstrous quality which inseparably belongs to the
> incomprehensible, one could even say the boundless. [. . .] When
> such an anxiety [*Angst*] begins to grow a reason [*Grund*] must
> quickly be found, as no one has the ability to live with it in its utter
> absence of reason [*Grundlosigkeit*]. Thus the neurotic, i.e. Everyman,
> may declare with great seriousness and in all awe that there is
> merely a minimal difference between God in heaven and a pain in
> the stomach. Since both emanate from one source and serve one
> purpose: to transform anxiety into fear.[1]

August 1936 was a particularly anxious time for Beckett. He had
been living in Dublin for about eight months, since returning from
London just before Christmas 1935, having broken off his two-year
course of psychoanalysis with Wilfred Bion. As James Knowlson
notes, Beckett had presented himself to Bion with 'severe anxiety
symptoms': 'a bursting, apparently arrhythmic heart, night sweats,
shudders, panic, breathlessness, and, at its most severe, total
paralysis'. However, the fact that these symptoms – which flared
up whenever he stayed with his mother in Dublin – continued to
plague him in early 1936 perhaps '[led] him to despair that nothing
had been resolved by two whole years of analysis'.[2] The fact that
the passage quoted above was written in German is significant: it
is one of Beckett's earliest attempts to express himself in a foreign
language, part of what Mark Nixon calls a 'personal and cultural

German complex' that was part of an ongoing effort 'to achieve a more personal and direct statement in his writing'.[3] Although its purpose is in part a linguistic exercise, it also articulates with admirable lucidity an insight that was clearly important to Beckett, coming as it does during a renewal of his anxiety attacks in the wake of an apparently failed course of psychoanalysis. Indeed, its displacement of anxiety from subjective pathology to ontological condition is inextricable from its German context: as Anna Wierzbicka notes, 'angst' denotes a 'peculiarly German concept', a notion confirmed by its use as a borrowed term in English.[4] Usually translated as 'anxiety', though some translators prefer 'dread', 'uneasiness' or even 'malaise',[5] 'angst' is used in English to specify a particular kind of anxiety, as a long-term, deep-seated existential condition, rather than a passing, and potentially treatable emotional state. In this chapter I wish to examine more closely the figuration of anxiety in Beckett's work, using as my primary example a passage from the opening of *Molloy*, in particular in so far as it sheds light on two broader questions: the role of 'feeling' in Beckett's writing, particularly in the postwar period, and Beckett's aesthetic preoccupation with the evocation of an unfathomable 'nothingness'.[6]

A significant debate in modern clinical psychology concerns the degree to which anxiety is treatable, curable. According to Stanley Rachman, 'anxiety' and 'fear' are usually distinguished on the basis that, whereas fear is brief and intense, 'an emotional reaction to a specific, perceived danger', anxiety is 'diffuse, objectless, unpleasant and persistent [. . .] grating along at a lower level of intensity'.[7] For these reasons, psychologists stake their therapeutic *raison d'être* on the notion 'that anxiety is potentially reducible to fear'.[8] Rachman continues:

> If the cause of the anxiety is potentially knowable and the focus is identifiable, then by diligent work [. . .] it should be possible to convert puzzling anxiety into clear-cut fear. Associated with this assumption [. . .] is the idea that fear is more manageable than anxiety.[9]

In other words, this is a reversal of Beckett's formulation: whereas Hippocratic optimism insists that the apparent objectlessness of anxiety should be traceable to a knowable and manageable object of fear, Beckett's German notebook entry suggests that fear is simply the displacement on to an object – whether 'God in heaven' or 'a pain in the stomach'– of a more fundamental anxiety whose object is precisely an unfathomable and unbearable nothingness.

It is known that Beckett read widely on the subject of anxiety. Shortly after he began psychotherapy with Bion in late 1933, he embarked on one of his periods of intensive reading and note-taking, compiling 54 typewritten pages of 'Psychology Notes' based on psychological and psychoanalytic texts by Karin Stephen, R. S. Woodworth, Ernest Jones, Sigmund Freud, Wilhelm Stekel, Alfred Adler and Otto Rank. As Matthew Feldman notes, the topic of 'acute anxiety states and accompanying symptoms' comprises 'the overwhelming majority of material transcribed'.[10] Of particular interest are Beckett's notes on Otto Rank's *The Trauma of Birth* (1923). The notion of birth as 'the first experience of anxiety, and thus the source and prototype of the affect of anxiety' comes originally from Freud's *Interpretation of Dreams*,[11] but in Rank's work the idea is expanded to become an all-encompassing theory whereby an individual's subsequent emotional life is significantly determined by their experience of the birth-event. Freud was later highly critical of the determinism of Rank's theory in *Inhibitions, Symptoms and Anxiety*.[12] Nevertheless, the notion of the trauma of birth as archetype of a lifelong anxiety clearly appealed to Beckett, echoing ideas of his own going back as far as Belacqua's 'womb-tomb' in *Dream of Fair to Middling Women*.[13] In an interview with James Knowlson in the last months of his life, Beckett claimed that during his sessions with Bion he 'came up with extraordinary memories of being in the womb. Intrauterine memories.'[14]

While the notion of birth as the origin of anxiety had a certain appeal to Beckett, however, it also attributes anxiety to a definite object, depriving it of its character as a confrontation with nothing-ness. We can read Beckett's German notebook entry as his attempt to formulate his own theory of anxiety, both as a means of self-analysis (or rather, as a means of marking his abandonment of a certain kind of self-analysis) and as part of an ongoing project to define, initially in theoretical terms, the key elements of his artistic vision. As Matthew Feldman observes, while Beckett's voracious 'notesnatching' of the 1930s seems to have begun as a Joycean accumulation of ostentatious erudition, the maturation of his artis-tic vision involved a process in which 'Beckett's allusions become increasingly opaque and embedded in his later writing, acting as ideas rather than erudite references'.[15]

The identification of a reified 'nothingness' at the heart of anxiety inevitably evokes the centrality of nothingness in Beckett's attempts at aesthetic self-definition through this period. In particular, it recalls the famous letter to Axel Kaun, written almost a year later on 9 July 1937 – once again in Dublin, once again in German – after Beckett had returned from his travels:

> More and more my own language appears to me like a veil that must be torn apart in order to get at the things (or the Nothingness) behind it. [. . .] To bore one hole after another in [language], until what lurks behind it – be it something or nothing – begins to seep through; I cannot imagine a higher goal for a writer today.[16]

If there remains an equivocation between 'something' and 'nothing' in this passage, it is a question soon to be decided in favour of the latter in Beckett's aesthetic, from the 'nothing to express' of the *Three Dialogues* to the question raised in the Addenda to *Watt*, of who may 'nothingness / in words enclose'.[17] Indeed, in a well-known 1967 letter to Sighle Kennedy, Beckett offers two different 'nothings' as interpretative keys to his writing: 'If I were in the unenviable position of having to study my work my points of departure would be the "Naught is more real . . ." and the "Ubi nihil vales . . ." both already in *Murphy* and neither very rational.'[18]

What is interesting about the passage in Beckett's German notebook is its association between a reified nothingness and an emotional state of unbearable anxiety. Compared with the truncated philosophical tags somewhat flippantly proffered in the 1967 letter, the earlier passage invests the experience of nothingness with an overwhelming affective urgency. It recalls perhaps the terms of a 'brutally honest, self-critical letter'[19] Beckett sent to Thomas MacGreevy in 1932, distinguishing between those of his poems that are '*facultatif*' (optional) and those that 'represent a necessity', between those 'that I would have been no worse off for not having written', and those 'that seem to have been drawn down against the really dirty weather of one of these fine days into the burrow of the "private life"'. Beckett's figure for the latter is the poem 'written above an abscess and not out of a cavity',[20] a corporeal metaphor for expression that cannot but recall Beckett's own psychosomatic afflictions of the period. While it is debatable whether one can or indeed should attempt to construct a coherent Beckettian aesthetic from his *obiter dicta*, particularly when they are scattered across private letters and notebooks, newspaper interviews and published writings over several decades, it is worth noting the persistence with which a kind of affective or even somatic necessity is invoked in Beckett's statements about his own writing. This is perhaps most starkly evident in Beckett's 1961 interview with Gabriel D'Aubarède:

> 'I never read philosophers.'
> 'Why not?'
> 'I never understand anything they write.'
> 'All the same, people have wondered if the existentialists' problem of being may afford a key to your works.'
> 'There's no key or problem. I wouldn't have had any reason to write my novels if I could have expressed their subject in philosophical terms.'
> 'What was your reason then?'
> 'I haven't the slightest idea. I'm no intellectual. All I am is feeling. "Molloy" and the others came to me the day I became aware of my own folly. Only then did I begin to write the things I feel.'[21]

On one level, Beckett's remark is clearly something of an evasive strategy, a wish to distance his writing from potentially schematic philosophical readings; certainly it is disingenuous for Beckett to claim he never read philosophers. The appeal to 'feeling' here suggests a desire to reposition his work in a domain of subjective inscrutability: 'all that inner space one never sees, the brain and the heart and other caverns where thought and feeling dance their sabbath'.[22] By the same token, however, it would be wrong to assume that this statement, or any other of the above statements, give licence to read Beckett, and particularly his postwar work, in narrowly autobiographical terms, simply as a form of confession – or worse, therapy – at either an explicit or an unconscious level. Nevertheless, I think there are good reasons for taking Beckett at his word here, and examining the role of 'feeling' in his work.

This is particularly timely because, despite the evident emotional intensity of Beckett's writing (or perhaps because of it), post-structuralist Beckett criticism has often been characterised, as Nicholas Allen observes, by 'a longstanding insistence to read Beckett in high abstraction'.[23] However, the Beckett Estate's relatively recent – and still incomplete – granting of scholarly access to the 'grey canon' of Beckett's manuscripts, notebooks and letters has stimulated a resurgence of biographical, empirical and genetic approaches to Beckett, approaches which nevertheless continue to 'productively overlap' with the 'abstraction' of more speculative, theoretical readings.[24] It is such a productive overlap of approaches I wish to adumbrate here, reading 'feeling' in Beckett's work – in this case, the feeling of anxiety – in a manner reducible to neither the biographical nor the theoretical, but seeking to draw out and explore the tension between them.

This approach is prompted by a wave of recent theoretical work on feeling, affect and emotion. We may provisionally define 'affect' as the physiological element of experience, 'emotion' as the (even minimal) cognitive interpretation of affect, and 'feeling' as 'a capacious term that connotes both physiological sensations (affects) and psychological states (emotions)'.[25] While recent approaches to affect and emotion differ widely, what they share is the hunch that paying attention to affect as a critical object has the capacity to disturb poststructuralist orthodoxies.

For example, Eve Kosofsky Sedgwick and Adam Frank draw on Silvan Tomkins's massive study *Affect, Imagery, Consciousness* to challenge what they see as the routine critical habits of post-structuralist theory: its *a priori* suspicion of 'biologism' or the notion of a biological (i.e. non-cultural) aspect of human experience; its privileging of language in its models of subjectivity; and its celebration of anti-essentialist models of difference.[26] Tomkins's insistence on 'eight (only sometimes it's nine) distinct affects hardwired into the human biological system' runs counter to contemporary theoretical suspicion of the 'natural' and the 'innate'.[27] However, Tomkins argues that the affect system, rather than the biological drive system usually seen to underpin it, is the primary motivator of human behaviour, whereby the 'apparent urgency'[28] of supposedly fundamental drives such as hunger, thirst or sexual arousal is in fact dependent on their 'co-assembly' with the affect system, which can act both to amplify and to weaken them. It is also worth noting, in relation to psychoanalytic models of subjectivity, that Tomkins relegates sexuality to 'the least imperious of the drives'.[29] In other words, Tomkins's affect system straddles the boundary between the biological and the social, according neither biological process nor social experience a primary role in explaining human motivation and behaviour.

Brian Massumi, following Deleuze and Guattari, more explicitly privileges 'affect' over 'emotion' as a means of undermining the post-structuralist model of discursively and linguistically constructed subjectivity. For Massumi, affects are non-subjective circulating flows of asignifying intensity – 'intensity is the unassimilable' – whereas emotions require a subject, and are given 'function and meaning' in a narrative and situational context: 'emotion and affect [. . .] follow different logics and pertain to different orders'.[30]

On the other hand, Rei Terada defends post-structuralism by arguing that, far from being glacially unemotional, 'poststructuralism is *directly* concerned with emotion',[31] since its primary theme – the decentring of subjectivity – is already evident in classical philosophical accounts of emotion. She argues that theorists such as Deleuze have a rhetorical investment in 'fixing the association between emotion and subjectivity', promoting the circular notion 'that subjects express emotions and emotions require subjects' in order to debunk it, when in fact the history of philosophy has repeatedly described emotion as 'non-subjective experience in the form of self-difference within cognition'. For Terada, 'the classical picture of emotion already contraindicates the idea of the subject': 'theories of emotion are always poststructuralist theories'.[32]

Here I wish to sidestep these oppositions between emotion and affect, subjective and non-subjective, discursive and biological, by drawing on the vaguer but also more suggestive term 'feeling', which can simultaneously and seemingly without contradiction evoke both physiological sensation and emotional experience (whether these are consciously registered or not) as well as the problem of the relation between them.[33] This is the approach favoured by theorists such as Sara Ahmed,[34] and in particular Sianne Ngai, whose study *Ugly Feelings* treats the distinction between affect and emotion as 'a modal difference of intensity or degree, rather than a formal difference of quality or kind'.[35] If the tendency of 'affect theorists' such as Massumi and Sedgwick is to insist, in Massumi's phrase, on the 'autonomy of affect', its quality of being 'unassimilable' to discursive, linguistic or psychoanalytic accounts of emotional experience,[36] Ngai sees affects as

> *less* formed and structured than emotions, but not lacking form or structure altogether; *less* 'sociolinguistically fixed', but by no means code-free or meaningless; *less* 'organised in response to our interpretations of situations', but by no means entirely devoid of organisation or diagnostic powers.[37]

Ngai describes *Ugly Feelings* as 'a series of studies in the aesthetics of negative emotions': not the 'vehement passions' of anger and fear – long-privileged topics of philosophical inquiry – but 'minor' and 'unprestigious' feelings such as irritation and envy, paranoia and, significantly, anxiety.[38] Ngai might be seen as taking heed of Sedgwick's and Frank's critique of Ann Cvetkovich's *Mixed Feelings*, where they allege that Cvetkovich deals in abstract terms with a 'reified substance called Affect', where 'there is no theoretical room for any difference between being, say, amused, disgusted, ashamed, and enraged'.[39] Accordingly, Ngai devotes a separate chapter to each of her particular 'ugly feelings', drawing out the ways different feelings are organised and expressed through distinctive spatial models or metaphors, in which the relationships between terms such as subjective and objective, inside and outside, surface and depth become the co-ordinates of a structure or arrangement that produces the distinctive 'tone' of each of these ugly feelings.

Ngai's chapter on 'Anxiety' is of particular interest here, not least because Ngai sees anxiety as having acquired a 'certain epistemological cachet' in Western intellectual history, having 'gradually replaced melancholia as the intellectual's signature sensibility', indeed becoming 'the distinctive "feeling-tone" of intellectual inquiry itself'.[40] Moreover, anxiety has a history of being gendered, not least through the influence of psychoanalysis, where the centrality of the castration complex ensures that 'only male subjects are capable of experiencing genuine anxiety or dread, whereas female subjects are allotted the less traumatic and therefore less profound (certainly more ignoble) affects of nostalgia and envy'.[41]

Indeed, anxiety emerges as a key concept in the existentialist tradition of Western philosophy Beckett seems at pains to distance himself from in the interview quoted above, especially in the work of Kierkegaard and Heidegger, and, although there is no evidence that Beckett had read either of them before August 1936, there are striking similarities between their formulations of anxiety and the ideas expressed in Beckett's German notebook.

In *The Concept of Anxiety*, Kierkegaard explicitly conceives of anxiety as a confrontation with nothingness: 'If we ask more particularly what the object of anxiety is, then the answer [. . .] must be that it is nothing'.[42] For Kierkegaard, this anxiety about nothing is not pathological, 'something that should be taken to the physician and if necessary suppressed with medication', but constitutive of our being in the world, and 'a primary resource for our spiritual education'.[43] It is the state of Adam in the Garden of Eden, aware of God's prohibition against eating the fruit of the Tree of Knowledge, but unable to comprehend it because he knows neither good nor evil nor the meaning of death. Adam's innocence gives rise to anxiety as 'the vague experience of being able and forbidden':[44]

> In this state [innocence] there is peace and repose, but there is simultaneously something else that is not contention and strife, for there is indeed nothing against which to strive. What, then, is it? Nothing. But what effect does nothing have? It begets anxiety. This is the profound secret of innocence, that it is at the same time anxiety.[45]

For Adam, as for humans in general, anxiety is 'the possibility of freedom'.[46] But the future-orientedness of anxiety also conceals its ultimately disempowering function. For if, according to an instrumentalist theory of emotion, emotions 'are closely connected with action',[47] then anxiety is the emotion of withheld action, of freedom experienced as 'entangled freedom, where freedom is not free in itself but entangled, not by necessity, but in itself'.[48]

So too, if emotions are often thought of as broadly categorisable in terms of attraction or repulsion, then anxiety, for Kierkegaard, is paradoxically in tension with itself, a *'sympathetic antipathy* and an *antipathetic sympathy'*:

> Anxiety is a desire for what one fears, a sympathetic antipathy, anxiety is an alien power which grips the individual, and yet one cannot tear himself free from it and does not want to, for one fears, but what he fears he desires. Anxiety makes the individual powerless.[49]

Kierkegaard's notion of anxiety as an ontological ground is taken up by Heidegger:

> When anxiety has subsided, then in our everyday way of talking we are accustomed to say that 'it was really nothing'. [. . .] Everyday discourse tends towards concerning itself with the ready-to-hand and talking about it. That in the face of which anxiety is anxious is nothing ready-to-hand within-the-world. But this 'nothing ready-to-hand', which only our everyday circumspective discourse understands, is not totally nothing. The 'nothing' of readiness-to-hand is grounded in the most primordial 'something' – in the *world*. Ontologically, however, the world belongs essentially to Dasein's Being as Being-in-the-world.

> So if the 'nothing' – that is, the world as such – exhibits itself as that in the face of which one has anxiety, this means that *Being-in-the-world itself is that in the face of which anxiety is anxious.*[50]

Anxiety functions here as a 'basic state-of-mind', a kind of degree-zero emotion that returns as soon as one relaxes one's involvement in the ready-to-hand and glimpses the underlying nothing that is the world as such, a world that 'has the character of completely lacking significance'.[51] For this reason, anxiety represents for Dasein 'one of the most far-reaching and most primordial possibilities of [self-] disclosure', and is thus a necessary precursor to authenticity: 'Anxiety throws Dasein back upon that which it is anxious about – its authentic potentiality-for-Being-in-the-world. Anxiety individualises Dasein for its ownmost Being-in-the-world.'[52] From this perspective, the ambition of psychology to convert indefinite and unmanageable anxiety into a definite and manageable fear must restrain itself at the point where anxiety 'bottoms out' as a condition of existence itself.[53]

Ngai's primary metaphor in her chapter on anxiety is the notion of *projection*, understood in a number of senses. First, given that anxiety is a fundamentally future-oriented emotion, projection clearly refers to the 'temporal dynamics of deferral and anticipation'. But the projection of anxiety has a spatial as well as a temporal aspect, 'as something "projected" onto others in the sense of an outward propulsion or displacement – that is, a quality or feeling the subject refuses to recognise in himself and attempts to locate in another person or thing (usually as a form of naïve or unconscious defense)'.[54] The link between projection and anxiety is central to Ngai's analysis of Hitchcock's *Vertigo*, where the film's fascination with verticality is read as an '"objective correlative" for Scottie's mindset',[55] such that his anxiety manifests itself in the specifically phobic form of a fear of heights. Ngai's argument, developing ideas from Jonathan Lear[56] and Sue Campbell[57], is that 'Scottie's anxiety "comes packaged" with its own logical (spatialized) explanation – it is an affect containing its own "theory" or formative principle'.[58] In other words, the experience of anxiety is produced and shaped by the very mode – projection – by which it is manifested and understood by the subject. The 'objective correlative', far from being an aesthetic formula for the evocation of a particular emotion in a work of art, as it was for T. S. Eliot,[59] becomes in this case a self-reflexive element of the emotion itself. That is, whereas Eliot's theory assumes 'that the expression of a psychological state is an instance of revealing or disclosing that state and is in no way formative of it',[60] Ngai argues that the experience of anxiety is shaped by the 'theory' one has about it and the mode by which it is expressed: '"Projection" in *Vertigo* thus does not designate a subjective operation whereby pre-existing feelings of the subject are displaced onto others, but rather designates the objective mechanism by which the feeling emerges.'[61]

Ngai's analysis is useful in its reading of projection as both constitutive and expressive of the feeling of anxiety. However, in tracing the influence of Beckett's formulation of a fundamentally ontological anxiety, I wish to add a further modification to her model. She notes in passing another spatial metaphor operative in *Vertigo*: 'For [Scottie's] notably anxious mindset could be described equally well in terms of a horizontal oscillation between two sites of feminine self-discontinuity, embodied in the figures of "Madeleine" and Judy.'[62] It is this figure of 'horizontal oscillation' I wish to dwell on here. Despite the main trajectory of Ngai's argument, it is the mode of projection as horizontal oscillation that is, I think, more expressive, more symptomatic of Scottie's anxiety than the film's more explicit vertical mode. The vertical mode lacks, significantly, that element of tension that is perhaps the primary characteristic of anxiety; for vertigo is a fear of something, and in the dysphoria of vertigo one is 'carried' by one's fear towards a course of action: avoidance. Anxiety, on the other hand, as an indefinite fear of nothing in particular, allows no escape through avoidance, just as it impels no specific course of action; it is a tension in which one remains free, but entangled in one's freedom: oscillating, vacillating, powerless to act.

This brings me to the opening of *Molloy*. Much has been made of the doubled quest structure of the novel, where Molloy's quest to reach his mother and Moran's quest to reach Molloy are read as expressive of fundamental drives or desires, or of a divided self embodied in the novel's openness as to whether Molloy and Moran may be in fact two aspects of the same person. What I wish to focus on here, however, are not the journeys but the anxious preludes that precede each character's departure. For Molloy, this revolves around the incident of A and C and occupies about eight pages of his narrative; for Moran, the laborious descriptions of the preparations for his journey take up thirty-six pages, or a little less than half of his narrative. What each of these passages deal with, I shall argue, is a movement that becomes characteristic of Beckett's work from this point on: the horizontal oscillation of anxiety.

In Moran's case, this involves the way he 'shirked the issue'[63] when given the order to find Molloy, and his narrative's restless focus on irrelevant detail is part of a movement of deferral of which Moran himself is only too bitterly aware:

> For in describing this day I am once more he who suffered it, who crammed it full of futile anxious life, with no other purpose than his own stultification and the means of not doing what he had to do. And as then my thoughts would have none of Molloy, so tonight my pen.[64]

Moran's foregrounding of his own anxiety inevitably recalls Ngai's claim that anxiety has become 'the distinctive "feeling-tone" of intellectual inquiry itself'. But if Moran is highly conscious of the objectless oscillation of his anxiety – 'Soon I would have to admit I was anxious'; 'I did nothing but go to and fro' – it is Molloy's prelude I wish to focus on here, and the incident of A and C.[65]

From his vantage point Molloy watches the meeting and subsequent parting of A and C, A returning to the town, C 'on by ways he hardly seemed to know'. Watching C recede, Molloy senses that 'the man was innocent, greatly innocent, he had nothing to fear, though he went in fear, he had nothing to fear'. As with Kierkegaard's Adam, innocence provokes a surge of anxiety:

> It seemed to me he wore a cocked hat. I remember being struck by it, as I wouldn't have been for example by a cap or by a bowler. I watched him recede, overtaken (myself) by his anxiety, at least by an anxiety which was not necessarily his, but of which as it were he partook. Who knows if it wasn't my own anxiety overtaking him.[66]

Molloy's anxiety here is clearly a projection, first as a displacement of his own anxiety on to C, and then as a self-conscious admission that this may be the case. This blurring of the boundary between inside and outside is signalled by the grammatical structure of the phrase, where the adjective 'overtaken' requires the disambiguation of the interpolation 'myself' to distinguish between first and third person, a disambiguation that is absent in the original French.[67] So too, even C's anxiety is not necessarily his own, but may be an external affect, an objective anxiety 'of which as it were he partook'. This blurring of first and third person, in what Molloy later calls 'the long confused emotion which was my life', is signalled in the opening of the scene: 'People pass too, hard to distinguish from yourself.'[68]

This confirms Ngai's observation that in feelings like anxiety 'confusion about feeling's objective or subjective status becomes *inherent* to the feeling'.[69] If the generally accepted distinction between emotion and affect is that 'the former requires a subject while the latter does not',[70] then anxiety hovers anxiously on the borderline between emotion and affect, both indubitably subjective, churning away in the gut, while also suspiciously out-there-in-the-world, a contagious, social emotion that can be 'caught' like a cold.

Molloy's pointed reference to C's hat, at the beginning of the passage quoted above, is significant, foreshadowing a materialisation of the metaphor of projection as horizontal oscillation. For Molloy's hat, as he later informs us, is fastened to the lapel of his greatcoat by a long lace. Later in the novel, when he removes his hat, it becomes just such an oscillating projectile: 'I threw it from me with a careless lavish gesture and back it came, at the end of its string or lace, and after a few throws came to rest against my side.'[71] So too, in the passage that we are concerned with here, he speculates that C's hat is attached 'by means of a string or an elastic'. This movement of projection and recoil is evoked in a startling metaphor when Molloy returns to the subject of C:

> I repeat I watched him recede, at grips (myself) with the temptation to get up and follow him, perhaps even to catch up with him one day, so as to know him better, be myself less lonely. But in spite of my soul's leap out to him, at the end of its elastic, I saw him only darkly, because of the dark and then because of the terrain, in the folds of which he disappeared from time to time, to re-emerge further on, but most of all I think because of other things calling me and towards which too one after the other my soul was straining, wildly.[72]

Here Molloy's anxiety in watching C recede is figured as 'my soul's leap out to him, at the end of its elastic', a horizontal oscillation in which the hat serves as synecdoche for the self, a figure already evident in the novella *The Expelled*, where the narrator's hat stands for an identity confirmed, and indeed conferred by the symbolic order:

When my head had attained I shall not say its definitive but its
maximum dimensions, my father said to me, Come, son, we are going
to buy your hat, as though it had pre-existed from time immemorial
in a pre-established place. He went straight to the hat. I personally
had no say in the matter, nor had the hatter. [. . .] It was forbidden
me, from that day forth, to go out bareheaded, my pretty brown hair
blowing in the wind. Sometimes, in a secluded street, I took it off
and held it in my hand, but trembling. [. . .] When my father died I
could have got rid of this hat, there was nothing more to prevent me,
but not I.[73]

Angela Moorjani suggests that the narrator's hat here functions
as the 'mark of the law of the father', a 'paternal imprint' that is
'indelible'.[74] So too in *Molloy*, Moran, who is so firmly committed to
the patriarchal order, arranges the elastic on his own hat such that
'however great my exertions, my boater stayed in its place, which
was on my head'.[75]

Of course it is possible to read the oscillation of anxiety not as a
fear of nothing, but as a fear, according to the Freudian model, of
a repressed instinct emerging into consciousness;[76] in such terms,
the ambivalence of anxiety is an expression of Kierkegaard's 'sympathetic antipathy', a distressing desire for what one fears and fear
of what one desires. Such indeed is Molloy's emotional response to
C, 'the fellow-convict you long to stop, embrace, suck, suckle and
whom you pass by, with hostile eyes, for fear of his familiarities'.[77]
This extreme ambivalence prefigures Molloy's encounter with the
charcoal burner, 'sick with solitude probably', whom Molloy admits
he 'might have loved [. . .] if I had been seventy years younger', but
whose attempts to keep Molloy near him result in Molloy giving
him a savage beating.[78]

Molloy's anxiety in watching C recede expresses precisely this
entangled freedom: 'I knew I could catch him, lame as I was. I had
only to want to. And yet no, for I did want to'. This wanting which
is a wanting-not-to is apparently ended the following morning by
a peremptory decision: 'But talking of the craving for a fellow let
me observe that having waked between eleven o'clock and midday
[. . .] I resolved to go and see my mother.' The quest narrative that
ensues represents, of course, an end to vacillation and thus a kind
of antidote to anxiety. But even then, in the midst of a journey
sustained by an imperative such that 'I seized with a trembling at
the mere idea of being hindered from going there', Molloy must

confront again the ambivalence of anxiety, the wanting-not-to at the heart of wanting:

> And in this command which faltered, then died, it was hard not to hear the unspoken entreaty, Don't do it Molloy. [. . .] And of myself, all my life, I think I had been going to my mother, with the purpose of establishing our relations on a less precarious footing. And when I was with her, and I often succeeded, I left her again without having done anything. And when I was no longer with her I was again on my way to her, hoping to do better the next time.[79]

Molloy's projected reunion with his mother is not, then, a home-coming, but merely the apogee of an oscillating trajectory, the moment of stillness at the apex of a throw.

This oscillating movement of projection and retraction might recall the famous *fort/da* game from 'Beyond the pleasure principle', where Freud describes watching his grandson playing with a spool of string, throwing the spool away with a cry of *o-o-o-o*, which Freud identifies as the German *fort*, meaning 'gone', and then retrieving it with a joyful *da*, 'here'. Freud speculates that the boy, who was very attached to his mother, was able to master the distressing experience of her departure by repeating it in the form of a game.[80] The child's playful re-enactment of a negative experience leads Freud to posit the notion of a death instinct, 'a compulsion to repeat [. . .] more primitive, more elementary, more instinctual than the pleasure principle which it over-rides'.[81]

However, while acknowledging the importance of the *fort/da* game as a structural element in Beckett's work[82] – indeed Moran himself draws attention to Freud's essay in his quip on 'the fatal pleasure principle' – there are significant differences between the *fort/da* game and the oscillation of anxiety I am concerned with here.[83] Most notably, whereas in the *fort/da* game the subject is fixed, mastering the coming and going of the loved one through projection and retraction of its surrogate, in anxiety it is the subject (or its surrogate) who is in motion, projected back and forth in an oscillation in which the fixed point is precisely the nothing-ness at the heart of anxiety. So too, where in the *fort/da* game the child desires the mother's presence, using the game as a means of coping with her absence, the forces that set the anxious subject in motion are more ambivalent: on the one hand a need to escape the 'utter unfathomableness' of anxiety, and on the other a deeply ambivalent relation to the object, the mingling of fear and desire at the heart of Molloy's 'craving for a fellow'.

The 'nothingness' of anxiety is thus the anchor-point of this oscillation, and the movement itself a means of disclosing a central absence. Beckett's claim 'All I am is feeling' might be seen as a way of saying that feeling (rather than reason, or language) is all there is to subjectivity, and that the ground zero of feeling, for Beckett as for Kierkegaard or Heidegger, is anxiety. Moreover, as a fundamentally projected feeling – a feeling structured by projection on to the outside of an inner tension that may in turn be merely the internalisation of an external affect – anxiety is notably unsuited to forming the basis of a stable subjectivity or a coherent ethical agency. Hence the importance of figures of oscillation in Beckett's later work, from the shuffling of *Footfalls* to the shuttling of *neither*, where the spatial structure of anxiety provides a means for disclosing the nothingness at its core, its 'unspeakable home'.[84] If anxiety endlessly seeks objects through which to convert itself into fear, fear of something as an escape from the unbearable fear of nothing, then the structure and the movement of anxiety must be capable, not of representing that nothingness, which by definition must remain unrepresentable, but of providing a kind of 'objective correlative', eliciting an emotional state in which that nothingness may be felt without being known.

Notes

1 Samuel Beckett, 'Clare St Notebook', Reading University Library MS 5003, 3r–4r. Translation by Mark Nixon from '"What a tourist I must have been": the German diaries of Samuel Beckett' (Ph.D. thesis, University of Reading, 2005), p. 50; emphasis in the original. The original German reads: 'Wie durchsichtig klar kommt mir dieser Mechanismus heute vor, dessen Prinzip heisst: Lieber um Etwas Angst haben, als um Nichts. Im ersten Fall wird nur ein Teil, im zweiten das Ganze bedroht, von dem Ungeheuren, welches zum Wesen des Unbegreiflichen, fast dürfte man des Unbegrenzten sagen, unzertrennlich gehört, nicht zu reden. [. . .] Wenn eine solche Angst zu steigen anfängt, muss ein Grund schleunigst dafür erfunden werden. Da es keinem gegönnt wird, mit ihr in ihrer absoluten Grundlosigkeit leben zu können. So mag der Neurotische, d.h. Jedermann, mit den grössten Ernst u. mit aller Ehrfurcht behaupten, dass zwischen Gott im Himmel u. Schmerz im Bauch der Unterschied bloss minimal ist.

Da beide von einer Quelle herrühren u. zum einen Zweck dienen: Angst in Furcht zu verwandeln.' Nixon, '"What a tourist"', p. 49. I wish to thank here Matthew Feldman and Mark Nixon for their assistance with details concerning Beckett's 'Clare St Notebook' and his readings in psychology. Any errors of fact or interpretation are, necessarily, my own.

2 James Knowlson, *Damned to Fame: The Life of Samuel Beckett* (London: Bloomsbury, 1996), pp.176 and 224.

3 Nixon, '"What a tourist"', p. ii.

4 Anna Wierzbicka, *Emotions across Languages and Cultures: Diversity and Universals* (Cambridge: Cambridge University Press, 1999), p. 123.

5 Martin Heidegger, *Being and Time*, trans. John Macquarie and Edward Robinson (Malden, MA: Blackwell, 2007), p. 227n.

6 This notion of anxiety as a fear without an object is famously challenged by Jacques Lacan, but interestingly through recourse to the notion of the unnameable: 'Look at everything that has ever been written about anxiety, it's always this that is insisted upon – fear has reference to an object, whereas anxiety is said to have no object. I say on the contrary that anxiety is not without an object. [. . .] It's very precisely the [. . .] I am unable to say the name, because, precisely, it's not a name. It's surplus *jouissance*, but it's not nameable, even if it's approximately nameable, translatable, in this way.' Jacques Lacan, *The Seminar of Jacques Lacan, Book XVII: The Other Side of Psychoanalysis*, trans. Russell Grigg (New York: Norton, 2007), p.147.

7 Stanley Rachman, *Anxiety* (Hove: Psychology Press, 1998), pp. 2–3 and 7.

8 Rachman, *Anxiety*, p. 7.

9 *Ibid.*

10 Matthew Feldman, *Beckett's Books: A Cultural History of Samuel Beckett's 'Interwar Notes'* (New York: Continuum, 2006), p. 96.

11 Sigmund Freud, *The Interpretation of Dreams*, trans. James Strachey (Harmondsworth: Penguin, 1982), p. 526n.

12 Sigmund Freud, *Inhibitions, Symptoms and Anxiety*, trans. Alix Strachey (London: Hogarth Press, 1948), pp. 131–6.

13 Samuel Beckett, *Dream of Fair to Middling Women* (London: Calder, 1993), p. 133.

14 Knowlson, *Damned to Fame*, p. 177.

15 Feldman, *Beckett's Books*, p. 113. See also John Pilling, *Beckett Before Godot* (Cambridge: Cambridge University Press, 1997) and Daniela Caselli, *Beckett's Dantes: Intertextuality in the Fiction and Criticism* (Manchester: Manchester University Press, 2005).

16 Samuel Beckett, *Disjecta: Miscellaneous Writings and a Dramatic Fragment*, ed. Ruby Cohn (London: Calder, 1983), p.172.

17 Samuel Beckett, *Proust and Three Dialogues with Georges Duthuit* (London: Calder, 1965), p. 103; Samuel Beckett, *Watt* (New York: Grove, 1953), p. 247.

18 Samuel Beckett, *Disjecta*, p. 113. 'Naught is more real . . .' alludes to Democritus of Abdera, as quoted in *Murphy*: 'Nothing, than which in the guffaw of the Abderite, naught is more real'. Samuel Beckett, *Murphy* (London: Picador, 1973), p. 138. 'Ubi nihil velis . . .' alludes to the 'beautiful Belgo-Latin of Arnold Geulincx: *Ubi nihil vales, ibi nihil velis*'. See again Beckett, *Murphy*, p. 101: 'Where you are worth nothing, there you should want nothing'. See also Shane Weller Chapter 6 above and his *A Taste for the Negative: Beckett and Nihilism* (Oxford: Legenda, 2005).

19 Knowlson, *Damned to Fame*, p. 222.

20 Samuel Beckett to Thomas MacGreevy, 18 October 1932, quoted in Knowlson, *Damned to Fame*, p. 222. See also Martha Dow Fehsenfeld and Lois More Overbeck (eds), *The Letters of Samuel Beckett: 1929–1940* (Cambridge: Cambridge University Press, 2009), p. 134, and Laura Salisbury, Chapter 12 below.

21 Gabriel D'Aubarède [1961], 'Interview with Samuel Beckett', in Lawrence Graver and Raymond Federman (eds), *Samuel Beckett: The Critical Heritage* (London: Routledge & Kegan Paul, 1979), p. 217.

22 Samuel Beckett, *Trilogy: Molloy, Malone Dies, and The Unnamable* (London: Calder, 1994), p. 10.

23 Nicholas Allen, 'Review of Paul Stewart's *Zone of Evaporation: Samuel Beckett's Disjunctions*', *Modern Fiction Studies*, 54:2 (2008), 445.

24 Ulrika Maude, 'Centennial Beckett: the gray canon and the fusion of horizons', *Modernism/Modernity*, 15:1 (2008), 180.

25 Rei Terada, *Feeling in Theory: Emotion after the 'Death of the Subject'* (Cambridge, MA: Harvard University Press, 2001), p. 4.

26 Eve Kosofsky Sedgwick and Adam Frank, 'Shame in the cybernetic fold: reading Silvan Tomkins', in Eve Kosofsky Sedgwick, *Touching Feeling: Affect, Pedagogy, Performativity* (Durham, NC: Duke University Press, 2003), pp. 93–4.

27 *Ibid.*, pp. 94 and 109.

28 Eve Kosofsky Sedgwick, 'Introduction', in *Touching Feeling*, p. 20.

29 Sedgwick, 'Introduction', pp. 21 and 20.

30 Brian Massumi, 'The autonomy of affect', in *Parables for the Virtual: Movement, Affect, Sensation* (Durham, NC: Duke University Press, 2002), pp. 28 and 27.

31 Terada, *Feeling in Theory*, p. 3.

32 *Ibid.*, pp. 7 and 3.

33 The subject of affect in Beckett's work is treated at length in *Samuel Beckett Today / Aujourd'hui: L'Affect dans l'oeuvre Beckettienne*, eds

Yann Mével and Michèle Touret, 10 (2000). However, the majority of these essays employ psychoanalytic methodologies, and are primarily concerned with the discursive, and especially linguistic, construction of subjectivity. The approach I am sketching out here, through focusing on the spatial metaphor of horizontal oscillation, seeks to understand affect primarily through a corporeal rather than a linguistic mode.

34 See especially Sara Ahmed, *The Cultural Politics of Emotion* (New York: Routledge, 2004), p. 40, n. 4.

35 Sianne Ngai, *Ugly Feelings* (Cambridge, MA: Harvard University Press, 2005), p. 27.

36 See Clare Hemmings, 'Invoking affect: cultural theory and the ontological turn', *Cultural Studies*, 19:5 (2005), 565.

37 Ngai, *Ugly Feelings*, p. 27.

38 *Ibid.*, pp. 1 and 6.

39 Sedgwick and Frank, 'Shame', pp. 111 and 110.

40 Ngai, *Ugly Feelings*, pp. 213–15.

41 *Ibid*, p. 213.

42 Søren Kierkegaard, *The Concept of Anxiety: A Simple Psychologically Orienting Deliberation on the Dogmatic Issue of Hereditary Sin*, ed. and trans. Reidar Thomte and Albert B. Anderson (Princeton: Princeton University Press, 1980), p. 96.

43 Gordon D. Marino, 'Anxiety in *The Concept of Anxiety*', in Alastair Hannay and Gordon D. Marino (eds), *The Cambridge Companion to Kierkegaard* (Cambridge: Cambridge University Press, 1998), p. 309.

44 Marino, 'Anxiety', p. 317.

45 Kierkegaard, *The Concept of Anxiety*, p. 41.

46 *Ibid.*, p. 155.

47 Martha Nussbaum, *Upheavals of Thought: The Intelligence of Emotions* (Cambridge: Cambridge University Press, 2001), p. 135.

48 Kierkegaard, *The Concept of Anxiety*, p. 49.

49 Søren Kierkegaard, *Søren Kierkegaard's Journals and Papers*, I–VII, ed. and trans. Howard V. Hong and Edna H. Hong (Bloomington: Indiana University Press, 1967), I: 42 and 39; quoted in Marino, 'Anxiety', p. 321.

50 Heidegger, *Being and Time*, pp. 231–2.

51 *Ibid.*, pp. 227 and 231.

52 *Ibid.*, pp. 226 and 232.

53 It is worth noting that Lacan, though he rejects the notion of anxiety as 'without an object', nevertheless insists on it as 'the central affect, the one around which everything is organised'. Lacan, *The Other Side*, p. 144. Indeed Lacan's *Seminar X* is dedicated entirely to anxiety, bearing the French title *L'Angoisse*.

54 Ngai, *Ugly Feelings*, p. 210.

55 *Ibid.*, p. 216.

56 Jonathan Lear, *Love and Its Place in Nature: A Philosophical Interpretation of Freudian Psychoanalysis* (New York: Farrar, Strauss and Giroux, 1990).

57 Sue Campbell, *Interpreting the Personal: Expression and the Formation of Feelings* (Ithaca, NY: Cornell University Press, 1997).

58 Ngai, *Ugly Feelings*, p. 222.

59 'The only way of expressing emotion in the form of art is by finding an "objective correlative"; in other words, a set of objects, a situation, a chain of events which shall be the formula of that *particular* emotion; such that when the external facts, which must terminate in sensory experience, are given, the emotion is immediately evoked'. T. S. Eliot, *The Sacred Wood: Essays on Poetry and Criticism* (London: Methuen, 1960), p. 100.

60 Campbell, *Interpreting the Personal*, p. 52.

61 Ngai, *Ugly Feelings*, p. 221.

62 *Ibid.*, p. 226

63 Samuel Beckett, *Trilogy: Molloy, Malone Dies, The Unnamable* (London: Calder, 1994), p. 132.

64 Beckett, *Molloy*, p. 122.

65 *Ibid.*, pp. 97 and 98.

66 *Ibid.*, pp. 9, 10–11.

67 Beckett, *Molloy* (Paris: Les Éditions de Minuit, 1951), p. 13.

68 Beckett, *Molloy*, pp. 25 and 9.

69 Ngai, *Ugly Feelings*, p. 19.

70 *Ibid.*, p. 24.

71 Beckett, *Molloy*, pp. 14 and 61.

72 Beckett, *Molloy*, pp. 14 and 11.

73 Samuel Beckett, *The Complete Short Prose, 1929–1989*, ed. S. E. Gontarski (New York: Grove, 1995), p. 48.

74 Angela Moorjani, *Abysmal Games in the Novels of Samuel Beckett* (Chapel Hill: University of North Carolina Press, 1982), pp. 109 and 110.

75 Beckett, *Molloy*, p. 127.

76 For Freud, 'phobias have the character of a projection in that they replace an internal, instinctual danger by an external, perceptual one'. By locating the object of fear in an external object, the subject can avoid that object, thus 'enabl[ing] the ego to cease producing anxiety': 'One cannot get rid of a father; he can appear whenever he chooses. But if he is replaced by an animal all one has to do is to avoid the sight of it [. . .] in order to be free from danger and anxiety'. Freud, *Inhibitions*, pp. 85–6.

77 Beckett, *Molloy*, p. 12.

78 *Ibid.*, pp. 83–4.

79 *Ibid.*, pp. 13, 16 and 87.

80 Sigmund Freud, 'Beyond the pleasure principle', trans. James Strachey, in *On Metapsychology: The Theory of Psychoanalysis*, Penguin Freud Library, vol. 11 (Harmondsworth: Penguin, 1991), pp. 284–7.

81 Freud, 'Beyond', p. 294.

82 Moorjani's *Abysmal Games* uses the structure of repetition-as-play as a key concept in an illuminating reading of Beckett's novels.

83 Beckett, *Molloy*, p. 99.

84 Beckett, *neither*, in *Complete Short Prose*, p. 258.

12

'Something or nothing': Beckett and the matter of language

Laura Salisbury

In 1981, Lawrence Shainberg sent Samuel Beckett a copy of his book about neurosurgery hoping it might be of interest. To Shainberg's surprise, Beckett replied almost straight away, and in their subsequent meetings, the younger author continued to be intrigued by Beckett's enthusiastic and particularised questions about the work of the brain surgeon:

> Whenever I saw him, he questioned me about neurosurgery, asking, for example, exactly how close I had stood to the brain while observing surgery, or how much pain a craniotomy entailed, or, one day during lunch at rehearsals: 'How is the skull removed?' and 'Where do they put the skull bone while they're working inside?'[1]

Perhaps this was nothing more than the curiosity of the interested amateur. Beckett's questions are given a particular resonance, however, because he went on to articulate to Shainberg an explicit connection between what we might term a metaphorics of the craniotomy and his own writing practice. In his written response to Shainberg's book, Beckett firmly stated: 'I have long believed that here in the end is the writer's best chance, gazing into the synaptic chasm'.[2]

If this was indeed a lasting belief, it might be productive to speculate on just how long Beckett had held the notion that it is within the brain, within the cleft between chemical synapses – those specialised junctions between which neuro-transmitters pass in order that the cells of the nervous system might signal to each other – that the writer's best chance may lie. For once one begins to look for it, it seems as though Beckett's fascination with the space inside the skull and the strangely materialised, perhaps even neurological, conception of language to be found there, can be traced as far back as the work of the 1930s. What lies behind textual images of the hard surface of the skull in Beckett's work is, of course, in the end, nothing but words – linguistic matter that describes cranial interiorities, wounded heads and a way of uttering traced through with lesions and disturbances. But there is a strange translation at work, here, a shuttling back and forth, in which language shapes the imagined appearance of a compulsively cranial space, but does so through an aesthetic seemingly bound to forms of signification scored through by an awareness of their emergence from a fraily material brain.

From that gap between the synapses that is peculiarly produc-tive and yet so easily disturbed, from this space which may indeed be no-thing but forms a connection (etymologically, *syn* 'together', *haptein* 'to clasp'), a space of emergence for language appears that is much more than a straightforward absence. One reason why it is suggestive that the later Beckett, so famously attracted to ideas of negation, silence, pause, should be specifically drawn to the functioning of the synapse and the cleft between neurons is that, within accounts of neurological function, the synaptic void is not any simple kind of 'nothing', despite having no material substance. When coining the term in 1897, Charles Sherrington was seeking to overturn the notion that nerve impulses pass from one excit-able cell to another in the brain through a continuously connected network of fibres.[3] He proposed instead a gap that enables chemi-cal neuro-transmitters to create particular conditions in the adja-cent neuronal receptors, increasing the likelihood that electrical impulses will be triggered in that neuron. So this gap, whilst being insubstantial, is the very condition for the production of message and information, for the emergence of all that 'something' of which the human subject experiences itself to be made. This is a gap that is the space of matter's translation into something that seems to transcend, to matter, more than the material.

The notion of a productive void that functions as the ground for signification and is to be found in the interstices of material pres-ence is, I will argue, central to Beckett's aesthetic. For although it is true that Beckett's work is persistently fascinated by the idea of silence and absence expressed in words, images and configurations of bodies and objects, it is plain that there can be no 'nothing' that would count as the 'work', except those shapes constructed and displaced by the material that is present. This is saying more than the obvious – that Beckett's oeuvre is made up of the texts that we have, the words printed or uttered and the bodies and objects presented on stage, rather than some imagined and ideal condition of silence to which his work is taken sometimes to point. It is saying that Beckett's work seems peculiarly concerned with using the material frame of what *is* there in the texts to determine and construct gaps, elisions and silences which become strangely porous; presence seems everywhere to be leaking into them, making them fecund, teeming with signification. For these are signifying voids in which information is constantly being exchanged between presence and absence; they are voids invaded by and replete with the conditions for the production of meaning rather than hermetically sealed spaces of nothing.

The argument here, though, is that this articulation of a peculiarly embodied and materially productive void that underpins the emergence of language and thought, does not itself come from nowhere – from the immateriality of Beckett's singular genius. Instead, it suggests that the 'synaptic chasm' illuminates something revealingly specific about an idea of language and signification experienced as issuing from a void that is the buzzing condition for a connection. For the synaptic chasm is a very particular kind of nothing that can be placed within a set of historical intellectual conditions in which language, cognition, and the subjectivities they subtend, are reconfigured as products of fundamentally material processes taking place in the nervous system. Returned to such a context, it is perhaps no surprise that Beckett's obsession with naggingly and sometimes abjectly fecund material voids, should undertake complex transactions with the work of signification seen to emerge from the interior of the cranium – a material brain figured as leaking language. Beckett finds within the cranium both a space for imagining writing and subjectivity nailed to a peculiar and estranging materiality, and a way of conceiving of linguistic signification as emergent from historically determined notions of the 'unseen vicissitudes' by which matter is translated into meaning.[4]

Skullscapes and deadheads

Beckett's late work is relatively well-known for its fascination with the interiority of the skullscape. Bound to scenes abstracted from recognisable geography and all but the most meagre particulars, a number of short prose texts written in the 1960s describe strangely cranial spaces. In *Imagination Dead Imagine*, bodies are confined within the space that compulsively imagines them. This space is described as a 'white rotunda', but its walls may in fact be more cranial than architectural, for they 'ring as in imagination the ring of bone'.[5] It is perhaps more than felicitous idiom that gathers *D'un ouvrage abandonné*, *Imagination morte imaginez*, *Bing* and *Assez*, in which the subject's memories obdurately persist as 'gleams in my skull',[6] into a collection published in 1967 in French as *Têtes-mortes*, or dead heads. But it is clear that this interest in the space inside the skull and its openings on to the world – 'that inner space one never sees, the brain and heart and other caverns where thought and feeling dance their sabbath' as *Molloy* has it –[7] can be traced further back into Beckett's work. C. J. Ackerley and S. E. Gontarski find the architecture of the cranium to be of sufficient significance across the oeuvre to offer up a section of their *Companion to Beckett* entitled 'skull'.[8] They note, amongst numerous examples, that in *Malone Dies* it seems to the narrator that he has become brain, he is 'in a head and [. . .] these eight, no, six, these six planes that enclose me are of solid bone',[9] whilst one of the Unnamable's 'vice existers'[10] similarly seeks comfort by imagining itself 'surrounded on all sides by massive bone'.[11]

This bone that might become a shield, impermeable to the exteriority of 'another's thoughts, lacerating my sky with harmless fires and noises signifying nothing',[12] seems to register the desire for the skull to be a last refuge ('crâne abri dernier').[13] A fantasy indeed appears in *The Unnamable* that the head and its interior could become a kind of kernel, something solid and essential – 'Yes, a head, but solid, solid bone, and you embedded in it, like a fossil in the rock.'[14] There is perhaps a hope that there might be a stable speaking subject to be found in this solid thinking head, something that is sufficiently substantial to bring the textual speculation to an end. But if this is so, there is a need to 'bung' up the 'streaming sockets' of the 'vice exister' so that it becomes 'round, solid and round [. . .] no asperities, no apertures'.[15] Of course, this is a vain hope: nothing ever does quite appear as itself in this text. Instead, little breaths of oxygen seep into the sealed space and the displacing and paradoxical effects of a morbidly aspirant language are produced: 'Air, air, I'll seek air, air in time, the air of time, and in space, in my head, that's how I'll go on.[16] The dilemma of being able to say the something of 'I' or nothing at all is a 'high class nut to crack',[17] and indeed it is precisely the cracking of the nut, the penetration of the cranium, of going deeper and further inside, that seems intuitively to get one nearer to a kernel of a graspable and stable subjectivity. But the opened skull only offers more language, and more information passing in and out, as internal material becomes frighteningly extended. Getting inside the head does not open up a smooth empty space, a cavern containing nothing on to whose walls immaterial shadows might be projected, although neither is it solid and substantial; rather, the head is bulging with matter. The policeman's skull penetrated in *Mercier and Camier* (begun in 1946) makes and takes an 'impression' precisely because of its abject materiality, the gelid firmness of the brain exposed '[l]ike a partly shelled hard-boiled egg'.[18] The perpetually refigured skulls in *The Unnamable* similarly refuse to be solid bowls – the casing for an empty space where imagination can play itself out in solitary joy –; instead, the cranium is pierced and the holes in it are 'streaming', reflexively oozing tears of 'liquified brain',[19] as they become sites of translation concerned with imbibing impressions and releasing torrents of language over which intention has only a tenuous hold.

Belacqua, in *Dream of Fair to Middling Women* (1931–32), speaks of the same desire to experience the mind as a curtained retreat:

> The mind, dim and hushed like a sick-room, like a chapelle ardente, thronged with shades; the mind at last its own asylum, disinterested, indifferent [. . .]; the mind suddenly reprieved, ceasing to be an annex of the restless body, the glare of understanding switched off. The lids of the aching mind close, there is suddenly gloom in the mind; not sleep, not yet, nor dream, with its sweats and terrors, but a waking ultra-cerebral obscurity.[20]

But this '[l]imbo from which the mistral of desire has been withdrawn', this 'tunnel, when the mind went wombtomb' cannot be sustained.[21] Sight and sound percolate and perforate through orifices in the cranium, disrupting the peace of its solipsism. And by the time of the *Trilogy*, the purity of the mind imagined as a monad no longer convinces; instead, mind is, as often as not, replaced and displaced by brain and body. The space inside the head is no longer self-sufficient, a windowless retreat, relieved of all engagement with exteriority. The head is, instead, a perforated container of recalcitrant substance, drinking in impressions and reflexively streaming language in ways that determinedly denude the text of a neatly intending or immaterial mind that could close its own curtains on the world.

Head wounds

In one sense it is hardly surprising that the *Trilogy*, so concerned with the vicissitudes of language and its relationship to the subject's sense of itself, should remain fascinated by the head and what it might mean to get inside it. For Beckett is writing in a historical period relatively newly certain that difficulties of cognition and language, alongside the concomitant torsions of subjectivity, could be localised in the materiality of the head, and even within particular areas of the brain. In *Dream*, a fine and rhythmic rhyme indeed appears that riffs on the fact that it is the brain rather than the soul, or even the mind, that is penetrated in the talking cure: here, it is 'a thalamus that by day folds up for psycho-analysis'.[22] As I have suggested elsewhere, Beckett's work indeed seems fascinated by language pathology and the distortions of expression, memory, cognition and mentation that bear useful comparison to the neurological dysfunctions that constellate in the symptom of aphasia.[23] There is certainly a sense that Beckett is writing in the wake of conceptions of language function rendered newly material and housed within the skull. After the 1860s debate all but ceased in medical discourse as to whether language was produced and represented within the materiality of the brain; discussion focused instead upon precisely how the relationship between physiology and function was to be theorised and modelled.[24] The faculty of language that had in the eighteenth and early nineteenth century been most commonly associated with the immaterial part of human nature, the unextended soul, was transfigured to appear as something that arose according to analysable anatomico-physiological conditions – conditions that were all too easily displaced and transformed by disease or wounding.

Although the idea of the cerebrum as the material home of language and the major proportion of higher mental functioning became something of a given in the twentieth century, Beckett was also aware of specific material on brain function through his reading of R. S. Woodworth's *Contemporary Schools of Psychology* in 1934–35. Beckett took down notes from Woodworth on the neurologist S. I. Franz (1874–1933), who worked to map 'sensory and motor areas of cortex, [and] studie[d] localization of higher functions'.[25] He might also have learnt that a golden age for work on the localisation of higher brain function in the 1920s was precipitated by a clear historical event. Woodworth asserts that the 'World War, with its numerous bullet and shrapnel wounds affecting small circumscribed spots of the cortex, gave abundant opportunity for testing these conclusions',[26] as a factory production line of relatively discrete head wounds allowed disabilities to be mapped on to the cortex from observable sites of penetration. War had thus produced the empirical testing of the relation between brain wound and symptom that it had not been possible to pre-cipitate experimentally in humans. Sixty years before the occlu-sions of the cranium would be dissolved by functional magnetic resonance imaging, it was penetrating head trauma that effected 'natural' experiments in the wounding of language; it was head trauma that enabled the shapes and distortions of a resolutely material language, and its concomitantly displaced subjectivity, to be observed.

So it is more than simply suggestive that Beckett's work accom-panies its experiments with estranged language and subjectivity with persistent images of penetrating the skull, that locked box of bone beneath the skin. In the late prose and poetry the skull is a reasonably smooth boundary, encasing an interior that is the textual home for experimentation; bone is something into which a neat hole can be bored by the narrator with surgical precision in order to anatomise what is inside. In the rotunda of *Imagination Dead Imagine*, for example, in which there is 'No way in', there is nevertheless the compulsion to 'go in, measure',[27] to delimit the contours of that something inside, and view and stage the interior machinations of perception, representation and affectivity. But the cranium in the *Trilogy* and the work that precedes it does not yield so easily to clean penetration. The surgical precision required to perform a craniotomy and to peer into the functioning of the living brain seems aesthetically unavailable; instead, as Woodworth notes of the wartime neurologist's gaze, getting into the living head can be effected only by a more thoroughgoing violence.

In *Malone Dies* one of the most striking assertions made by the narrator is that he might be living in a 'kind of coma'. He seems vaguely to recall some of events of the earlier *Molloy* and wonders whether 'I was stunned by a blow, on the head, in a forest perhaps.'[28] The 'creature', reminiscent of Molloy, that Malone invents as a protagonist for his stories also wears a hat that is 'as hard as iron, superbly domed above its narrow guttered rim, [. . .] marred by a wide crack or rent extending in front from the crown down and intended probably to facilitate the introduction of the skull'.[29] For Lemuel, the homicidal figure who tends the disabled and indigent Malone, self-inflicted head-trauma actually has its comforts: 'the part he struck most readily, with his hammer, was the head [. . .] for it too is a bony part, and sensitive, and difficult to miss, and the seat of all the shit and misery, so you rain blows upon it, with more pleasure than on the leg for example, which never did you any harm, it's only human'.[30] It is the cranium, then, the newly determined 'seat of all the shit and misery', that persistently becomes the site of Beckett's experimental wounding. Of course, Beckett's characters need more injuries like they need holes in the head: skull trauma is just one more entry in the catalogue of wounds, disabilities and decrepitudes they are forced to endure and perhaps even enjoy. The repetition of violent skull trauma in Beckett's texts of this period is particularly significant, however, because the effects of penetrating head wounds are also articulated. These works indeed seem to play out, through textual experimentation, the deficits of articulation, cognition and perception that can be read according to the neurological damage that a penetrating head wound might inflict. And within that symptom, although language and the subjectivity it subtends are disabled and reshaped, they are, significantly, never reduced to nothing.

Aphasia can be defined, somewhat unsatisfactorily, as a 'loss of speech, partial or total, or loss of power to understand written or spoken language, as a result of disorder of the cerebral speech centres' (*OED*). The emphasis on loss, the reduction of areas of linguistic ability to nothing, in this definition accords with the aphasiology of a classical localisationist such as Carl Wernicke. In the 1870s, Wernicke produced models and diagrams that reconstructed language as a process of purely mechanical communication of sensory-motor units along 'association fibres' in the brain. Damage was thus synonymous with negation: 'If certain letters are missing in the apparatus, specific errors would be consistently repeated in the message'.[31] But the complexity of the symptom of aphasia, which did not, in fact, submit itself placidly to Wernicke's mapping of determinedly localised lesions on to relatively predictable symptoms, began to demand more complex accounts of the emergence of language than the simple firing of punctate areas of the cortex. For the aphasic symptom, as the dictionary definition implies, very rarely results in the complete wordlessness one would expect if there were a wholly localisable speech centre. John Hughlings Jackson was the first to emphasise in 1897 that aphasia is not a disorder that manifests silence or wordlessness; it is, instead, a form of propositional speechlessness, with emotional (the more automatic) language being preserved where there is a loss of intellectual (the more voluntary) qualities of speech.[32] The neurologist Kurt Goldstein, who worked primarily with soldiers in the aftermath of the First World War, notes approvingly that it was Jackson who emphasised that aphasic speech was disturbed and displaced rather than absent: 'The patients have not lost words, but the words are not available for the higher service of propositional expressions, i.e., for some special purpose of the individual. Aphasia, for Jackson, is one expression of a defect of basic mental function, similar to what I later called abstract attitude.'[33]

Although Goldstein is not mentioned by Woodworth, *Contemporary Schools of Psychology* demonstrates a profound intellectual sympathy with the German clinician's position, derived from Gestalt psychology, that the brain is not a fleshly typewriter whose keys may be broken to produce specific and repeatable errors in the message. Woodworth implies that particular areas of the cortex do not fire according to the push and pull of reflex arcs, as classical aphasiologists such as Wernicke had thought; instead, the brain 'functions in wide-spreading patterns or dynamic systems and not in sharply localized centres'.[34] Indeed, Woodworth asserts that the brain works, as Beckett notes down, through a '[p]rinciple of equipotentiality – any part of the cortex (exclusive to motor and sensory areas) potentially the same as any other in its ability to participate in an sort of learned performance [. . .] the cortex acts as a whole'.[35] For Goldstein, this explains the complexity of the aphasic symptom, as the brain produces displacements that are 'positive', linked to a reorientation of function, rather than simple records of loss and negation.

Gestalt psychology attempted to reconfigure the classical,

mechanistic conception of the brain/mind relation by demonstrating empirically, using the apparatus of psychophysics and experimental psychology, that lived reality was not produced according
to the random generation, perception and subsequent ordering of
meaningless elements in a mechanically associating brain. Instead,
the human mind was constructed according to a latent orientation
of function towards the perception of patterns of order. Goldstein
translated this notion into a theory of neurological function, noting
from his observation and treatment of wounded soldiers that the
underlying and universal disturbance in all brain injury was a
defect in the ability to perceive pattern and meaning, Gestalts,
from a background sea of phenomena – a defect in the 'figure
ground function'.[36] Language use, if it was non-pathological, was
similarly orientated towards the perception and categorisation of
Gestalts: 'A word becomes meaningful from the context in which
it appears; the meaning of a thought is conditioned by a vast contextual background.'[37] But brain-damaged language is born from 'a
general levelling or intermingling of figures and background' which
leads inexorably to an impairment of the 'abstract attitude'.[38] What
is damaged in the aphasic symptom is precisely language's ability
to function in a predictably intentional, purposive fashion – to
affirm what counts as something and what can recede into the
background as nothing substantial.

As a number of critics have suggested, Beckett's explicit and
parodic use of Gestalt psychology's fascination with the 'figure-
ground' problem can be found in *Murphy*.[39] In his Woodworth
notes, Beckett transcribes the Gestaltist position: 'Nature runs to
<u>organized</u> wholes [. . .] The figure stands out naturally from the
ground in virtue of the fundamental distinction between them'.[40]
But in *Murphy*, this 'natural' relationship has become disturbed:
'[n]o sooner had Miss Dwyer [. . .] made Neary as happy as a man
could desire, than she became one with the ground against which
she had figured so prettily. Neary wrote to Herr Kurt Koffka [a
Gestalt psychologist mentioned by Woodworth and associated with
Goldstein] demanding an explanation. He had not yet received an
answer.'[41] Instead of an answer that could emerge from language
working according to an 'abstract attitude', figure and ground
convert into one another, mirroring the disorganisation of brain
damage. Like those articulating brains bored into by the bullets of
the First World War, or the subjects of penetrating head wounds

in which Beckett's *Trilogy* delights, the language towards which Beckett begins to gesture in the 1930s is not one that is transcended in or as silence; instead, it is language written to its material limit. Stable signification reveals itself to be a figure that is only ever contingently separated from the noise and nonsense of sounds and signifiers which are language's Ur-condition and into which it threatens to merge. So although 'divine aphasia' is the phrase used by Lucky in *Waiting for Godot* to describe God's incommunicativeness, this 'personal God quaquaquaqua with white beard quaquaquaqua' does not appear in an immaculate silence in which language is transcended;[42] instead, the divine Word is garbled, rendered as an unintelligible quacking, a noisy 'quaquaqua' in which message and noise cannot be fully distinguished. Lucky's very mode of expression is in fact closer to certain configurations of aphasic language than any silence would be. For, disarticulated from the 'abstract attitude', the measure and seeming intentional transparency of 'normal' language use, Lucky stutters rather than reduces words to nothing, stammering 'the skull the skull the skull the skull in Connemara'.[43]

Boring Beckett

In 1937 Beckett wrote to Axel Kaun what is often taken to be his most explicit theoretical statement about language:

> And more and more my own language appears to me like a veil that must be torn apart in order to get at the things (or the Nothingness) behind it [. . .] As we cannot eliminate language all at once, we should at least leave nothing undone that might contribute to its falling into disrepute. To bore one hole after another into it, until what lurks behind it – be it something or nothing – begins to seep through; I cannot imagine a higher goal for a writer today. Or is literature alone to remain behind in the old lazy ways that have so long ago been abandoned by music and painting? Is there something paralysingly holy in the vicious nature of the word that is not found in the elements of the other arts? Is there any reason why that terrible materiality of the word surface should not be capable of being dissolved, like for example the sound surface, torn by enormous pauses, of Beethoven's seventh Symphony, so that through whole pages we can perceive nothing but a path of sounds suspended in giddy heights, linking unfathomable abysses of silence?[44]

Beckett seems, at first glance, to be following Stéphane Mallarmé's sense of the imperfection of language, which, in its current condition, can be matched in univocal harmony neither with the 'things' nor perhaps the 'Nothingness' (the more suspicious Beckett insists), to which signs point.[45] In 'Crisis in poetry' Mallarmé speaks of a necessary 'fluttering of the temple's veil – meaningful folds and even a little tearing',[46] and the creation of a signifying fissure in the fabric of language to which Beckett's letter seems clearly to allude. But where Mallarmé finds reparation and 'atonement' 'for the sins of language' in tearing the veil,[47] in the rhythmic penetration and disruption of the sound surface in such a way as to allow a glimpse of revelation, Beckett's letter insists that all it can do is console itself with '*sinning* willy-nilly against a foreign language' (my emphasis),[48] insisting upon the compulsive and involuntary (this sinning is 'unwillkürlich')[49] poking of a tongue into the tender cavities of words to explore and widen their gaps and crannies.

So Beckett moves beyond Mallarmé's metaphor of rending the veil of language to 'bor[ing] one hole after another into it',[50] which seems more like an acknowledgement of an obdurately 'vicious' and 'terrible materiality' than its transcendence – the suggestion of the possibility of revelation. For both Mallarmé and Beckett, the metaphor of the veil is redolent of Christian conceptions of the Word made flesh, as appears it in Hebrews 10.20. Christ offers 'a new and living way, which he hath consecrated for us, through the veil, that is to say, his flesh', with the crucifixion representing both a tearing apart of the veil of corporeality and a rupturing of the orthodoxy of the Temple as the only conduit to God: 'the veil of the temple was rent in twain from the top to the bottom' (Matthew 27.51). Beckett's insistence on boring holes into the paralysing holiness of language, whilst cleaving to the elision of word and flesh, is decidedly untranscendent, however; it seems more suggestive of sexual penetration, which would accord with the metaphorics of desire that runs throughout the text and Beckett's insistence that his language must throw off the outdated modesty of 'the Victorian bathing suit'.[51] But if such metaphors return us to the space of language's embodiment, perhaps it is not too tendentious to suggest that the instrument used to bore holes into the word made flesh need not simply be bound to sexual desire and penetration, but might be related to other modes of piercing the flesh and exploring the body's interiority.

There is nothing in the letter that specifically links the 'terrible materiality of the word surface' into which holes must be bored to the brain and its containing cranium; nevertheless, as we have seen, if language is material, in this period the head becomes its most obvious home. One could argue, then, that the Beckett who had subjected his own skull to penetration under the psychotherapy of Wilfred Bion only two years previously might be reconfiguring his linguistic method not through analytical structures but as a kind of textual trepanning in which disarticulated language becomes both the instrument and effect of an experimental head wound. Etymologically linked to the action of 'boring' (derived from the Greek *trypanon*), trepanning is metaphorically suggestive for Beckett's textual experiments because it evokes the creation of a new cranial orifice of perception and expression through which something other than the normative self might form itself and speak. Accounts of trepanning tend to concur that although it is performed for a variety of medical and mystical purposes, its underlying aim is to create a new aperture in the skull because the given ways in and out of the cranium are somehow insufficient either to let something out – be it pus, pressure, vapours, spirits – or to let something in – air, inspiration or the gods.[52] The most clear textual link between Beckett's writing and a form of ritual trepanning is to be found in Beckett's transcription of a practice undertaken by Tibetan lamas in his *Whoroscope Notebook* in the early 1930s. Beckett notes:

> 'hik!' followed by 'phat'
> spiritual ejaculations whereby the spirit of the dying leaves the body by hole in skull (very important), pronounced by lamas, or by dying man himself, if he has the leisure.
> Suicide by hik! phat![53]

The source is uncertain, but could be Alexandra David-Neel's *Magic and Mystery in Tibet*, published first in French in 1929, which details that '*hik!*', '*Phat!*' 'is the ritualistic cry that the officiating lama shouts beside a man who has just died, in order to free the "spirit" and cause it to leave the body through a hole that this magic syllable opens in the summit of the skull'.[54] She goes on to state, as does Beckett in more ironic terms, that if these sounds are uttered by the lama without the presence of a dying person, the lama himself will effect a precipitate and deadly separation of spirit and body. Language itself becomes the trepan, then, a 'magic syllable' that can bore a hole through the materiality of the skull in a suggestive convertibility of instrument and effect.[55]

If the boring of holes is framed in terms of skull trauma, the German letter seems to be using words as an instrument of penetration to create a new orifice that mouths and forces the emergence of a profoundly un-normative language – a language which, in turn, persists in piercing and distorting itself, bringing itself into disrepute. The hole bored in the word surface, like the orifice torn into the blank blackness of the theatre in *Not I*, streams a language denuded of much of its securely intending, propositional qualities. Of course, Mouth's organ and utterances are possessed of an excessive materiality and presence that has no truck with silence. On a closer reading, however, what appears through the newly made holes in the German letter is not muteness but the whisper of a peculiarly Beckettian form of silence that is characterised as sound rather than its negation, something rather than nothing. More akin to propositional speechlessness, as Hughlings Jackson might have had it, rather than wordlessness, this 'silence' is audible, articulating itself as a murmur, the '*whisper* of that final music *or* silence that underlies All' (emphasis mine);[56] it is a kind of detuned signification in which the muttering interference of the unsorted, the unintended, the involuntary, can be heard. Beckett equivocates, wondering whether what seeps through after boring a hole into language really is 'something or nothing'. This hesitation is everything. For what emerges from a pierced language that becomes both an instrument and its wounded effect is a 'literature of the unword' in which it is precisely what counts as something and what as nothing, what is figure and what is the ground, that cannot finally be determined.

The work of the abscess

In a letter to Mary Manning written two days after the one to Kaun, Beckett repeats that one must sin against the putative holiness of language. Again, the aim is not that language should be dematerialised but that its embodied materiality could be strained so that its occluded substance would begin to extrude. 'I am starting a Logoclasts league', he writes to Manning, 'I am the only member at present. The idea is ruptured writing, so that the void may protrude, like a hernia.'[57] From strain and a little tearing of the surface of words there will be a protrusion of tissue, or an organ, through the fabric of the muscle or membrane that is supposed to contain it. To imagine a void linked to language as a hernia suggests an urging, unwilled, probing presence rather than absence and, by association, a remarkably embodied and substantial form of nothing. In terms of the persistent emphasis on the materiality of words, it becomes revealing to read Beckett's insistence on a linguistic hole, alongside the hernia that pokes through it, as part of the system that Evelyne Grossman describes as an aesthetic of the abscess that preoccupies Beckett in the 1930s.[58] Suffering from cysts, boils, herpes, and lancing his own infected finger with a needle and razor blade,[59] Beckett indeed returns repeatedly in this period to a vision of language bound to the swellings of the abject and to an eventual dehiscence in which the surface of the artwork is ruptured and something bursts forth from behind. This void from which language appears, like the synaptic chasm, is not an arid absence; here it takes the shape of a teeming, oozing fecundity. Mercier asks Camier, 'how is your cyst?'; the reply is '[d]ormant [. . .] but under the surface mischief is brewing'.[60]

In 1932, however, the abscess seems to stand for another kind of anxiety that is precisely the obverse of the unwilled accumulation of abject material imaged in the shape of a hernia. Beckett writes to MacGreevy, complaining that his unsuccessful work seems forced, overly-willed; his writing is 'all frigged up, in terram, faute d'orifice [for want of an orifice] [. . .] – the work of the abscess', instead of having the involuntary 'integrity of the eyelids coming down before the brain knows there is grit in the wind'.[61] Here, then, the abscess is associated with masturbation; it is 'frigged up',[62] emerging as a strangely embodied form of intentionality bound to a frotted self-involvement. Physiologically, the work of the abscess is the body's creation of a cavity in its tissue, which it then fills with its own materials, with pus, in order to encase an infection and control its spread. According to its etymology, '(*abs* away + *cede-ere* to go), to move away, to lose contact' (*OED*), the abscess and its cavity are part of an embodied process of holding things apart; so it is perhaps appropriate that it should be aligned in Beckett's formulation with masturbation and a momentary refusal to meet with otherness. In this work there is not yet an orifice of emission that would enable the boil to be lanced and a passage between interiority and exteriority to be formed.

Beckett's own boils and cysts, alongside the tortured relationship with his mother, had led him to psychotherapist Wilfred Bion in 1934. And, writing many years later in 1957, it is Bion who offers up a model that associates a form of psychological 'encysting' with a refusal of the outside world and the exteriority of otherness. Bion suggests that there is a tendency for psychotic parts of the personality to split themselves and the world into autistic and persecutory islands of experience: 'the psychotic splits his objects [the people and objects with which he interacts and exists], and contemporaneously all that part of his personality, which would make him aware of the reality he hates, into exceedingly minute fragments'. Using the Kleinian concept of projective identification – an omnipotent phantasy that one is able to split off temporarily undesired, though sometimes valued, parts of the psyche and put them into an object – he continues: 'consciousness of sense impressions, attention, memory, judgement, thought, have brought against them [. . .] the sadistic splitting eviscerating attacks that lead to their being minutely fragmented and then expelled from the personality to penetrate, or encyst, objects'.[63] For Bion, projective identification should exist in tandem with an introjective activity, in which experience of the external world can be taken back into the self to allow the formation of good internal objects. But in the excessive projective identification of the psychotic state, '[t]he object, angered at being engulfed, swells up, so to speak, and suffuses and controls the piece of personality that engulfs it' (48). As such, the object cannot be taken back into the mind and integrated with it, although neither can it remain safely encysted.

In 'Attacks on linking' (1959), Bion describes how it is language itself that is often the subject of such splitting attacks, owing to its capacity to effect cognitive and symbolic links and integrations between areas of the mind that were seemingly cleanly dissociated.[64] Such a model of the encysted mind and the work of the abscess as an attack on linking is suggestive for reading the fantasy of the monad in Beckett's early work, in which, as we have seen, 'the mind at last its own asylum' hopes to insist, safe from contamination. The letter from 1932 of course suggests a desire that pulls in the other direction. There is hope for an artwork written 'above an abscess and not out of a cavity',[65] a poetry that would refuse the omnipotence of the purely voluntary denuded of any external contact. It is significant, though, that another version of the abscess and the cyst keeps festering in Beckett's texts of the 1930s, and in this model the idea of art and language as an infected lump no longer stands just for the encystic elements of the voluntary in which linking is attacked. For the assault on language in the German letter is indeed not simply an attempt to keep things in their own containers; instead, the violent attack on words through words that Beckett imagines leads to a penetration of something that seems redolent of an abscess, as the perforation of language as flesh – the epidermal veil – leads to the creation of a new expressive orifice and a linguistic leaking, an involuntary oozing. As the veil is punctured, the voluntary work of the abscess cedes authority to an unwilled dehiscence. Of course, in Bion's model, it is precisely the attack on linking that, whilst hoping safely to encyst, brews up mischief, bad objects that will threaten to burst forth and engulf the mind. In Beckett's German letter, the attack on language also punctures the abscess, causing a hole in its material fabric that allows inside to ooze into outside as the interiority of the cavity becomes topologically continuous with the surface of the skin. In imaging language as both containing skin and dehiscent pus, produced and seeping from a teeming void, Beckett reveals the frightening and involuntary fecundity within words, figured according to their ability to couple, connect and contaminate.

The word 'dehiscence', or the opening of a pod at maturity, that Beckett copied into his *Dream Notebook* from Pierre Garnier's *Onanisme seul et à deux* (1894), appears in *Dream* in relation to the production of the aesthetic. The narrator invokes the 'the dehiscing, the dynamic décousu [unstitchedness], of a Rembrandt' that threatens to invade the surface of the art as a 'disfaction, a désuni, an Ungebund, a flottement, a tremblement, a tremor, a tremolo, a disaggregating, a disintegrating, efflorescence, a breaking down and multiplication of tissue, the corrosive ground-swell of Art'.[66] In opposition to an art that is intentionally stitched into an impermeable container, the involuntary urging of the hernia or a dehiscence appears in which material pushes from behind the surface of language, rupturing its limits. The narrator goes on to speak of Beethoven's work in *Dream* as something which takes musical punctuation, spacing and pause, back to its etymological root in the punctum, the bringing to a point. Here, punctuation becomes a piercing in which all begins to come unstitched, rather than a mode of suture:

> [Beethoven] incorporates a punctuation of dehiscence, flottements,
> the coherence gone to pieces, the continuity bitched to hell because
> the units of continuity have abdicated their unity, they have gone
> multiple, they fall apart, the notes fly about, a blizzard of electrons;
> and then vespertine compositions eaten away with terrible silences,
> [. . .] pitted with dire stroms of silence [. . .] And I think of the
> ultimately unprevisible atom come asunder.[67]

This seems at first glance to be a repetition of the earlier notion
of an 'incoherent continuum as expressed by, say, Rimbaud and
Beethoven [. . .] whose audibilities are no more than punctuation
in a statement of silences'.[68] But what is significant here is that
punctuation or pauses are, at one moment, the 'stroms of silence'
between the phrases as they might appear in music or spoken language, and at another the articulation of 'audibilities', the presence
of a punctuation mark.

For Belacqua, the distinction between punctuation as presence
and absence, something and nothing, becomes lost as the book's
'whole fabric come[s] unstitched, [. . .] The music comes to pieces.
The notes fly about all over the place, a cyclone of electrons.'[69] This is
art subject to dehiscence, the very opposite of a textual monad; it is
pierced, leaking signification in and out, so that what becomes figure
and what remains ground is blurred and dispersed in a material swell
of signifying marks and phenomena. Earlier, the narrator speaks of
the night sky as, first of all, a metaphor for the absolute transcendence of art: 'The night firmament is abstract density of music, symphony without end, illumination without end.' But in this vision
any blackness, or complete illumination, is soon compromised by
observations of intermittence – the 'crazy stippling of stars'.[70] Again,
involuntary states are lauded as part of the capacity to burrow away
from the involuted 'work of the abscess', the cystic work of a particular kind of thought that attacks the wild disorganisation of language
as 'blizzard' or 'cyclone' – language as an unbounded linking:

> The tense passional intelligence, when arithmetic abates, tunnels,
> skymole, surely and blindly (if only we thought so!) [. . .] in a
> network of loci that will never be co-ordinate. The inviolable crite-
> rion of poetry and music, the non-principle of their punctuation, is
> figured in the demented perforation of the night colander.[71]

The narrator insists, though, that the process by which such
art might be made is no longer a process of 'going wombtomb',

retreating inwards into the quarantined and curtained 'sick room'
of the intending mind; instead, the drapes find themselves being
ripped apart, the windows of the subjective and textual monad
are punched through towards exteriority: 'The mind suddenly
entombed, then active in an anger and a rhapsody of energy, in a
scurrying and plunging towards exitus, such is the ultimate mode
and factor of the creative integrity, its proton, incommunicable.'[72]
It is this 'scurrying and plunging towards exitus' which produces a
particular kind of text in which an 'insistent, invisible rat, fidgeting
behind the astral incoherence of the art surface' can make its way
out – tunnelling 'skymole' rather than 'wombtomb'. Art appears as
something within which a writhing life, drawn from images of sup-
purating fecundity, swells in its frame, its container, bursts forth
and is lanced, and then swells again.

When Beckett returns to Beethoven in the German letter, to 'the
sound surface, torn by enormous pauses, so that through whole
pages we can perceive nothing but a path of sounds suspended in
giddy heights, linking unfathomable abysses of silence',[73] the very
fact that pause and silence emerge from a peculiarly embodied
act of boring, in which both presence and absence become leaky
vessels, is suggestive of a conception of language and artwork as
'demented colanders' rather than impermeable containers. Beckett
goes on to call for the longed-for formation of a 'Literatur des
Unworts';[74] and his turn to a neologism, or *Unwort*, is revealing
because of its particular attitude to negation. Literature and words
are not transcended in the turn to the 'unword'; rather, the word
surface is perforated. This does not announce the appearance of
something completely other; instead, as with a hernia, something
from within extrudes and is displaced from its proper shape,
marking the very contingency of normative syntactical and lexical
forms. Gilles Deleuze suggests in 'He stuttered' that the symptom
manifested in Beckett's language is indeed a straining of the grammatical limit. Beckett's language proceeds according to 'inclusive
disjunctions', Deleuze affirms, as the different lexical and syntactical possibilities that are the creative conditions from which any
singular utterance appears are folded back into the texture of the
message rather than excluded or rendered redundant – as nothing.
He states: 'Every word is divided, but into itself [. . .]; and every
word is combined, but with itself [. . .] Beckett took this art of inclusive disjunctions to its highest point, an art that no longer selects

but affirms the disjointed terms through their distance, without limiting one by the other or excluding one from the other.'[75] It certainly seems that the unwordly quality of the 'unword' comes from the peculiar agrammaticality of an 'inclusive disjunction' (in German as in English).[76] For 'un' can be used as a prefix to negate verbs, adjectives or adverbs, but not nouns. The 'un' pushes the noun into disequilibrium, makes it do and describe an action of negation; it thus forms a nagging presence rather than announces the transformation of something into nothing – word become nonword. The 'un' adds rather than subtracts; it adds action and quality, and takes something of the 'ground' of the material noise and redundancy that should be excluded if the word is to function in a clearly intentional, singular fashion, back into the distorted shape of the figure.

In 'The exhausted', Deleuze writes that the signature of Beckett's words is their ability to 'pierce themselves and turn against themselves so as to reveal their own outside',[77] as he reaffirms, in a refrain from 'He stuttered', that to 'strain' utterance and writing in this way is to 'push language as a whole to its limit, to its outside, to its silence – this would be like the *boom* and the *crash*'.[78] The void protruding like a hernia through words so strained, or the pierced and penetrated cyst bursting so that the cavity is exposed and what seems like interiority seeps out to become one with the surface of the skin, suggests an illegitimate topology in which inside and outside leak into one another. And what emerges from language figured in these terms is a new work of the abscess. This work, though anxious about its legitimacy, begins to undo the attack on linking that marks the putative outside of language – that definitive sorting of something from nothing – to render a sense of words as emergent from the abjectly productive groundswell, from the urging and uncontainable noise that aphasiology began to hear as part of the Ur-condition of language that shapes itself in a fragile material brain. Such noise in the German letter offers up precisely that paradoxical 'silence' that nevertheless whispers, a silence that, in Deleuze's initially illogical terms, 'would be like the *boom* and the *crash*'. So in the letter to Axel Kaun of 1937, Beckett's language states its aim: to render audible within words the condition of noise in which something *and* nothing seep into one another, and to pierce the abscess, the 'frigged up' cavity of the voluntary. By returning words to their commerce with the automatic, to their propensity to proceed according to the non-propositional and through sets of teeming and fertile links, what would normally be figured as the outside of language shows itself to have been immanent all along. It only takes a piercing of the head or a disreputable straining of the word for it to whisper its way back in.

Notes

1 Lawrence Shainberg, 'Exorcising Beckett', *Paris Review*, 104 (1987), 102.
2 *Ibid.*, 102.
3 Don Todman, 'Synapse', *European Neurology*, 61 (2009), 190–1.
4 Beckett noted down the phrase 'unseen vicissitudes of matter' in his *Whoroscope* Notebook. Reading University Library MS 3000/84.
5 Samuel Beckett, *The Complete Short Prose 1929–1989* (New York: Grove Press, 1995), p. 182.
6 *Ibid.*, p. 187.
7 Samuel Beckett, *Trilogy: Molloy, Malone Dies, The Unnamable* (London: John Calder, 1994), p. 10.
8 C. J. Ackerley and S. E. Gontarski, *The Grove Companion to Beckett* (New York: Grove, 2004), pp. 530–1.
9 Beckett, *Trilogy*, p. 222.
10 *Ibid.*, p. 317.
11 *Ibid.*, p. 350.
12 *Ibid.*, p. 350.
13 Samuel Beckett, *Poems: 1930–1989* (London: Calder Publications, 2002), p. 62.
14 Beckett, *Trilogy*, pp. 396–7.
15 *Ibid.*, p. 307.
16 *Ibid.*, p. 397.
17 *Ibid.*, p. 314.
18 Beckett, *Mercier and Camier* (London: John Calder, 1974), p. 93.
19 Beckett, *Trilogy*, p. 269.
20 Samuel Beckett, *Dream of Fair to Middling Women* (London: John Calder, 1996), p. 44.
21 *Ibid.*, p. 45.
22 *Ibid.*, p. 149.
23 See Laura Salisbury, '"What is the Word": Beckett's aphasic modernism', *Journal of Beckett Studies*, 17 (2008), 78–126.
24 For an account of this see Laura Salisbury, 'Sounds of silence: aphasiology and the subject of modernity', in Laura Salisbury and Andrew Shail (eds), *Neurology and Modernity* (Basingstoke: Palgrave, 2009).
25 Trinity College Dublin 10971/7/10.

26 Robert S. Woodworth, *Contemporary Schools of Psychology* (London: Methuen, 1931), p. 90.
27 Beckett, *Complete Short Prose*, p. 182.
28 Beckett, *Trilogy*, p. 184.
29 Beckett, *Trilogy*, p. 229. The holograph notebook of *Malone meurt* also contains a doodle of a head with what appears to be a small hatchet or hammer embedded in it.
30 Beckett, *Trilogy*, p. 269.
31 Carl Wernicke, 'The motor speech path and the relation of aphasia to anarthia' (1884), in Gertrude H Eggert (ed.), *Wernicke's Works on Aphasia: A Sourcebook and Review* (The Hague: Mouten, 1977), pp. 152–3.
32 John Hughlings Jackson, 'On affections of speech from disease of the brain' (1897), in Paul Eling (ed.), *Reader in the History of Aphasia* (Amsterdam: John Benjamins, 1994), p. 152.
33 Kurt Goldstein, *Language and Language Disturbances* (New York: Grune and Stratton, 1948), p. 22.
34 Woodworth, *Contemporary Schools*, pp. 92–3.
35 Trinity College Dublin 10971/7/10.
36 Goldstein, *Language*, p. 5.
37 *ibid.*, p. 5.
38 *ibid.*, p. 5.
39 See, in particular, C. J. Ackerley, *Demented Particulars: The Annotated Murphy* (Tallahassee: Journal of Beckett Studies Books, 2004), p. 37.
40 Trinity College Dublin MS 10971/7/12.
41 Samuel Beckett, *Murphy* (London: Picador, 1973), p. 31.
42 Samuel Beckett, *The Complete Dramatic Works* (London: Faber & Faber, 1990), p. 42.
43 *ibid.*, p. 43.
44 Beckett, *Disjecta*, pp. 171–2.
45 John Pilling notes that Beckett seems to be alluding to Mallarmé in the letter, although he does not make the reference explicit. John Pilling, *Beckett Before Godot* (Cambridge: Cambridge University Press, 1997), p. 153.
46 Stéphane Mallarmé, *Mallarmé: Selected Prose Poems, Essays, and Letters*, trans. Bradford Cook (Baltimore: Johns Hopkins Press, 1956), p. 34.
47 Mallarmé, *Selected*, p. 38.
48 Beckett, *Disjecta*, p. 173.
49 *ibid.*, p. 54.
50 *ibid.*, p. 172.
51 *ibid.*, p. 171.

52 See Edward L. Margetts, 'Trepanation of the skull by the medicine men of primitive cultures, with particular reference to present-day East African practice', in Donald R. Brothwell and A. T. Sandison (eds), *Diseases in Antiquity*, (Springfield: Charles C. Thomas, 1967), pp. 673–701.

53 Reading University Library MS 3000/78.

54 Alexandra David-Neel, *Magic and Mystery in Tibet* (Escondido: Book Tree, 2000), p. 14.

55 David-Neel notes that it is known that a lama has achieved the capacity to perform this feat when, after shouting '*hik!*', 'a straw stuck in the skull stands up straight for as long as desired' p. 14.

56 Beckett, *Disjecta*, p. 172.

57 Samuel Beckett to Mary Manning, 11 July 1937, Harry Ransom Humanities Research Center, University of Texas at Austin, Box 8, Folder 10. Quoted in Martha Fehsenfeld and Lois More Overbeck (eds), *The Letters of Samuel Beckett 1929–1940* (Cambridge: Cambridge University Press, 2009), p. 521.

58 Evelyne Grossman, *L'Esthetique de Beckett* (Liège: SEDES, 1998), pp. 37–40.

59 James Knowlson, *Damned to Fame: The Life of Samuel Beckett* (London: Bloomsbury, 1996), p. 241.

60 Beckett, *Mercier and Camier*, p. 30

61 Samuel Beckett to Thomas MacGreevy, 18 October 1932. Fehsenfeld and Overbeck, *Letters*, pp. 134–5.

62 It seems more likely that this word is 'frigged' rather than Fehsenfeld and Overbeck's 'trigged'. 'Frigged' is not only less arcane, it works as the obverse of the desired aesthetic of spontaneous ejaculation referred to in the same paragraph as 'the integrity of a pendu's [hanged man's] emission of semen'. John Pilling has also suggested to me that Fehsenfeld and Overbeck's 'in terrain' should read 'in terram'.

63 Wilfred Bion, 'Differentiation of the psychotic from the non-psychotic personalities', in *Second Thoughts* (London: Karnac, 1984), p. 47.

64 Wilfred Bion, 'Attacks on linking', in *Second Thoughts*, p. 94.

65 Fehsenfeld and Overbeck, *Letters*, p. 134.

66 Beckett, *Dream*, pp. 138–9.

67 *ibid.*, p. 139.

68 *ibid.*, p. 102.

69 *ibid.*, p. 113.

70 *ibid.*, p. 16.

71 *ibid.*, p. 16.

72 *ibid.*, pp. 16–17.

73 Beckett, *Disjecta*, p. 172.

74 *ibid.*, p. 173.

75 Gilles Deleuze, 'He stuttered', in *Essays Critical and Clinical*, trans. Daniel W. Smith and Michael A. Greco (London: Verso, 1998), pp. 110–11.

76 The exception which perhaps proves the rule would be neologisms like the uncanny (*das Unheimlich*) or the undead, both of which seem to take something of their spooky quality precisely from the grammatical violation. On the uncanny, see also Thomson, Chapter 4 above.

77 Deleuze, 'The exhausted', *Essays*, p. 173.

78 Deleuze, 'He stuttered', *Essays*, p. 113.

Coda:
The no-thing that knows no name and the Beckett envelope, blissfully reconsidered

Enoch Brater

I love talking about nothing. It is the only thing I know anything
about. (Oscar Wilde, *An Ideal Husband*)

In July 1974, when Maurice Beebe planned to edit a special number
of the *Journal of Modern Literature* to interrogate (as we *didn't* say
at the time) a sea change that was taking place in the cultural landscape all around us, he already knew that such a consideration was
long overdue. 'From modernism to post-modernism', as the 200-
page issue of *JML* was called, served as an early and modest and
now mostly forgotten contribution to an academic discussion that
was to have major repercussions in the decades to come. Thirteen
years later Linda Hutcheon published her landmark study, *A
Poetics of Postmodernism: History, Theory, Fiction*, soon followed
in 1991 by Fredric Jameson's provocative and influential response
entitled *Postmodernism: The Cultural Logic of Late Capitalism*. At
about the same time Marjorie Perloff and others began to wonder
whether one could effectively talk about 'postmodern genres',
while Deborah Geis speculated on the specifically theatrical potential of 'postmodern theatric[k]s' in contemporary American drama.
Somewhat later, critics like H. Porter Abbott would centre this
discussion on Beckett. Could his work be properly situated in the
broad and less contentious context of 'late modernism'? Richard
Begam went even further, describing how Beckett's fiction anticipates many of the defining themes and ideas of Barthes, Foucault
and Derrida in moving us toward 'the end of modernity'.[1]

By contrast, Beebe's authors were far more tentative in the
approaches they pursued, though it should be noted here that
they were equally concerned, albeit in embryonic form, with the

interrelated questions of aesthetics, Marxism, literary form and culture – though in this case it is probably fair to say that theirs was more observation than critique. Looking back on the period when these accomplished essays were written in the early 1970s seems like a glance at a lost innocence, soon to be characterised as nothing short of critical naivety; for the special issue appeared in print in the fleeting moment just before literary theory took over English departments with a vengeance. Translators from the French were working overtime. Modernism, ill-defined, and postmodernism, even more so – the latter term continues its vexed reign, this despite the consolations derived from those ambitious studies cited above – was a tempting though still ambiguous borderline for the *JML* authors, centring their attention as they did on an uncontested canonical space of 'primary' texts: Eliot, Pound, Williams, Wyndham Lewis, Lawrence and Gertrude Stein loom large. 'The remarks that follow', Beebe wrote cautiously in his introduction, 'are therefore intended to be more suggestive than definitive'.[2]

My own contribution to the volume was a short piece that served, as this one does, as the final entry but not the final word on an intellectual dilemma that was at best both playful and profound. 'The empty can: Samuel Beckett and Andy Warhol', composed soon after completing my Ph.D. during the time when I was still trying to figure out how *not* to write about this most formidable of Irish playwrights, ended, *pace* Cleanth Brooks,[3] like this:

> The well-wrought urn may have indeed become the empty can, but in the transformational historical process this anxiety between object and audience has become a terrifying metaphor for the anxiety the world imposes on us as we approach the final quarter of twentieth-century aesthetics.[4]

Shades of Harold Rosenberg, self-quotation notwithstanding. In his 1964 study, *The Anxious Object: Art Today and Its Audience*, Rosenberg made a persuasive case for an unenviable condition Beckett had earlier problematized in his novel *Watt*: 'But what was this pursuit of meaning, in this indifference to meaning? And to what did it tend? These are delicate questions.'[5] A Beckett play – *Endgame*, for example – and a series of Warhol silkscreens, both filled with alarming and mysterious suggestion, might be seen as objects 'anxious' for a definition nowhere to be found. In terms of audience reception, nothing might indeed be more *sur*-real than nothing.

The 1970s was also an important decade for a change – nothing less than a paradigm shift – that was swiftly taking place in Beckett's creative activity. His late style for the theatre achieved a startling new dimension with Jessica Tandy's performance of *Not I* at Lincoln Center in New York in 1972. This was followed a few months later by Billie Whitelaw's legendary interpretation at the Royal Court in London (this well-known version was shot in close-up sharp focus and broadcast on the BBC as part of a program called 'Shades' in 1976). Beckett had written a remarkable play about a mouth in conflict with a stubborn pronoun, first-person, then – even more terrifying, '. . . she . . . SHE! . . .'. Other body parts were soon on display. Beckett's next play, *That Time*, featured a disembodied head in a work the playwright himself character-ised as the 'brother to *Not I*.[6] The play was produced in 1976 on a double bill, also at the Royal Court Theatre, with an even more enigmatic piece, *Footfalls*. In the second of the play's three related movements, an offstage voice intones fragments of a story that seem to objectify the haunting soundscape we encounter on stage as a female figure paces back and forth:

> I say the floor here, now bare, this strip of floor, once was carpeted, a deep pile. Till one night, while still little more than a child, she called her mother and said, Mother, this is not enough. The mother: Not enough? May – the child's given name – May: Not enough. The mother: What do you mean, May, not enough? May: I mean, Mother, that I must hear the feet, however faint they fall. The mother: The motion alone is not enough? May: No, Mother, the motion alone is not enough, I must hear the feet, however faint they fall.[7]

In the next section the shrouded figure, '*chime a little fainter still*', narrates her own 'semblance' of a highly charged but none the less compromised back-story:

> Mrs W: You yourself observed nothing . . . strange? Amy: No, Mother, I myself did not, to put it mildly. Mrs W: What do you mean Amy, to put it mildly, what can you possibly mean, Amy, to put it mildly? Amy: I mean, Mother, that to say I observed nothing . . . strange is indeed to put it mildly. For I observed nothing, of any kind, strange or otherwise. I saw nothing, heard nothing, of any kind. I was not there. Mrs W: Not there? Amy: Not there.[8]

Beckett's short prose published in the same period, written in an eccentric 'grammar for being elsewhere',[9] was in some ways even more elliptical – and nothing if not downright 'strange'. It was difficult to tell at the time whether these short pieces were discrete works of their own, works in progress, or fragments of some larger opus yet to emerge, re: Joyce. Several were composed in the mid-1960s. *Lessness*, the author's dynamic translation of French *Sans*, was printed on a single page of the *New Statesman* on 1 May 1970. Its 120 sentences are in reality only 60, each one organized into six statement groups containing a mere ten. Each of the two 'orders' is assigned a different paragraph structure, the whole arranged in '2 × 12 = 24 paragraphs'. *Make sense who may.* Beckett said he handwrote each of the 60 sentences on a separate piece of paper, mixed them all in a container, then drew them out in random order twice.[10]

With so many parallels to Dada composition, echoes of James Joyce, and resonances to the 'midget grammar' of Gertrude Stein,[11] it has always been difficult to know where to place Beckett on the great modernist/postmodernist divide. Somewhere beyond minimalism, his work explores the vast terrain that separates nothing from nothingness, and both from the far more intriguing *nothing in particular*. How can 'worsening words', Beckett's literary métier, be structured, repositioned and retooled so that they 'enclose' – embrace really – something as contagious and all-encompassing as:

> this this –
> this this here –
> all this this here –[12]

In the early 1970s 'The empty can' proposed looking elsewhere, outside of literature perhaps, for the appropriate artistic climate of spontaneity that seemed so central to Beckett's relentless 'work-in-regress'.[13]

Undaunted by such considerations, as well as several others, Beebe mailed a copy of the journal to Beckett. A few weeks later he called to say that an airmail letter addressed to me c/o the *Journal of Modern Literature*, Temple University, Philadelphia, had just arrived at his office, posted from Paris. But there was something odd about this: what he held in his hand was only an empty envelope, *nothing* enclosed. Perhaps, he offered, a letter had slipped out? Interesting: I asked if the envelope looked as though it had

9 The empty envelope sent by Beckett to Brater

been sealed. Apparently not. Did I want it sent to me anyway? I told the journal editor to dispatch it sans delay.

The Beckett envelope arrived by fast-mail the very next day. I recognised the ironic hand behind the handwriting immediately. The void never looked quite so promising before, especially so for a young scholar who was beginning to find his way through so much 'mental thuggee'. *A pox on void.*[14]

Such was my first contact with Samuel Beckett: nothingness enclosed indeed. Yet what the receipt of his non-correspondence

10 The empty envelope sent by Beckett to Brater

makes clear, finally, is something much more substantial and ful-
filling than the provenance of some empty can: fashions of critical
definition come and go, yet the encounter with Beckett's magnifi-
cent void, 'that MINE', is still out there somewhere waiting for his
Reader, as for his Listener – somehow, 'nohow',[15] always already
not there.

Notes

1 For discussions of modernist and postmodernist perspectives, see Linda Hutcheon, *A Poetics of Postmodernism: History, Theory, Fiction* (London: Routledge, 1987); Fredric Jameson, *Postmodernism: The Cultural Logic of Late Capitalism* (Durham, NC: Duke University Press, 1991); Marjorie Perloff, ed., *Postmodern Genres* (Norman: University of Oklahoma Press, 1988); Deborah R. Geis, *Postmodern Theatric[k]s: Monologue in Contemporary American Drama* (Ann Arbor: University of Michigan Press, 1993); H. Porter Abbott, 'Late modernism: Samuel Beckett and the art of the oeuvre,' in Enoch Brater and Ruby Cohn (eds), *Around the Absurd: Essays on Modern and Postmodern Drama* (Ann Arbor: University of Michigan Press, 1990), pp. 75–96; and Richard Begam, *Samuel Beckett and the End of Modernity* (Stanford: Stanford University Press, 1996).

2 Maurice Beebe, 'What modernism was', *Journal of Modern Literature*, 3:5 (July 1974), 1065–84, p. 1065.

3 Cleanth Brooks, *The Well Wrought Urn: Studies in the Structure of Poetry* (New York: Harcourt, Brace and World, 1947).

4 Enoch Brater, 'The empty can: Samuel Beckett and Andy Warhol', *Journal of Modern Literature* (July 1974), 1255–64.

5 See Harold Rosenberg, *The Anxious Object: Art Today and Its Audience* (New York: Horizon, 1964); and Samuel Beckett, *Watt* (New York: Grove Press, 1959), p. 75.

6 Quoted by Enoch Brater in *Why Beckett* (London: Thames & Hudson, 1989), p. 110.

7 Samuel Beckett, *Footfalls*, in *The Collected Shorter Plays of Samuel Beckett* (New York: Grove Press, 1984), p. 241.

8 *Ibid.*, p. 243.

9 H. Porter Abbott, 'A Grammar for being elsewhere', *Journal of Modern Literature* (February 1977), 39–46.

10 Enoch Brater, *The Drama in the Text: Beckett's Late Fiction* (New York: Oxford University Press, 1994), pp. 93–4; and Samuel Beckett, *What Where*, in *Collected Shorter Plays*, p. 316.

11 See Susan D. Brienza, *Samuel Beckett's New Worlds: Style in Metafiction* (Norman: University of Oklahoma Press, 1987), p. 88.

12 Samuel Beckett, *Worstward Ho* (New York; Grove Press, 1983), pp. 28–9; and 'what is the word', in *As the Story Was Told: Uncollected and Late Prose* (London: John Calder, 1990), p. 132. For 'nothingness / in words enclose', see the Addenda to *Watt*, p. 247.

13 Beckett used the phrase 'work in regress' on a postcard addressed to Ruby Cohn on 14 December 1971. Since the early 1970s there have been a number of useful studies linking Beckett's work to the

non-literary arts. See in particular Lois Oppenheim, *The Painted Word: Samuel Beckett's Dialogue with Art* (Ann Arbor: University of Michigan Press, 2000); Mary Bryden (ed.), *Samuel Beckett and Music* (Oxford: Oxford University Press, 1998); and Lois Oppenheim (ed.), *Samuel Beckett and the Arts: Music, Visual Arts, and Non-print Media* (New York: Garland, 1999).

14 Samuel Beckett, *Eh Joe* in *Collected Shorter Plays*, p. 203; and *Worstward Ho*, p. 43.

15 Samuel Beckett, . . . *but the clouds* . . . and *Ohio Impromptu*, in *Collected Shorter Plays*, pp. 261 and 285; and *Worstward Ho*, p. 47.

Bibliography

Samuel Beckett

Works in English

As the Story Was Told: Uncollected and Late Prose (London: John Calder, 1999).

The Beckett Trilogy: Molloy, Malone Dies, The Unnamable (London: Picador, 1979).

Cascando and Other Short Dramatic Pieces (New York: Grove Press, 1968).

Collected Poems in English and French (London: John Calder, 1977, 1986).

Collected Poems in English and French (New York: Grove Press, 1977).

Collected Poems in English and French (London: John Calder, 1977, 1986).

Collected Shorter Plays (London: Faber & Faber, 1984).

Company, Ill Seen Ill Said, Worstward Ho (London: John Calder, 1992).

The Complete Dramatic Works (London: Faber & Faber, 1986, 1990, 2006).

The Complete Short Prose 1929–1989, ed. S. E. Gontarski (New York: Grove Press, 1986).

Disjecta: Miscellaneous Writings and a Dramatic Fragment, ed. Ruby Cohn (London: John Calder, 1983).

Disjecta: Miscellaneous Writings and a Dramatic Fragment, ed. Ruby Cohn (New York: Grove Press, 1984).

Dream of Fair to Middling Women, ed. Eoin O'Brien and Edith Fournier (Dublin: Black Cat, 1992).

Dream of Fair to Middling Women (London: John Calder, 1995, 1996).

Eh Joe and Other Writings (London: Faber & Faber, 1966).

The Expelled and Other Novellas (Harmondsworth: Penguin, 1980).

Film (New York: Grove Press, 1969).
Ill Seen Ill Said (London: John Calder, 1982).
Mercier and Camier (London: John Calder, 1974).
Murphy (London: George Routledge & Sons, 1938).
Murphy (London: Picador, 1973).
No Author Better Served: The Correspondence of Samuel Beckett and Alan Schneider, ed. Maurice Harmon (London: Harvard University Press, 1998).
No's Knife (London: Calder and Boyars, 1967).
Proust and Three Dialogues with Georges Dathuit (London: Calder & Boyars, [1955] 1970).
Stories and Texts for Nothing (New York: Grove Press, 1967).
The Theatrical Notebooks of Samuel Beckett Vol. IV *The Shorter Plays* ed. by S.E. Gontarski (London: Faber & Faber, 1999).
Trilogy: Molloy, Malone Dies, The Unnamable (London: John Calder, 1959, 1994).
The Unnamable (London: Calder & Boyars, 1951).
Waiting for Godot (London: Faber & Faber, [1956] 1957).
Watt (London: John Calder [1963], 1976, 1981).
The Way, first published as 'Crisscross to infinity' in *College Literature*, 8:3 (1981).
'What is the Word', *Grand Street*, 9:2 (1990), 17–18.
Worstward Ho (London: John Calder, 1983).
Worstward Ho (New York: Grove Press, 1983).

Works in French
Comédie et actes divers (Paris: Les Éditions de Minuit, 1966).
L'Innommable (Paris: Les Éditions de Minuit, 1953).
Molloy (Paris: Les Éditionds de Minuit, 1951).
Murphy (Paris: Les Éditions de Minuit, 1965).
Nouvelles et textes pour rien (Paris: Les Éditions de Minuit, 1955).
Pas, suivi de quatre esquisses (Paris: Les Éditions de Minuit, 1978).
Watt (Paris: Olympia Press, [1953] 1958).

Unpublished works
Samuel Beckett, *German Diaries 4*, entry of 18 January 1937.
TCD (Trinity College Dublin) MS 10971
UoR (Reading University Library) MS 3000
UoR MS 3218
UoR MS 3458
UoR MS 2957
UoR MS 5003

Critical works on Beckett

Abbott, H. Porter, 'Late Modernism: Samuel Beckett and the art of the oeuvre', in Enoch Brater and Ruby Cohn (eds), *Around the Absurd: Essays on Modern and Postmodern Drama* (Ann Arbor: University of Michigan Press, 1990), pp. 75–96.

—— 'A grammar for being elsewhere', *Journal of Modern Literature: Samuel Beckett number*, 6:1 (February 1977), 39–46.

Ackerley, C. J., *Obscure Locks, Simple Keys: The Annotated Watt* (Tallahassee, FL: Journal of Beckett Studies Books, 2005).

—— *Demented Particulars: The Annotated Murphy* (Tallahassee: Journal of Beckett Studies Books, 2004).

Ackerley, C. J. and S. E. Gontarski, *The Grove Companion to Samuel Beckett* (New York: Grove Press, 2004).

Adders, Rose, *The Bored @ Work Doodle Book* (London: Carlton, 2008).

Addyman, David, 'Samuel Beckett and the treatment of place' (Ph.D. thesis, Royal Holloway, University of London, 2008).

Adorno, Theodor, 'Trying to understand *Endgame*', in Theodor Adorno, *Notes to Literature*, 2 vols, vol. 1, trans. Shierry Weber Nicholsen (New York: Columbia University Press, 1991).

A. H. [unsigned review], '*Film*: Keaton joue Beckett', *Le Quotidien de Paris* (7 March 1984).

Ahmed, Sara, *The Cultural Politics of Emotion* (New York: Routledge, 2004).

Alexander, Archibald B. D., *A Short History of Philosophy*, 3rd edn (Glasgow: Maclehose, Jackson & Co., 1922).

Allen, Nicholas, 'Review of Paul Stewart's *Zone of Evaporation: Samuel Beckett's Disjunctions*', *Modern Fiction Studies*, 54:2 (2008).

Asmus, Walter D., *Footfalls*, directed by Walter Asmus, filmed in Ardmore Studios April 2000, with Susan Fitzgerald and Joan O'Hara. *Beckett on Film*, produced by Michael Colgan and Alan Moloney (Blue Angel Films / Tyrone Productions for Radio Telefís Éireann & Channel 4: 2001).

—— 'Practical aspects of theatre, radio and television: rehearsal notes for the German première of Beckett's *That Time* and *Footfalls* at the Schiller Theater Werkstatt, Berlin', *Journal of Beckett Studies*, 2 (Summer 1977), 82–95.

B. G. [unsigned review], '*Film*: Godot ne viendra plus', *Télérama*, 1782 (7 March 1984).

Badiou, Alain, *Beckett: l'increvable désir* (Paris: Hachette, 1995).

—— 'L'Écriture du générique: Samuel Beckett', *Conditions* (Paris: Seuil, 1992).

Baldwin, Hélène L., *Samuel Beckett's Real Silence* (Philadelphia: Pennsylvania University Press, 1981).

Ballmer, Karl, *Aber Herr Heidegger!* (Basel: Rudolf Geering, 1933).

Barfield, Steve, 'Beckett and Heidegger: a critical survey', in Richard Lane (ed.), *Beckett and Philosophy* (Basingstoke: Palgrave Macmillan, 2002), pp. 154–65.

Barrow, John D., *The Book of Nothing* (London: Jonathan Cape, 2000).

Barry, Elizabeth, *Beckett and Authority: The Uses of Cliché* (Basingstoke: Palgrave Macmillan, 2006).

Beebe, Maurice, 'What modernism was', *Journal of Modern Literature*, 3:5 (July 1974), 1065–84.

Begam, Richard, *Samuel Beckett and the End of Modernity* (Stanford: Stanford University Press, 1996).

Ben-Zvi, Linda, 'Samuel Beckett's media plays', *Modern Drama*, 28:1 (1985), 22–37.

Bergson, Henri, *Matter and Memory*, trans. N. Paul and W. Palmer (New York: Macmillan, 1912).

Bernstein, Susan, 'It walks: the ambulatory uncanny', *Modern Language Notes*, 118:5 (2003), 1111–39.

Bignell, Jonathan, *Beckett on Screen: The Television Plays* (Manchester: Manchester University Press, 2009).

—— 'Beckett at the BBC: the production and reception of Samuel Beckett's plays for television', in L. Ben-Zvi (ed.), *Drawing on Beckett: Portraits, Performances, and Cultural Contexts* (Tel Aviv: Assaph, 2003), pp. 165–82.

—— 'Questions of authorship: Samuel Beckett and *Film*', in Jonathan Bignell (ed.), *Writing and Cinema* (Harlow: Longman, 1999), pp. 29–42.

Bion, Wilfred, *Second Thoughts* (London: Karnac, 1984).

Birkett, Jennifer, and Kate Ince (eds), *Samuel Beckett: Longman Critical Reader* (London: Longman, 2000).

Blanchot, Maurice 'Where now? Who now?', in Gabriel Josipovici (ed.), *The Siren's Song* (Brighton, Harvester, 1982).

Borchardt-Hume, Achim, *Doris Salcedo: Shibboleth* (London: Tate, 2007).

Bowley, A. H. et al., *Psychology: The Study of Man's Mind* (London: Odhams Press, 1949).

Boxall, Peter, *Contemporary Writers in the Wake of Modernism* (London: Continuum, 2009).

—— *Samuel Beckett:* Waiting for Godot *and* Endgame (Basingstoke: Palgrave Macmillan, 2000).

—— 'Beckett's negative geography: fictional space in Beckett's prose' (Ph.D. thesis, University of Sussex, 1996).

Brater, Enoch, *The Drama in the Text: Beckett's Late Fiction* (Oxford: Oxford University Press, 1994).

—— *Why Beckett* (London: Thames & Hudson, 1989).

—— *Beyond Minimalism: Beckett's Late Style in the Theatre* (Oxford and New York: Oxford University Press, 1987).

—— 'The empty can: Samuel Beckett and Andy Warhol', *Journal of Modern Literature* (July 1974), 1255–64.

Brienza, Susan D., *Samuel Beckett's New Worlds: Style in Metafiction* (Norman: University of Oklahoma Press, 1987).

Brooks, Cleanth, *The Well Wrought Urn: Studies in the Structure of Poetry* (New York: Harcourt, Brace and World, 1947).

Brundson, Charlotte, 'Problems with quality', *Screen*, 31:1 (1990), 67–90.

Bryden, Mary (ed.), *Samuel Beckett and Music* (Oxford: Clarendon Press, 1998).

Burnet, John, *Greek Philosophy, Part I: Thales to Plato* (London: Macmillan, 1914).

C., J. -L. [unsigned review], 'Retour à Tours ou Vanité du portrait', in *Cahiers du Cinéma*, 177 (April 1965), 17–19.

Cage, John, *Empty Words* (London: Marion Boyars, 1980).

—— *Silence* (London: Marion Boyars, 1978).

Campbell, Sue, *Interpreting the Personal: Expression and the Formation of Feelings* (Ithaca, NY: Cornell University Press, 1997).

Caselli, Daniela, *Beckett's Dantes: Intertextuality in the Fiction and Criticism* (Manchester: Manchester University Press, 2005).

—— 'The promise of Dante in Beckett's manuscripts', *Samuel Beckett Today / Aujourd'hui: Notes diverse holo*, eds Matthijs Engelberts, Everett Frost and Jane Maxwell, 16 (2006), 37–57.

Caselli, Daniela, Steven Connor and Laura Salisbury (eds), *Journal of Beckett Studies*, 10:1 and 2 (Fall 2000/Spring 2001). Reprinted as *Other Becketts* (Tallahassee FL: Journal of Beckett Studies Books, 2002).

Cavell, Stanley, *Must We Mean What We Say? A Book of Essays* (Cambridge: Cambridge University Press, 2002).

Cixous, Hélène, *Le Voisin de zéro: Sam Beckett* (Paris: Galilée, 2007). Forthcoming in English as *Zero's Neighbour*, trans. Laurent Milesi (Cambridge: Polity, 2009).

Coe, Richard, *Beckett* (London: Oliver & Boyd, 1964).

Coetzee, J.M., 'Eight ways of looking at Samuel Beckett', in *Samuel Beckett Today / Aujourd'hui: Borderless Beckett / Beckett sans frontiers*, eds Minako Okamuro et al., 18 (2008).

—— *Slow Man* (London: Secker and Warburg, 2006).

Cohn, Ruby, *A Beckett Canon* (Ann Arbor: University of Michigan Press, 2001).

—— *Just Play: Beckett's Theatre* (Princeton: Princeton University Press, 1980).

—— 'Philosophical fragments in the works of Samuel Beckett', in Martin Esslin (ed.), *Samuel Beckett: A Collection of Critical Essays* (Englewood Cliffs, NJ: Prentice Hall, 1965), pp. 169–77.

—— *Samuel Beckett: The Comic Gamut* (New Brunswick: Rutgers University Press, 1962).

Connor, Steven, *The Book of Skin* (Ithaca, NY: Cornell University Press, 2003).

—— 'The doubling of presence in *Waiting for Godot* and *Endgame*', in Steven Connor (ed.), *New Casebooks:* Waiting for Godot *and* Endgame (Basingstoke: Macmillan, 1992).

—— *Samuel Beckett: Repetition, Theory and Text* (Oxford: Blackwell, 1988).

—— 'Scribbledehobbles: Writing Jewish-Irish feet', unpublished, online at http://www.stevenconnor.com/scribble/.

Critchley, Simon, *Very Little . . . Almost Nothing: Death Philosophy Literature* (London: Routledge, [1997] 2004).

Crowther, Bosley, 'Bette Davis and Keaton movies are shown', *New York Times* (15 September 1965), 41:1.

Cunningham, David, 'Ascetism against colour, or modernism, abstraction and the lateness of Beckett', *New Formations*, 55 (Spring 2005), 104–19.

—— 'Trying (not) to understand: Adorno and the work of Beckett', in Richard Lane (ed.), *Beckett and Philosophy* (Basingstoke: Palgrave Macmillan, 2002), pp. 125–39.

D'Aubarède, Gabriel, 'Interview with Samuel Beckett', in Lawrence Graver and Raymond Federman (eds), *Samuel Beckett: The Critical Heritage* (London: Routledge & Kegan Paul, [1961] 1979).

David-Neel, Alexandra, *Magic and Mystery in Tibet* (Escondido: Book Tree, 2000).

Deleuze, Gilles, *Essays Critical and Clinical*, trans. Daniel W. Smoth and Michael A. Greco (London: Verso, 1998; Minneapolis: University of Minnesota Press, 1997).

Denora, Tia, *Beethoven and the Construction of Genius* (Berkeley, Los Angles and London: University of California Press, 1995).

Derrida, Jacques, *Papier machine* (Paris: Galilée, 2001).

—— '"This strange institution called literature": an interview with Jacques Derrida', in *Acts of Literature*, ed. Derek Attridge (London: Routledge, 1992), pp. 33–75.

—— *Acts of Literature*, ed. Derek Attridge (New York: Routledge, 1991).

—— *Speech and Phenomena*, trans. David B. Allison (Evanston: Northwestern University Press, 1973).

Derrida, Jacques and Geoffrey Bennington, *Jacques Derrida* (Chicago: Chicago University Press, 1993).

Dickinson, Emily, *The Poems of Emily Dickinson: Reading Edition*, ed. R. W. Franklin (Cambridge, MA: Harvard University Press, 1998).

Dolar, Mladen, *A Voice and Nothing More* (Cambridge, MA: MIT Press, 2006).

Dowd, Garin, *Abstract Machines: Beckett and Philosophy after Deleuze and Guattari* (Amsterdam: Rodopi, 2007).

Drew, Elizabeth, 'Head to footsteps: "fundamental sounds" in "dread nay" and "Roundelay"', *Samuel Beckett Today / Aujourd-hui*, eds Angela Moorjani and Carola Veit, 11, pp. 295–6.

Driver, Tom, 'Beckett by the Madeleine', *Columbia University Forum*, 4:3 (1961).

Duras, Marguerite, *India Song* (Paris, Gallimard 1973).

Dwyer, John, 'In the shadows with Feldman and Beckett', *Lively Arts, Buffalo News*, 27 (November 1976).

Eliot, T. S., *The Sacred Wood: Essays on Poetry and Criticism* (London: Methuen, 1960).

Elliott, Kamilla, 'Novels, films, and the word/image wars', in Robert Stam and Alessandra Raengo (eds), *A Companion to Literature and Film* (Malden: Blackwell, 2004), pp. 1–22.

—— *Rethinking the Novel/Film Debate* (Cambridge: Cambridge University Press, 2003).

Engelberts, Matthijs, '*Film* and *Film*: Beckett and early film theory', in Linda Ben-Zvi and Angela Moorjani (eds), *Beckett at 100: Revolving It All* (New York: Oxford University Press, 2008), pp. 152–76.

Engelberts, Matthijs, '*Film* et *Film*: Beckett et les premières théories cinématographiques', in *Samuel Beckett Today / Aujourd'hui: Présence de Samuel Beckett / Presence of Samuel Beckett'*, ed. Sjef Houppermans, 17 (2006), 331–50.

Everett Frost, and Jane Maxwell (eds), *Samuel Beckett Today / Aujourd'hui. Notes Diverse Holo*, 16 (Amsterdam: Rodopi, 2006).

Ehrenzweig, Anton, *The Hidden Order of Art* (Berkeley: University of California Press, 1967).

Fehsenfeld, Martha Dow, and Lois More Overbeck (eds), *The Letters of Samuel Beckett 1929–1940* (Cambridge: Cambridge University Press, 2009).

Feldman, Matthew, *Beckett's Books: A Cultural History of Samuel Beckett's 'Interwar Notes'* (London: Continuum, 2006).

—— 'Beckett and Popper, or "what stink of artifice": some notes on methodology, falsifiability, and criticism in Beckett Studies', *Samuel Beckett Today / Aujourd'hui Notes diverse holo*, eds Matthijs Engelberts, Everett Frost and Jane Maxwell, 16 (2006), 372–91.

Feldman, Matthew, and Mark Nixon (eds), *Beckett's Literary Legacies* (Newcastle: Cambridge Scholars Publishing, 2006).

Feldman, Morton, '"The note man on the word man": interview with Everett Frost', in Chris Villars (ed.), *Morton Feldman Says: Selected Interviews and Lectures 1964–1987* (London: Hyphen Press, 2006).

—— *Neither: An Opera in One Act on a Text by Samuel Beckett for Soprano and Orchestra* (London: Universal Edition, 1977).

Fieschi, Jean-André and André Téchiné, '*Film* de Samuel Beckett et Alan Schneider (U.S.A.)', *Cahiers du Cinéma* (Dossier 'Venise 65'), 171 (October 1965), 48–9.

Fletcher, Beryl, John Fletcher, Barry Smith and Walter Bechem, *A Student's Guide to the Plays of Samuel Beckett* (London: Faber & Faber, 1978).

Fletcher, John, 'The private pain and the whey of words: a survey of Beckett's verse', in Martin Esslin (ed.), *Samuel Beckett: A Collection of Critical Essays* (Englewood Cliffs, NJ: Prentice Hall, 1965), pp. 23–32.

Foster, Paul, *Beckett and Zen* (London: Wisdom, 1989).

Freud, Sigmund, 'Jokes and their relation to the unconscious' (1905), *Standard Edition of the Complete Psychological Works of Sigmund Freud*, ed. James Strachey, vol. 8 (London: Hogarth Press, 1964).

—— *The Interpretation of Dreams*, trans. James Strachey (Harmondsworth: Penguin, 1982).

—— *Inhibitions, Symptoms and Anxiety*, trans. Alix Strachey (London: Hogarth Press, 1948).

—— 'Beyond the pleasure principle', trans. James Strachey, in *On Metapsychology: The Theory of Psychoanalysis*, vol. 11 (Harmondsworth: Penguin, 1991).

Geis, Deborah R., *Postmodern Theatric[k]s: Monologue in Contemporary American Drama* (Ann Arbor: University of Michigan Press, 1993).

Geulincx Arnold, *Ethics*, trans. Martin Wilson, eds Han Van Ruler, Anthony Uhlmann and Martin Wilson (Leiden and Boston: Brill, 2006).

—— *Metaphysics*, trans. Martin Wilson (Wisbech: Christoffel, 1999).

Gibson, Andrew, *Beckett and Badiou: The Pathos of Intermittency* (Oxford: Oxford University Press, 2006).

Gigante, Denise, 'The endgame of taste: Keats, Sartre, Beckett', in Timothy Morton (ed.), *Cultures of Taste / Theories of Appetite: Eating Romanticism* (Basingstoke: Palgrave Macmillan, 2004), pp. 183–202.

Goldstein, Kurt, *Language and Language Disturbances* (New York: Grune and Stratton, 1948).

Gombrich, E. H., *The Uses of Images* (London: Phaidon, 1999).

Gontarski, S. E., 'Staging himself, or Beckett's late style in the theatre', *Samuel Beckett Today / Aujourd'hui: Crossroads and Borderlines / L'œuvre carrefour / L'œuvre limite*, eds Marius Buning, Matthijs Engelberts and Sjef Houperman, guest editor Emmanuel Jacquart, 6 (Amsterdam: Rodopi, 1997), 87–97.

—— 'From unabandoned works: Samuel Beckett's short prose', in *Samuel Beckett: The Complete Short Prose 1929–1989* (New York: Grove Press, 1995).

—— 'Editing Beckett', *Twentieth Century Literature*, 41:2 (1995), 190–207.

Gontarski, S. E. and Anthony Uhlmann (eds), *Beckett After Beckett* (Gainesville: University Press of Florida, 2006).

Graver, Lawrence, and Raymond Federman, *Samuel Beckett: The Critical Heritage* (London: Routledge and Kegan Paul, 1979).

Grossman, Evelyne, *L'Esthetique de Beckett* (Liège: SEDES, 1998).

Gruen, John, 'Samuel Beckett talks about Beckett', *Vogue*, 127:2 (February 1970), 108.

Heath, Stephen, and Gillian Skirrow, 'Television: a world in action', *Screen*, 18:2 (1977), 7–59.

Heidegger, Martin, *Pathmarks*, trans. and ed. William McNeill (Cambridge: Cambridge University Press, 1998); *Wegmarken*, second edition (Frankfurt am Main: Klostermann, 1978).

—— *Being and Time*, trans. John Macquarrie and Edward Robinson (Oxford: Blackwell, [1962]; 1999); *Sein und Zeit*, second edition (Halle: Max Niemeyer, 1929).

—— *The Fundamental Concepts of Metaphysics*, trans. W. McNeill and N. Walker (Bloomington: Indiana University Press, 1995).

—— *Introduction to Metaphysics*, trans. Gregory Fried and Richard Polt (New Haven, CT: Yale University Press, 2000).

Hemmings, Clare, 'Invoking affect: cultural theory and the ontological turn', *Cultural Studies*, 19:5 (2005).

Herren, Graley, *Samuel Beckett's Plays on Film and Television* (New York and Basingstoke: Palgrave Macmillan, 2007).

—— '*Nacht und Träume* as Beckett's *agony in the garden*', *Journal of Beckett Studies*, 11:1 (2001), 54–70.

—— 'Splitting images: Samuel Beckett's *Nacht und Träume*', *Modern Drama*, 43 (2000), 182–91.

Hill, Leslie, *Beckett's Fiction: In Different Words* (Cambridge: Cambridge University Press, 1990).

Hughlings Jackson, John, 'On affections of speech from disease of the brain' (1897), in Paul Eling (ed.), *Reader in the History of Aphasia* (Amsterdam: John Benjamins, 1994).

Hume, David, *A Treatise of Human Nature* (London: Routledge, 1985).

Hutcheon, Linda, *A Poetics of Postmodernism: History, Theory, Fiction* (London: Routledge, 1987).

Iser, Wolfgang, *The Implied Reader: Patterns of Communication in Prose Fiction from Bunyan to Beckett* (Baltimore: Johns Hopkins University Press, 1974).

Jameson, Fredric, *Postmodernism: The Cultural Logic of Late Capitalism* (Durham, NC: Duke University Press, 1991).

Jaurretche, Colleen (ed.), *Beckett, Joyce and the Art of the Negative*: *European Joyce Studies* 16 (Amsterdam: Rodopi, 2005).

Juliet, Charles, *Conversations with Samuel Beckett and Bram van Velde*, trans. Janey Tucker (Leiden: Academic Press Leiden, 1995).

Kalb, Jonathn, 'The mediated Quixote: the radio and television plays, and *Film*', in J. Pilling (ed.), *The Cambridge Companion to Beckett* (Cambridge: Cambridge University Press ,1994), pp. 124–44.

—— *Beckett in Performance* (Cambridge: Cambridge University Press, 1989).

Katz, Daniel, *Saying I No More: Subjectivity and Consciousness in the Prose of Samuel Beckett* (Evanston, IL: Northwestern University Press, 1999).

Kierkegaard, Søren, *The Concept of Anxiety: A Simple Psychologically Orienting Deliberation on the Dogmatic Issue of Hereditary Sin*, ed. and trans. Reidar Thomte and Albert B. Anderson (Princeton: Princeton University Press, 1980).

—— *Søren Kierkegaard's Journals and Papers*, I–VII, ed. and trans. Howard V. Hong and Edna H. Hong (Bloomington: Indiana University Press, 1967).

King, William, *Sermon on Predestination* (Dublin, 1709), in *Archbishop King's Sermon on Predestination*, ed. Andrew Carpenter (Dublin: Cadenus Press, 1976).

Knowlson, James, *Damned to Fame: The Life of Samuel Beckett* (London: Bloomsbury, 1996).

Krauss, Rosalind, *The Originality of the Avant-Garde and Other Modernist Myths* (Cambridge, MA: The MIT Press, 1986).

L. M. [unsigned review], '*Film*, d'Alan Schneider et *L'Enfant invisible*, d'André Lindon', *Le Monde* (21 March 1984).

Lacan, Jacques, *The Seminar of Jacques Lacan, Book XVII: The Other Side of Psychoanalysis*, trans. Russell Grigg (New York: Norton, 2007).

—— *Le Sinthome* (*Le Séminaire XXIII*) (Paris: Seuil, 2005).

Laing, R. D., *Knots* (London: Tavistock, 1970; reprinted London: Penguin, 1972).

Lane, Richard, (ed.), *Beckett and Philosophy* (Basingstoke: Palgrave, 2002).

Laws, Catherine, *'Headaches Among the Overtones': Music in Beckett, Beckett in Music* (New York and Amsterdam: Rodopi, 2009).

—— 'Beethoven's haunting of Beckett's *Ghost Trio*', in Linda Ben-Zvi (ed.), *Drawing on Beckett: Portraits, Performances, and Cultural Contexts* (Tel Aviv: Assaph, 2003), pp. 197–214.

—— 'Morton Feldman's *Neither*: a musical translation of Beckett's text', in Mary Bryden (ed.), *Samuel Beckett and Music* (Oxford: Clarendon Press, 1988).

Lear, Jonathan, *Love and Its Place in Nature: A Philosophical Interpretation of Freudian Psychoanalysis* (New York: Farrar, Strauss and Giroux, 1990).

Levy, Shimon, *Samuel Beckett's Self-Referential Drama: The Sensitive Chaos* (Eastbourne: Sussex Academic Press, 2002).

Locatelli, Carla, 'Delogocentering silence: Beckett's ultimate unwording', in Enoch Brater (ed.), *The Theatrical Gamut: Notes for a Post-Beckettian Stage* (Ann Arbor: University of Michigan Press, 2005).

—— *Unwording the Word: Samuel Beckett Prose Works after the Nobel Prize* (Philadelphia: University of Pennsylvania Press, 1990).

Losseff, Nicky, and Jenny Doctor (eds), *Silence, Music, Silent Music* (Aldershot: Ashgate, 2007).

Lyotard, Jean-François, *The Differend*, trans. Georges Van Den Abbeele (Manchester: Manchester University Press, 1988).

Maclagan, David, 'Between the aesthetic and the psychological', *Inscape* 2 (1994).

—— 'Freud and the figurative', *Inscape* (October 1983).

—— 'Solitude and communication: beyond the doodle', *Raw Vision* (Summer 1990), 33–38.

Maclay, W. S. E. Guttmann and W. Margus-Gross, 'Spontaneous drawings as an approach to some problems of psychopathiology', *Proceedings of the Royal Society of Medicine*, XXXI (1938), 1337–50.

McMullan, Anna, *Theatre on Trial: Samuel Beckett's Later Drama* (London: Routledge, 1993).

McMullan, Anna, and S. E. Wilmer (eds), *Reflections on Beckett: A Centenary Celebration* (Ann Arbor: University of Michigan Press, 2009).

McQueeny, Terence, 'Samuel Beckett as critic of Proust and Joyce' (Ph.D. thesis, University of North Carolina, 1977).

Maier, Michael, '*Geistertrio*: Beethoven's music in Samuel Beckett's *Ghost Trio*: part one', *Samuel Beckett Today / Aujourd-hui: Endlessness in the Year 2000*, eds Angela Moorjani and Carola Veit, 11 (2001), 267–78.

Mallarmé, Stéphane, *Mallarmé: Selected Prose Poems, Essays, and Letters*, trans. Bradford Cook (Baltimore: Johns Hopkins Press, 1956).

Malraux, André, *Man's Fate*, trans. Stuart Gilbert (New York: Random House, 1961).

—— *La Condition humaine*, in *Romans*, Bibliothèque de la Pléiade (Paris: Gallimard, 1947).

Margetts, Edward L., 'Trepanation of the skull by the medicine men of primitive cultures, with particular reference to present-day East African practice', in Donald R. Brothwell and A. T. Sandison (eds), *Diseases in Antiquity*, (Springfield: Charles C. Thomas, 1967), pp. 673–701.

Marino, Gordon D., 'Anxiety in *The Concept of Anxiety*', in Alastair Hannay and Gordon D. Marino (eds), *The Cambridge Companion to Kierkegaard* (Cambridge: Cambridge University Press, 1998).

Martin, Elaine, 'Re-reading Adorno: the "after-Auschwitz" aporia', *Forum*, 2 (2006), 1–13.

Massumi, Brian, *Parables for the Virtual: Movement, Affect, Sensation* (Durham, N.C.: Duke University Press, 2002).

Maude, Ulrika, 'Centennial Beckett: the gray canon and the fusion of horizons', *Modernism/Modernity*, 15:1 (2008).

—— 'The body of memory: Beckett and Merleau-Ponty', in Richard Lane (ed.), *Beckett and Philosophy* (Basingstoke: Palgrave Macmillan, 2002), pp. 108–22.

Mauthner, Fritz, *Beiträge zu einer Kritik der Sprache*, vol. 2 (Leipzig: Felix Meiner, 1923).

Mengham, Rod, '"Failing better": Salcedo's trajectory', in *Doris Salcedo: Neither* (London: Jay Jopling / White Cube, 2004), pp. 9–11.

Melville, Herman, *Moby Dick* (Oxford: Oxford University Press, 1988).

Merewether, Charles, 'To bear witness', in Dan Cameron and Charles Merewether (eds), *Doris Salcedo* (New York: New Museum of Contemporary Art, 1998).

Merleau-Ponty, Maurice, *The Phenomenology of Perception*, trans. Colin Smith (London: Routledge & Kegan Paul, [1962] 1981); Maurice Merleau-Ponty, *La Phénoménologie de la perception* (Paris: Gallimard, 1945).

Mercier, Vivien, 'The uneventful event', *Irish Times* (18 February 1956).

Mével, Yann, and Michèle Touret (eds), special issue of *Samuel Beckett Today / Aujourd'hui: L'Affect dans l'oeuvre Beckettienne*, 10 (Amsterdam: Rodopi, 2000).

Milton, John, *Paradise Lost*, ed. Alastair Fowler (Harlow: Pearson Longman, 2007).

Moorjani, Angela, *The Aesthetics of Loss and Lessness* (Basingstoke: Palgrave Macmillan, 1991).

—— *Abysmal Games in the Novels of Samuel Beckett* (Chapel Hill: University of North Carolina Press, 1982).

Moran, Dermot, 'Wandering from the path: *navigatio* in the philosophy of John Scottus Eriugena', *The Crane Bag Book of Studies*, 2:1 and 2 (Dublin, Blackwater Press, 1978), pp. 244–51.

Muller, R., 'Coffee without brandy', *Observer* (1 September 1996).

Murphy, P. J., *Beckett's Dedalus: Dialogical Engagements with Joyce in Beckett's Fiction* (Toronto: University of Toronto Press, 2009).

Ngai, Sianne, *Ugly Feelings* (Cambridge, MA: Harvard University Press, 2005).

Nixon, Mark '"What a tourist I must have been": the German diaries of Samuel Beckett' (Ph.D., University of Reading, 2005).

Northcott, Bayan, 'Review of Morton Feldman's *Neither*', The *Sunday Telegraph* June 26, (1977).

Nussbaum, Martha, *Upheavals of Thought: The Intelligence of Emotions* (Cambridge: Cambridge University Press, 2001).

O'Hara, J. D., 'Beckett's Schopenhauerian reading of Proust: the will as whirled in re-presentation', in Eric van der Luft (ed.), *Schopenhauer: New Essays in Honor of His 200th Birthday* (Lewiston, Queenston and Lampeter: The Edwin Mellon Press, 1988), pp. 273–92.

The Onion, 42:17 (26 April 2006).

Oppenheim, Lois, *The Painted Word: Samuel Beckett's Dialogue with Art* (Ann Arbor: University of Michigan Press, 2000).

—— (ed.), *Samuel Beckett and the Arts: Music, Visual Arts, and Non-Print Media* (New York: Garland, 1999).

Overbeck, Lois More, and Martha Fehsenfeld, 'In defense of the integral text', *Samuel Beckett Today / Aujourd'hui: Notes diverse holo*, eds Matthijs Engelberts, Everett Frost and Jane Maxwell, 16 (2006), 347–71.

Pardo, Enrique, 'The theatres of boredom and depression: two gateways to imagination', *Spring 1988* (1988), 166–76.

Parrott, Jeremy '"Nothing neatly named": the Beckettian aesthetic and negative theology', *Samuel Beckett Today / Aujourd'hui:* Three Dialogues *revisited / Les* Trois dialogues *revisités*, eds Marius Buning, Matthijs Engelberts, Sjef Houppermans, and Danièle de Ruyter-Tgnotti, 13 (2003), 91–101.

Perloff, Marjorie (ed.), *Postmodern Genres* (Norman: University of Oklahoma Press, 1988).

Peters, J. D., *Speaking into the Air: A History of the Idea of Communication* (Chicago: University of Chicago Press, 1999).

Phillips, Adam, *On Kissing, Tickling and Being Bored* (London: Faber & Faber, 1993).

Pilling, John, *A Samuel Beckett Chronology* (Basingstoke: Palgrave Macmillan, 2006).

—— '"For interpolation": Beckett and English literature', *Samuel Beckett Today / Aujourd'hui: Notes diverse holo*, eds Matthijs Engelberts, Everett Frost and Jane Maxwell, 16 (2006), 220–21.

—— (ed.), *Beckett's 'Dream' Notebook* (Reading: Beckett International Foundation, 1999).

—— *A Companion to 'Dream of Fair to Middling Women'* (Tallahassee, FL: Journal of Beckett Studies Books, 2004).

Pinter, Harold, *The Proust Screenplay: A la recherche du temps perdu* (New York: Grove, 1977).

Princenthal, Nancy, Carlos Basualdo and Andreas Huyssen (eds), *Doris Salcedo* (London: Phaidon, 2000).

'Project One', *Sight & Sound*, 34:2 (Spring 1965), 61–2.

Poe, Edgar Allan, *The Fall of the House of Usher and Other Writings*, rev. edn (Harmondsworth: Penguin, 2003).

Rachman, Stanley, *Anxiety* (Hove: Psychology Press, 1998).

Revault d'Allonnes, Fabrice, 'Buster Keaton rencontre Samuel Beckett: 1er avril 1964', in *Cahiers du Cinéma* numéro spécial '100 journées qui ont fait le cinéma' (hors série, January 1995), 48–9.

Ricks, Christopher, *Beckett's Dying Words* (Oxford: Oxford University Press, 1995)

Riley, Denise, *Impersonal Passion: Language as Affect* (Durham: Duke University Press, 2005).

Riskin, Robert, 'Mr. Deeds Goes to Town', in P. McGilligan (ed.), *Six Screenplays by Robert Riskin* (Berkeley: University of California Press, 1997).

Rosenberg, Harold, *The Anxious Object: Art Today and Its Audience* (New York: Horizon, 1964).

Roy, Jean, 'Film', *L'Humanité* (14 March 1984).

Sacks, Oliver, *An Anthropologist on Mars* (London: Picador, 1995).

Salisbury, Laura, 'Sounds of silence: aphasiology and the subject of modernity', in Laura Salisbury and Andrew Shail (eds), *Neurology and Modernity* (Basingstoke: Palgrave, 2009).

—— '"What is the word": Beckett's aphasic modernism', *Journal of Beckett Studies*, 17 (2009 forthcoming).

Sardin, Pascale, 'Beckett et la religion au travers du prisme de quelques textes courts auto-traduits', *Samuel Beckett Today / Aujourd'hui: Beckett and Religion / Beckett / Aesthetics / Politics*, eds Mary Bryden and Lance St John Butler, 9 (2000), 199–206.

Sarris, Andrew, 'New York', *Movie*, 12 (April 1965), 41.

Sartre, Jean-Paul, *Being and Nothingness: An Essay on Phenomenological Ontology* (London and New York: Routledge, [1943] 2003).

—— *La Nausée* (Paris: Livre de Poche, 1968).

Scannell, Paddy, 'Love and communication: a review essay', *Westminster Papers in Communication and Culture*, 1:1 (2004), 93–102.

Schneider, Alan, 'On directing *Film*', in *Samuel Beckett Today / Aujourd'hui: The Savage Eye / L'œil fauve*, ed. Catharine Wulf, 4, (1995), 31–40.

Schopenhauer, Arthur, *The World as Will and Representation*, trans. E. F. J. Payne, 2 vols (New York: Dover, 1969).

Schwab, Gabriele, 'The politics of small differences: Beckett's *The Unnamable*', in Henry Sussman and Christopher Devenney (eds), *Engagement and Indifference: Beckett and the political* (Albany: State University of New York Press, 2001).

Sconce, Jeffrey, *Haunted Media: Electronic Presence from Telegraphy to Television* (Durham, NC: Duke University Press, 2000).

Sebald, W. G., *Austerlitz*, trans. Anthea Bell (London: Penguin, 2001).

Sebald, W. G., and Jan Peter Tripp, *Unrecounted*, trans. Michael Hamburger (New York: New Directions, 2004).

Sedgwick, Eve Kosofsky, *Touching Feeling: Affect, Pedagogy, Performativity* (Durham, NC: Duke University Press, 2003).

Shainberg, Lawrence, 'Exorcising Beckett', *Paris Review*, 104 (1987), 102.

Simmer, Stephen, 'The academy of the dead: on boredom, writer's block, footnotes and deadlines', *Spring 1981* (1981), 91.

Simon, Alfred, *Samuel Beckett* (Paris: Belfond, 1963).

Skempton, Howard, 'Beckett as librettist', in Chris Villars (ed.), *Morton Feldman Says: Selected Interviews and Lectures 1964–1987* (London: Hyphen Press, 2006).

Sontag, Susan, 'The aesthetics of silence', in *Styles of Radical Will* (New York: Picador, 2002).

—— 'Against interpretation', in *A Susan Sontag Reader* (London: Penguin, 1983), pp. 95–104.

Stevens, Wallace, *Selected Poems* (London: Faber and Faber, 1965).

Tahiri, Yoshiki, *Samuel Beckett and the Prosthetic Body: The Organs and Senses in Modernism* (Basingstoke: Palgrave Macmillan, 2006).

Terada, Rei, *Feeling in Theory: Emotion after the 'Death of the Subject'* (Cambridge, MA: Harvard University Press, 2001).

Thevenaz, Pierre, *What Is Phenomenology?*, trans. J. M. Edie, C. Courtney and P. Brockelman (Chicago: Quadrangle, 1962).

Todman, Don, 'Synapse', *European Neurology*, 61 (2009), 190–1.

Tonning, Erik, *Samuel Beckett's Abstract Drama: Works for Stage and Screen 1962–1985* (Oxford: Peter Lang, 2007).

Tuttle, Raymond, 'Neither' (Review), *Classical Net* 2001, http://www.classical.net/music/recs/reviews/c/col20081a.php.

Uhlmann, Anthony, *Samuel Beckett and the Philosophical Image* (Cambridge: Cambridge University Press, 2006).

—— *Beckett and Poststructuralism* (Cambridge: Cambridge University Press, 1999).

Van Hulle, Dirk, *Manuscript Genetics: Joyce's Know-how, Beckett's Nohow* (Gainsville, FL: University Press of Florida, 2008).

—— (ed.), *Beckett the European* (Tallahassee, FL: Journal of Beckett Studies Books, 2005).

Voigts-Virchow, Ekart, 'Face values: Beckett Inc., the camera plays and cultural liminality', *Journal of Beckett Studies*, 10:1/2 (2000–1), 119–35.

—— 'Exhausted cameras: Beckett in the TV-zoo', in J. Jeffers (ed.), *Samuel Beckett: A Casebook* (New York: Garland, 1998), pp. 225–49.

Walker, J. A., *Arts TV: A History of Arts Television in Britain* (London: John Libbey, 1993).

Wall, John, 'Murphy, Belacqua, Schopenhauer and Descartes: metaphysical reflections on the body', *Journal of Beckett Studies*, 9:2 (Spring 2000), 21–61.

Wang, Stephen, 'Aquinas on human happiness and the natural desire for God', *New Blackfriars*, 88:1015 (May 2007), 322–34.

Weaver, William, 'Review of Morton Feldmans *Neither*', *International Herald Tribune* (14 June 1977).

Weiler, A. H., 'Now cinema!', *New York Times* (9 April 1968).

Weller, Shane, '"Gnawing to be naught": Beckett and Pre-Socratic nihilism', *Samuel Beckett Today / Aujourd'hui*, 20 (2008), 307–19.

— 'The politics of body language: the Beckett embrace', in Thomas Baldwin, James Fowler and Shane Weller (eds), *The Flesh in the Text* (Oxford: Peter Lang, 2007), pp. 141–59.

— *A Taste for the Negative: Beckett and Nihilism* (Oxford: Legenda, 2005).

Wernicke, Carl, 'The motor speech path and the relation of aphasia to anarthia' (1884), in Gertrude H. Eggert (ed.), *Wernicke's Works on Aphasia: A Sourcebook and Review* (The Hague: Mouten, 1977).

Whitelaw, Billie, *Billie Whitelaw . . . Who He?* (London: Hodder & Stoughton 1995).

Wierzbicka, Anna, *Emotions across Languages and Cultures: Diversity and Universals* (Cambridge: Cambridge University Press, 1999).

Windelband, Wilhelm, *A History of Philosophy, with Especial Reference to the Formation and Development of Its Problems and Conceptions*, trans. James H. Tufts (London: Macmillan, 1893).

Winnicott, Donald Woods, *Playing and Reality* (London: Tavistock, 1971).

Woodworth, Robert S., *Contemporary Schools of Psychology* (London: Methuen, 1931).

Wright, Joseph (ed.), *The English Dialect Dictionary* (London: Frowde, 1900).

Zurbrugg, Nicholas, *Beckett and Proust* (Gerrards Cross: Colin Smythe, 1988).

Index

Lightning Source UK Ltd.
Milton Keynes UK
UKOW02f0623230815

257370UK00004B/48/P